# GNVQ Intermediate
# Information
# Technology

## Peter Hodson and Mike Watkins

Letts Educational
Aldine Place
LONDON W12 8AW
0181 740 2266
1996

# Acknowledgements

The authors thank all of their colleagues who have generated ideas throughout the development of the text. Catherine Tilley at Letts has also been a source of encouragement to us.

Some material created for the Advanced level book has been adopted in this text and the authors thank their colleagues at this time, especially Geoff Foot at BTEC.

The various examples used throughout the text have been prepared using Microsoft Office products, all of which provide an ideal platform for the GNVQ IT programme.

Any errors remain the authors' responsibility and any feedback would be welcome, especially recommendations on changes or re-emphasis.

Finally we would like to thank our families for their continuing patience.

*A CIP catalogue record for this book is available from the British Library*

ISBN 1 85805 193 2
Copyright P.J. Hodson & M. Watkins © 1996

First edition 1996
Reprinted 1997

Typeset by Elizabeth Elwin, London and Kai Typesetting, Nottingham

Printed in Great Britain by
Nuffield Press, Abingdon

Letts Educational is the trading name of BPP (Letts Educational) Ltd

# *About the authors*

The authors are both staff at The University of Glamorgan and are active in the delivery of BTEC or GNVQ programmes.

**Peter Hodson** is Head of the Department of Computer Studies, University of Glamorgan. He has been involved in the developments of Advanced Level GNVQ in IT during the original writing of the unit specifications and has worked with NCVQ on monitoring the pilot year in test centres.

**Mike Watkins** has worked in computing for twenty-seven years. He is currently a Principal Lecturer at the University of Glamorgan and is course leader on the HND Computing Scheme. The major areas of interest include data modelling, database implementation and information engineering. His research interests are in computer based learning.

# Lecturers' Preface

This book provides comprehensive coverage of the four mandatory units in GNVQ Intermediate Information Technology

The text is structured to follow the GNVQ unit definitions as closely as possible, with each unit dealt with in a separate chapter, and each element given a separate section in that chapter. As individual colleges or schools will tackle the units in a different sequence, the units in the text have been written to allow this, and each is as independent of the others as the topic allows. Where appropriate, cross-referencing of material has been undertaken. Where material has been fully covered in another unit, it is not rigorously treated on a subsequent occasion.

## How to use this book with your students

The text is designed to support units taught through a combination of lectures and practical sessions. The text follows the GNVQ specification closely and can therefore form an underpinning framework for the course, enabling students to see clearly how the topics they are being taught meet the requirements of the course.

## Assessment material

Throughout the text are embedded short questions (with answers at the unit ends) that can be used in class or by students themselves to check they have understood the basic points being made. These are intended to confirm the learning process only.

Each unit also contains a series of in-text tasks that provide a scheme of activities necessary to generate the evidence required for each student's portfolio. Some tasks are practical in nature and will require the student to spend time on a computer system. Others require students to undertake on-site visits or to review a case study. Each task is referenced to the particular performance criteria it addresses, and, if appropriate, to a core skills criteria too. The Lecturers' Supplement (see below for full details) gives answers and guidance to the tasks.

At the end of each unit is a specimen external test paper in the style of the multi-choice questions of the actual papers. Answers are also in the Lecturers' Supplement.

## Lecturers' Supplement

A supplement to the book is available to lecturers, which contains answers to tasks and tests papers, guidance on delivering the unit and on meeting some of the requirements of the specification. It is free to lecturers adopting the text as a course text (please apply on college headed paper giving details of the course and likely bookshop supplier) and can be supplied for a charge of £3 to lecturers who are using it as a reference text.

# *Students' Introduction*

### Studying a GNVQ

GNVQs have been introduced to give a work-related qualification that is broadly based. It also provides a route towards more advanced and into Higher Education. The programme consists of four mandatory units plus two optional units. Careful choice of optional units will help you get a job in your preferred area.

You will also be assessed in three Core Skills, which are specified as Communication, Application of Number and Information Technology. It is assumed that the core skill in Information Technology will be automatically covered in this programme, so only Communication and Application of Number skills are addressed (see under *How to get the most out of this book*). Core skills may be renamed Key skills in the future.

The key terms used in a GNVQ programme need a little explanation:

❏ A **unit** is an area of study. To achieve a GNVQ you will be tested on 6 units plus the core skills.

❏ An **element** is a topic of study within a unit. There are typically 3 or 4 elements in each unit.

❏ **Performance criteria** (PCs) are the essential skills and knowledge you need to gain and understand for each element. Each element consists of a number of performance criteria and you have to demonstrate your competence in each of these.

❏ **Range statements** exist within each element, defining the area or extent of knowledge specified by the performance criteria.

❏ **Evidence indicators** represent the work you have undertaken in demonstrating that you have acquired the necessary skills to meet the performance criteria. They are the proof you need to be assessed as competent in the element/unit.

❏ **Assessment** is the measure of how well you have met the performance criteria. For the mandatory units assessment will be a combination of reviewing your portfolio of evidence containing your work plus an externally set test. All the work you have undertaken in a unit, such as coursework and project assignments are aimed at providing the evidence indicators needed. Each performance criterion needs to be completed, with all the range covered, before a pass is recorded. You should carefully keep all your work in your Portfolio of Evidence, since it may be reviewed by staff who are involved in the quality assurance issues relating to verification of evidence.

## How to get the most out of this book

The book is organised in exactly the same way as the four mandatory units of the GNVQ Intermediate Information Technology. It is designed to support a combination of lectures and practical sessions. Each *unit* is separately identified, with each *element* presented as a separate section of a chapter. Embedded, short self-assessed questions are introduced which allow you to check whether you have understood the basic points being made. These questions are not part of the formal assessment and are there to give you an early feedback on how well you have understood the material. Suggested answers to these questions are provided at the end of each unit.

Within each unit is a series of tasks which cover all the performance criteria of that unit. These are intended to provide a framework of activities necessary for you to assemble the evidence required for your portfolio. Each task is clearly labelled with the performance criteria (PC) that it addresses. Completion of each of the tasks will put you well on your way to completing this aspect of assessment. Remember to file your work from these tasks carefully in your portfolio.

The top right-hand corner of certain tasks indicates which core skills may be assessed during completion of that task. We have used a nomenclature of C to represent communication skills and N a numeracy skill. They are all level 2 core skills with 4 elements in the communication skills and 3 elements in the application of numbers. Hence C2.2 means a communication skill at level 2 with element 2 evidence.

At the end of each unit is a specimen test paper based on multi-choice questions. The style of each paper is similar to that which you will take with your Examining Body, although they may structure the paper into topics rather than randomly fire questions at you.

## Completing the tasks

The work you undertake in collecting the evidence of your skills and competence is supported by the task structure. The approach you need to take should be varied to suit the particular requirements. Some tasks are practical in nature and need time on computer systems. Others require you to undertake on-site visits or to review a case study. This style of investigation should be carefully documented and contribute to an active-learning approach.

*Peter Hodson*
*Mike Watkins*

*August 1996*

# Contents

# Contents

by **Mike Watkins**

# Introduction to information technology

**Information technology (IT)** is about using computers to carry out tasks found in commerce and industry. Today we are witnessing an IT revolution – the computer is changing the way we do business, communicate, control things and learn. Many jobs today cannot be carried out effectively unless a computer is available. The advent of the microchip and the subsequent reduction in costs of **personal computers (PCs)**, coupled to the availability of **graphic user-friendly interfaces (GUI)**, has provided 'computers for everyone'.

This unit introduces IT systems within the context of commercial (business) applications (e.g. supermarket checkout or payroll systems) and industrial applications (e.g. robotic manufacturing or washing machine programmes). In these situations, IT has been used to benefit the user and the organisation, but its use also has some limitations.

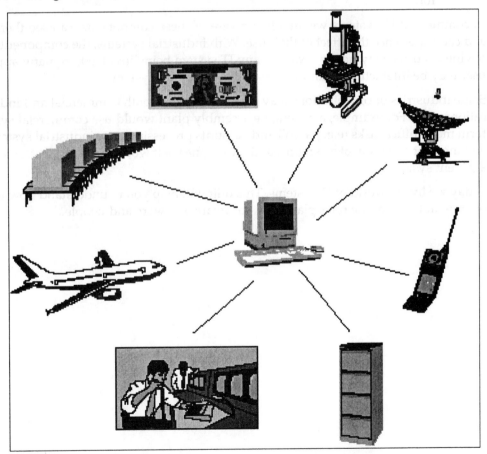

*Figure 1.1 Applications of IT*

Computerised IT system applications can be divided into two categories as follows.

- **Commercial systems** are primarily concerned with business or organisation data-processing activities, where the computer is used as tool by the user (a person) to carry out some task. These systems include: administrative applications (e.g. payroll, accounts, order processing), competitive advantage applications (e.g. automated checkout, holiday bookings, banking automated teller), office automation applications (e.g. wordprocessing, electronic diaries, electronic mail).
- **Industrial systems** are primarily concerned with controlling a machine or system of devices that automatically accomplish some task within the home, in the workplace or in our environment with little or no user interaction. These systems include: vehicle systems for engine management and in-car displays, home appliance systems (e.g. burglar alarms, satellite TV decoders/receivers, washing machines), manufacturing systems using robotics and process control, systems to assist the disabled.

An IT system will be composed of:

- **hardware** – the physical components that make up a computer system;
- **software** – the programs that logically controls the hardware to make it perform specific tasks;
- **people** – the users of the system that interact with it (using the hardware under the control of the software);
- **procedures** – that describe how to use a system effectively for the purpose it was built for.

In commercial IT systems we are often aware of these components, can see them being used and can experience the effect of their use. With industrial systems, the components may be less obvious and we may not be aware of any IT system being involved, in many applications the user may be interacting unknowingly with a computer system.

Some industries or organisations may require the use of both commercial and industrial applications of IT. For example, a car engine assembly plant would use commercial systems to perform many office tasks (e.g. payroll and accounts processing), use industrial systems to control and monitor assembly of an engine, and the engine itself would have an electronic engine management system.

Today we live in world of IT systems. This unit will help you to understand how these systems operate in terms of the roles played by hardware, software and people.

# *Examine industrial and commercial information technology systems*

## 1.1.1  Commercial systems

**Commercial systems** are concerned with the computerisation of business or organisation data processing systems. Many of these system activities have been done manually by people without the use of a computer. They usually involve carrying out repetitive administrative or office desk tasks that require extensive paperwork and often involve duplication of effort. Other commercial systems have changed how businesses operate by providing information and services that were not available in the past.

Early examples of such commercial applications are concerned with the computerisation the traditional central administrative tasks that are common to most organisations that employ people to produce goods or provide a service (e.g. payroll and accounts). More recent applications have used IT to assist the organisation in gaining some competitive advantage over its market place competitors and these tend to be more industry specific. In the retail industry automated checkouts at supermarkets help provide a better customer service through speeding up the checkout processing and enabling lower prices. Office automation is a direct result of the reduction in costs and increase in power of typical micro computers which provide IT tools to assist with general office work (e.g wordprocessing and electronic mail).

Today, businesses, education at all levels, and the general public at home, are being urged to hook up to the information superhighway and enter cyber space by connecting to the **Internet** and making use of the **world wide web (www)**. This facility covers the globe. It gives its users access to a huge source of data and information on practically any subject made available by providers at sites around the world. Many TV advertisements in the USA now carry the web address of the products company. To use this facility today requires a personal computer, in the next year or so new cheaper gadgets will be produced that will provide the same facilities using a TV set.

## Payroll

Payroll is one of the oldest and most common applications to be computerised. Today it will be one of the first, if not **the** first, IT application developed by a newly-formed organisation, apart from office automation applications. Payroll is a sensitive application in that employees expect to be paid correctly and on time, mistakes cannot be tolerated, reliability of processing cannot be questioned, inaccuracies and delay can cause tension and potential conflict.

A payroll system must be able to do the following.

- Process the pay of all employees of an organisation, whether they are paid weekly, monthly, salaried or paid by the hour.

- Take into account the components that make up gross pay (e.g. basic, overtime, back pay, bonus, expenses), the authorised deductions from gross pay that apply to each individual employee (e.g. personal pension, staff clubs, trade union subscriptions), the statutory deductions such as national insurance and income tax (calculated correctly using the employee's tax code) and finally produce the correct basic pay due.

- Produce a printed pay slip that shows the earnings and deductions for the current pay period and also cumulative figures for the current tax year to date.

- Handle different forms of payment to employees (e.g. cash or cheque or direct to the employee's bank). If payment is by cash, a coinage analysis can be produced for each employee to help make up each person's pay, and a cumulative analysis can be used to order cash from the bank. Payment by cheque will involve printing the basic pay amount in words and figures on pre-printed cheque stationary. Payment direct to the bank is an example of **electronic funds transfer (EFT)** and does away with the need for cash or pay cheques.

- Keep pay records for each employee up-to-date (e.g. records change to tax codes and cumulative year to date values). This pay record is used at the end of the tax year to produce an annual summary, a P60 for each employee.

- Automatically generate and produce various reports necessary for management or required by external agencies such as the inland revenue.

## Benefits

There are many benefits to a computerised payroll system. Manual payroll systems are labour intensive, requiring repeated calculations that are highly error prone – the activity is an ideal one for a computer. Computerised payroll will enable faster processing of payroll data, and the system can produce employee pay slips and payments earlier. It has the capability to produce a variety of reports for management or government with little labour or delay. Manual preparation of such reports could take days or weeks. Accuracy of processing of payroll records is improved, payments are made on time with no missing payments. It is easier to meet government requirements and to produce a payroll analysis for management.

## Limitations

The computerised payroll system, however, has some limitations. Where an off-the-shelf payroll package is used, the organisation may need to amend its documents (such as pay slip format) to meet those of the package. Staff will require training in the use of the package. If the staff who regularly use the system are absent for any reason, a stand-in must be readily available. Changes in government statutory requirements may require the software to be updated. A computerised payroll imposes rigidity on payroll procedures and will be unable to accommodate odd situations or special cases. Security of payroll data is an important concern, only authorised access to data is allowed, any changes should be audited, unauthorised activities may be prosecuted under the Computer Misuse Act 1990. Extensive use of a computer terminal may result in illness such as repetitive strain injury, and the design and use of such equipment should be planned to minimise any problems. Employers are subject to the Health and Safety at Work Act 1974 and there are several recent European Union directives that apply specifically to computer terminal use.

# Supermarket system

The grocery retail business is one of the most price-sensitive markets in many countries today. For example, one supermarket chain will attract customers away from a competitor by offering lower prices and/or by providing a better level of service such as quicker checkout of goods purchased leading to shorter queues at the checkouts. Cheaper prices are achieved by increasing the volume of sales and/or achieving a reduction in costs. In order to reduce operational costs while maintaining or improving customer service, many supermarkets have introduced automated checkouts that require very little operator action. This type of system utilises the universal product code in the form of a barcode printed on each individual product or pack. The barcode is read when passed over a fixed laser-scanner built into the checkout station, although products such as loose fruit and vegetables will not be barcoded and will need the operator to key in their data. These systems provide an opportunity to capture information on goods sold direct from the checkout 'till'. Similar systems are also used in many DIY stores, but here the variable size of products sold requires the use of a more portable laser wand.

*Figure 1.2 Bar code and laser wand or light pen*

A supermarket system must have the following features.

- It must have a database of all products available for sale; each product record will be identified by its product code, and other details kept will include its price and current stock level (which changes as items are sold), and new stocks delivered from suppliers. The system may trigger automatically the re-ordering of products when their in-stock quantity falls below some set level.
- It must tally the purchases and produce an itemised bill for the customer.
- It must be able to handle a variety of payment methods by the customer, e.g. cash, credit card, debit card, tokens and also any customer club scheme.
- It must provide facilities to handle special offers that the supermarket puts on from time to time, 'buy three get an extra one free'.
- It must provide facilities for management to monitor stock levels and produce reports for local and head-office management.

Some supermarket chains have recently started allowing customers to checkout their own trolley or basket of goods and then take their bill for payment to a central payments' desk. Spot checks are used to combat any attempt at fiddling by the customer.

## Benefits

The main benefits of a supermarket computerised system are labour saving, while providing a better customer service. Checkout productivity is increased, mistakes minimised, while the customer receives an itemised bill and overall improved service. Cash flow is also improved. Goods can be re-ordered automatically and re-pricing of any product line is easier as the system requires no price labels being attached to each individual item, although shelf labels will require change. Several retail organisations have 'club' or 'membership' cards that are used when making purchases and provide discounts or points. Such cards attract the customer to return and at the same time the company has access to very useful marketing information that can be used to mail-shot customers about new or coming shopping events.

### Limitations

The advantages of a supermarket computerised system can only be achieved providing the system is reliable and readily available. Should the store's computer system fail, then it would be virtually impossible for it to operate. Non barcoded products (like fruit and vegetables) can be accommodated, but require increased checkout operator action. Use of such systems may also require an expensive initial investment to re-equip stores and re-train the personnel in its use.

## Booking systems

A computerised booking system is commonplace today throughout the travel and holiday industry. It is central to the operation of most airlines, vehicle hire companies, sea ferry operators, holiday companies, hotels and the associated travel agencies. Customers may use the services of a travel agency to gather the relevant information regarding a journey or holiday, they can also contact travel and holiday companies direct by telephone and make their own arrangements.

Whatever method is used the IT booking system provides the following on-line service.

- It provides information about the availability of seats or places on flights, hotels, or some holiday package.
- It easily turns initial enquiries into a provisional booking, identified by a unique booking reference number, which can be held for the customer for several days.
- It allows the customer to confirm the booking by paying a deposit (paid by cash or credit card) and the payment is recorded on the system. Credit card deposits can easily be paid over the telephone, although some companies will require the customer to accompany the deposit with a completed booking form as confirmation.
- It produces invoices for full payment. Later, usually eight to ten weeks prior to departure, the system will produce an invoice to the customer for the balance due, and payment can again be made by telephone using a credit card.
- It produces travel tickets and hotel vouchers, or triggers the sending of them. Just prior to departure (within two weeks), tickets and other necessary documents will be sent to the customer for them to use on their journey or holiday.
- It produces management reports showing booking and other statistics.

### Benefits

A computerised booking system provides the company with up-to-date availability, enabling them to operate at higher occupancy levels. They are also able to provide an improved customer service by reducing the chances of over or double booking. Customers may make and pay for holidays by telephone.

### Limitations

The information held on the booking system must be up to date and reflect the current offerings of the company. Many companies rely heavily on electronic communications to do their business on-line and so customers may experience severe delays when trying to make a telephone connection in order to make a booking or enquiry. As the data for such systems is on-line, they must be secure to prevent unauthorised access and any customer data should be confidential. For system operators the usability of the system will have health and safety implications.

## Mail-order systems

A computerised mail-order system is a particular example of a sales order processing system common to most businesses that sell goods or services. Although mail-order is different in that it is accessible to the general public. Like the booking systems described earlier, these systems can operate via an agency or by direct contact with the customer. Orders can be made direct by telephone and processed immediately or by completing a paper order-form that is then posted to the company and processed on receipt.

Whether by telephone or by paper, the order is processed by an operator using a computer terminal that:

- provides on-line access to product and customer data;
- records the current stock level of any item is readily available – customers can be immediately advised if any item is out of stock and therefore unavailable, and the operator may be able to suggest an alternative that is in stock and available;
- produces the necessary paper documentation after the order is accepted, which will accompany the items when they are delivered to the customer;
- updates customer accounts – payment may be required with the order, although some customers will have an account which is updated with the order details;
- produces invoices and statements to account customers requesting payment;
- produces management reports, particularly for marketing.

### Benefits

The benefits of a computerised mail-order system are similar to those for on-line booking systems, in that an improved customer service is provided enabling shopping from the house. The customer details provide an on-line customer base for marketing mailshots.

### Limitations

The limitations of a computerised mail-order system are largely concerned with the reliability and availability of the computer system. As with booking systems, security of the system from unauthorised access and the operators health and safety aspects are important features.

## Electronic funds transfer (EFT)

**Electronic funds transfer (EFT)** is used in many of the above systems. Retail outlets can allow the customer to pay for their goods or services using 'plastic' payment card (such as a credit or direct debit card) via an **electronic point of sale terminal (EPOS)**. Payroll systems use the **Banks Automated Clearing System (BACS)**, to enable payment of an employee's salary directly to their bank account. Holiday booking invoices, mail order invoices and other household payments can be made by giving payment card details over the telephone.

Such systems debit the payer's account and credits the payee's account, using electronic transactions that flow between the respective computer systems holding the accounts of the store and the credit card company, or the employee and the employer.

With an EPOS system, the card is swiped through a reader. Communications line contact is made with the payment card company and the respective account (identified by the card). The total value of the sale is transmitted through to the card's account. A receipt is provided for the customer, who signs it, and the transaction is listed on a monthly statement to be received by the customer from the payment card company. Petrol forecourts have pumps that allow the driver to choose a method of payment, by payment card at the pump or by any method at the kiosk.

## Benefits

Electronic funds transfer systems have the following benefits. EFT systems reduce paperwork and can improve security. In payroll systems there is no need to make up pay-packets or produce pay-cheques. The employee need not visit their bank to pay in their salary, and the amount is credited to the employee's account on a particular day each month. Payment cards reduce the quantity of cash that must be handled by a retail outlet. They make paying easier for the customer who need not carry large amounts of cash but may also encourage customers to spend more. On petrol forecourts pump payment can result in quicker service.

## Limitations

Accuracy and correct data are import requirements of EFT systems, they are also open to electronic fraud, so security is another important consideration. The Barings Bank collapse is an excellent example of using a computer system to obtain vast amounts of money and to cover up misdealings. Stolen payment cards can be used by others to make purchases, however once reported stolen, EPOS may reduce the possibility of fraudulent use. However, credit card fraud is a major crime industry.

*Modern DIY retail stores have checkouts where laser-operated wands are used to scan bar codes on products.*

## Question 1.1

*Which is the main benefit of these checkouts to the customer?*

*A   it is faster to go through the checkout*

*B   there is more choice of products*

*C   prices are cheaper*

*D   shelves are never empty*

## Question 1.2

Which is the main benefit to the DIY store?

A   products are re-ordered immediately

B   staff enjoy using the computers

C   shelves are never empty

D   checkout operators need less training

## Question 1.3

A customer may pay for purchases using a payment card. Which IT development has made this possible?

A   stock control systems

B   electronic funds transfer

C   order processing

D   booking systems

## Task 1.1   PC 1

Make arrangements to visit a local private company that uses IT, e.g. a travel agent, vehicle hire company, music store, or supermarket. Observe how the IT is used, interview staff, management and operators about their use of IT. Prepare a report that describes benefits and limitations of one particular commercial IT system, the company may have several. The report should present points of view from both the customer and the company perspective.

## Task 1.2   PC 1

Make arrangements to visit a local 'public' organisation, e.g. the local authority offices, a school, college, or utility (electricity, gas, water) company. Observe how IT is used, interview staff at all levels about their use of IT. Prepare a report that describes the benefits and limitations of one particular commercial IT system (the organisation is likely to have many). The report should present points of view from both the customer/user perspective and the company perspective.

## 1.1.2 Industrial systems

Industrial computerised systems are involved with industrial activities concerned with manufacturing and process control. As with commercial systems, many of these system activities have been done manually by people without the use of a computer. They usually involve carrying out repetitive assembly and other factory shop-floor tasks or the monitoring of processes by observation and manual control. The availability of such systems has changed how some processes are carried out, and given greater flexibility and reliability of process monitoring and control, while providing information and services that were not available in the past. The techniques used also have application within the home where embedded systems control their appliance.

Early examples of such computerised industrial applications are the use of robots in the manufacturing process, a common domestic example is the control of washing machine by a small embedded computer system.

## Design systems

The drawing office, where technicians produced high quality drawings using pencil and paper, has all but disappeared from most manufacturing companies. The skills required remain, but the tools used today are computers using sophisticated drawing and design tools called a **Computer Aided Design (CAD)** software package.

CAD has traditionally been associated with engineers and scientists to design industrial equipment and state-of-the-art products, but today it is associated with all types of design work. Examples of the use of CAD are 'wire frame' diagrams that can be rotated and viewed from all angles – these have often featured on TV programs showing how some new product, car or aeroplane was conceived and designed. The 'wire frame' image can also be filled in by the CAD package to produce a three-dimensional object. CAD packages are very powerful systems and require extensive computer power to perform some of their actions. The increase in power of the PC has enabled CAD packages, like AutoCAD, to be widely used. CAD is also used to design such things as company logos, initial introductory frames of TV programs, buildings, road bridges, kitchens and printed circuit-board layouts.

Once a design has been produced using CAD it can be tested using computer-based simulation that models the operating conditions under which the product will be used. The aerodynamics of a car design or the visual impact of a road bridge design can both be simulated and useful data or feedback obtained. Other related CAD products can produce high quality pictures of finished household products (such as HiFi units) that simulate the appearance of many materials used in their construction.

### Benefits

The CAD system provides its user with an extensive array of tools to enable high quality two- and three-dimensional drawings to be produced accurately and efficiently. The drawings are easily changed and allow quick viewing of alternative designs, designs may also be projected into a simulated environment allowing the designer to view its effect. Designs produced can be saved, re-loaded and amended as required.

### Limitations

CAD systems require a great deal of computer power and are heavy users of the processor for calculations, and until recently required the use of expensive specialised hardware. However, the increase in power of the microcomputer and the fall in hardware costs has meant that the initial costs of such systems are no longer such a limitation. Special purpose hardware (such as high-resolution large-screen monitors, digitising tablets and plotters) are still required, and do push up the price of a complete system. Given an increasing market due to the greater availability of the hardware, software prices have also fallen. Special training in the use of the package will also be required. Dependence on a computer system for CAD means that system reliability and backup is a major requirement for such systems. In a competitive world, where new designs are highly secret, security and prevention of unauthorised access is also a requirement.

## Publishing

Newspaper, magazine and book production has been revolutionised by the use of IT. **Desktop publishing (DTP)** uses the computer to produce near typeset quality copy that can be printed immediately using a laser printer to produce paper copy or a printing plate for use in the actual printing process. Such systems do away with the need for the traditional typesetting and paste-up process of 'newspaper' production. A DTP package allows documents to be physically pasted together and rearranged. The documents can contain text in columns and of varying fonts and size, photographs or pictures that have been scanned into the computer, and artwork designed using a graphics or CAD package. The finished page can be viewed prior to printing using WYSIWYG ('What You See Is What You Get') and any adjustments made. The DTP software will provide camera-ready copy for all types of printed document.

### Benefits

Document composition involves bringing together text, graphics and pictures into a designed document layout, and using a DTP package does this effectively and efficiently. DTP allows professional-looking documents to be produced within an organisation without having to use the services of a specialised printer. For newspapers, such systems coupled to image-setters enable 'hold the front page' to become an eleventh hour reality that enables them to accommodate late breaking news events. Such systems allow the re-scheduling of 'stories' to later editions.

### Limitations

Extended use of DTP in the publishing industry will require investment in expensive additional hardware, however this capital outlay will usually pay for itself within a couple of years. Such packages have many features and training in its use is essential. Document design is a highly creative and imaginative 'art' and not all users of DTP systems possess these aesthetic skills.

## Process control

A process control system uses IT to monitor and control the operation of some system – the inputs, outputs and flows within the system are monitored by sensors and regulated as necessary. The IT system influences the outcomes or conditions of the system it controls. The process is constantly monitored by the IT system and should it begin to deviate from the norm, the IT system will trigger some corrective action or raise an alarm! Such systems are used extensively in the petro-chemical industry, electricity generation, gas and water supply industries, and to fly passenger aeroplanes. In a long haul flight from London to Tokyo the pilot may only actually fly the plane for say twenty minutes, for the first ten minutes after takeoff and the last ten minutes prior to landing. In between times the aeroplane is under the control of the pre-programmed in-flight computer that monitors progress, controls the engines, maintains altitude and communicates with satellite navigation aids. However, the pilot does have the ability to intervene to take control of the aeroplane, say to alter course or altitude to avoid a storm. Domestic examples that use small embedded IT systems are central heating control systems, security alarms and washing machine programs.

### Benefits

Process control systems require less human intervention and allow the process to take place unsupervised. The washing machine can be used at night while the family sleeps. In safety systems the continuous monitoring by the computer should improve the chances of detecting any malfunction early.

### Limitations

For small-scale domestic systems the disadvantages are that when things go wrong with the piece of electronic gadgetry it usually cannot be repaired, and a complete replacement will be needed, which may be expensive. For large-scale industrial applications, the initial investment will be costly and require specialist installation. Where malfunctions of equipment on such systems are frequent and cause false alarms, a real warning may be ignored at first. Where a system has a high degree of control it may trigger off a sequence of events that make matters worse or overreact. There are examples of automatic monitoring systems in the financial markets overreacting in this way.

## Robotics

The integration of IT with robotics is, in reality, generally associated with the manufacturing process. Industrial robots are basically a mechanical arm under the control of a computer system. The arm has components similar to the human arm (e.g. elbow, forearm, wrist) and can perform motions and actions similar to those of the human arm, but with much greater precision and without getting tired. They are also very useful for working in hazardous environments. The car industry uses robots on assembly lines for assembly of engines, paint spraying and welding, the electronics industry uses them in the assembly of circuit boards. Robots can also be used in combination with process control systems to select and remove reject items. In warehouse systems, robot 'storemen' can be used to store and retrieve items from computerised racking systems that use 'vision' and 'sensing' systems.

### Benefits

Robotic systems provide a reliable and dependable workforce that is punctual, seldom sick, and doesn't complain or answer back. They can reduce labour costs by making production or the service cheaper. They often result in improving productivity and quality of the product made or job done.

### Limitations

The cost of an initial investment in robotics will be high, however they may have quite a long working life which should enable a healthy payback on this initial outlay. The introduction of robots is often poorly received by the workforce who feel that their jobs are under threat and this leads to industrial unrest. Robots perform single specific tasks in prescribed sequences and must be 'trained' to perform that task. They, like any other electronic equipment, may malfunction and need repair or replacement.

## Health care

Hospitals are major users of IT. Having commercial systems for patient records and other administrative tasks; and industrial systems that control machines and monitor patients. Many life-support machines are computer-controlled and can be set up to suit the requirements of individual patients. During a theatre operation, particularly one involving complex surgery, patients are wired up to computers that monitor their condition and constantly display this to theatre staff. Using IT in this way has reduced the risk associated with many of these operations. During recovery after an operation, computers are used to monitor the patient and alert staff should any problems arise.

IT is used extensively in diagnostic equipment, such as CAT and MR scanners that provide video pictures of the inside or cross-section of a body. Such information enable doctors to take better informed decisions regarding the treatment of their patient's condition.

### Benefits

The benefits of such systems will be in improved health care and service for patients.

### Limitations

The equipment used in the health service is some of the most expensive, often costing hundreds of thousands of pounds for one machine. As new machines become available to carry out new tasks, so specialist personnel must be trained to use them. There have been many instances of a hospital being unable to use expensive equipment due to the unavailability of suitably trained staff. The health and safety features of such machines are important issues that affect both the patient and the staff who operate them throughout each day.

## Vehicle and traffic systems

On-board computers are common in many cars today. Digital display devices provide the driver with information, such as the inside and outside temperature, current miles per gallon and battery charging voltage. In addition, many car engines are controlled by computers to help them maintain optimum performance, and these can also be connected to diagnostic computers when being serviced to help trace faults. Companies running fleets of lorries can use on-board IT and satellite communications to track where each truck is. There are plans to give each vehicle on the road an electronic identification tag that can trigger road-side sensors and accumulate data on individual vehicle road use. Emergency vehicles could be fitted with map display devices that would show their current position and help the find the quickest route to where their assistance is needed.

Road vehicles are beginning to use satellite navigation systems. Shipping and aircraft have been big users of such systems for many years, as 'there are no signposts at sea or in the air'. A recent experiment has utilised satellite navigation linked to a local computer for a blind person, who is fitted with a transceiver to aid travelling on foot about town.

Traffic lights are controlled by computers that can to react to changing traffic conditions. On main roads of a city the lights can be set to speed incoming traffic flow in the early morning 'rush hour' prior to 9 am, revert to 'normal' status during the working day, then be reset to speed outgoing traffic in the evening 'rush hour' to 6 pm. Many police forces use speed cameras to monitor vehicle speeds on urban roads and motorways – these take snap shots of vehicles recording the date, time and speed. Providing the registration number is visible on the photograph, drivers breaking the speed limit can be 'caught' and fined, and they may not be aware of it!

## Benefits

On-board vehicle systems can provide improved information for the driver in the same way that aircraft systems have for pilots. Engine management systems improve engine performance, can aid maintenance and help trace faults. Route planners and map display devices can save money in transport costs. Computerised traffic control systems can react to local events and smooth the traffic flow.

## Limitations

Adding computerised systems to vehicles increases their cost and can result in increased maintenance. The vehicle systems can become reliant on the electronic devices – when these devices fail it can result in total loss of information to the driver which may make the engine inoperable. Failure of the traffic lights computer may cause havoc over the whole area controlled by it. The installation of traffic control hardware may have an impact on the environment with the need to provide gantries and wire connections.

 *A car manufacturer intends installing robots on its production line to help build its cars and to use CAD to design new cars.*

## *Question 1.4*

*Which is the main advantage of using robots for the car manufacturing company?*

*A  car production is cheaper*

*B  cars are safer*

*C  cars are available in more colours*

*D  car production takes less space*

## Question 1.5

Which is the main advantage of using robots for the car worker?

A they work shorter hours

B they do more interesting work

C they do less hazardous work

D they get paid more

## Question 1.6

Which is the main limitation of using robots on the production line?

A efficiency

B cost

C security

D accuracy

## Question 1.7

What benefit will the CAD system have for the manufacturer's designers?

A fewer design staff are required

B designs are easier to change

C fewer models have to be designed

D choice of colour scheme is automated

## Question 1.8

What is the main disadvantage of a CAD system?

A designers take longer to design a car

B fewer design options are available

C hardware and software are expensive

D fewer designers are employed

## Task 1.3  PC 2

*Make arrangements to visit a local organisation that uses industrial IT systems, e.g. a local hospital, factory, newspaper, printer or utility company. Observe how the industrial IT system is used, interview staff, management and operators about their use of IT. Prepare a report that describes the benefits and limitations of one particular industrial IT system (the company may have several). The report should present points of view from both the process and the company perspective.*

## Task 1.4  PC 2

*Observe how IT systems are used within your house or a friend's house. Prepare a report that describes the benefits and limitations for the householder of one particular IT system (the house may have several).*

### 1.1.3  Features of commercial systems

An IT commercial system will in general have **data** that is processed, **hardware** that does the physical processing, **people** who operate the hardware, **processing activities** that carry out specific tasks, and **software** that logically controls the hardware and processing activities. The systems will seek to perform in an effective manner and meet the requirements of its users and exist for a specified purpose.

Data is processed by the computer and can be divided into three categories as follows.

- **Input data** is captured by the system. This is usually a **transaction** record, e.g. the product code in the supermarket system, the clock card data in a payroll system, the customer and holiday details in a system booking, and the cheque details in a banking system.

- **Stored** or **file data** is referenced and updated during the processing of the input data. This data is often stored in **master files**, e.g. the product stock file containing its price, the employee payroll record containing a tax code and year to date values, holiday file containing availability data, bank account file holding current balance and other details.

- **Output data** is produced from the system in the form of screen displays or hard copy printed document, report or list, e.g. the itemised till roll, the weekly payslip, the holiday invoice, a bank statement.

## Question 1.9

*A requisition note, filled out to obtain an item from stores within a factory, is an example of what?*

*A  output data*

*B  stored data*

*C  input data*

*D  auxiliary data*

### Question 1.10

*An employee weekly payslip is an example of what?*

*A output data*

*B stored data*

*C input data*

*D auxiliary data*

### Question 1.11

*A customer account record held in a bank is an example of what?*

*A output data*

*B stored data*

*C input data*

*D auxiliary data*

## Hardware

Hardware comprises the physical components or devices of the IT system and can be divided into the following.

- **Input** or **data capture devices**, that provide a means for entering or capturing data into the computer system, the laser scanner of the supermarket checkout reads the product barcodes, a keyboard will be used to enter clock-card data for the payroll, a magnetic ink character reader for scanning cheques;

- **main processor unit**, this carries out the actual data processing under the control of software. It consists of a central processing unit or chip and memory for holding software instructions and data. In the supermarket this unit will be located in the administrative offices of the store and will be connected to each checkout;

- **output devices**, that produce results from the processing of data, on display screens or paper. Hard copy printers may use different technologies to produce the printed image, the traditional (noisy) impact using a ribbon and character 'hammers', today many offices use the laser or ink-jet technology that are not only quieter but provide many extra facilities. In the supermarket details of each individual item scanned is displayed on a small digital screen and on completion a printed receipt is produced detailing each item and tallying the total. In a payroll system an impact printer will usually print payslips and pay-cheques on special continuous stationery;

- **data storage devices**, that are able to store data permanently or temporally for later use by software. A large capacity disk storage system would be used to keep the product file for the supermarket system. Magnetic disks, the portable floppy or the built in hard Winchester disk of many PC systems are the most common form of data storage, other forms include CD-ROM, magnetic tape in cassette form or larger spool and video tape.

# People

People are largely involved in operating the computer systems, either as users where the use of the computer is an essential part of their job duties, or as computer operations personnel responsible for keeping the system going and performing general housekeeping operations.

- **Data capture personnel** make up a very large body of people who operate the data capture equipment of a commercial system, usually to perform a specific task. In a supermarket system the checkout operator in one such person, in a holiday booking system it will be the travel agency employee.

- **End-user personnel** perform similar activities to the data capture staff, however, they tend to use the computer system to carry out a variety of different tasks usually within the office environment.

- **Operations personnel** are people who are responsible for the day-to-day running and administration of a computer system. Many systems today require very little 'operator' intervention. In some systems these tasks may be undertaken by someone from the user group, whereas for large corporate systems or distributed systems there will be a team of people carrying out operations tasks. Operations tasks will involve loading printers with special stationery, taking security backups and configuring system hardware and software.

- **Analysis, designer** and **development personnel** are the 'computer people' who are responsible for the overall development of a computerised system to meet the requirements of its users. These are the systems analyst and computer programmers who have special skills that enable them to produce reliable systems that can be used by the user group.

## Question 1.12

A network manager is which type of IT person?

A data capture

B end-user

C operations

D development

## Question 1.13

A travel agent clerk is which type of IT person?

A data capture

B end-user

C operations

D development

## Question 1.14

*A computer programmer is which type of IT person?*

*A  data capture*

*B  end-user*

*C  operations*

*D  development*

## Question 1.15

*The electricity and gas companies often ask their customers to complete meter reading cards and post them to the company. What type of activity is the customer performing?*

*A  data capture*

*B  file update*

*C  system development*

*D  data storage*

## Processing activities

Processing activities within a commercial system will depend on the system's function. The system will have to process transactions input and used to **update** or **maintain** the master data files stored in the system. Some transaction activities (whether they are manual or computerised) must be carried out in a particular sequence if the system is to function correctly. In order for any computer system to function effectively, its users must follow a set procedure. This is usually a checklist of tasks to be carried out on one transaction or group of transactions, in a particular time sequence. Once entered into the system, a transaction will be processed and will normally be used to update one or more stored data files within the system. Other activities may involve **sorting, merging** and **collating** of input data or output results.

In a payroll system, a transaction would be an amendment to an employee pay record (e.g. a tax code change), all such amendments should be applied to the master payroll file prior to starting the main payroll processing-run.

In a supermarket system, one type of transaction would be a product price change. All of the price changes must have been applied to the product records before processing the first product they apply to. Each product passed through the checkout will generate a transaction that updates the systems data files.

**Batch processing** is where data to be input to a system may need collating and manual controls applied before entry to the system as a batch of transactions, e.g. on completion of processing hard-copy printed documents or reports will need to be distributed to relevant personnel. Accounting systems often handle sales and purchase data in batches collated daily.

**On-line processing** is where systems process transactions on-line, handling each one immediately as it occurs, output may be immediate or later in a report. A stores system will often immediately update the master stock file with issues from and receipts to stock as they occur, producing a summarised stock movements report at the end of each day.

## Question 1.16

*Booking an airline seat using a travel agent is an example of which type of processing?*

*A batch*

*B on-line*

*C sorting*

*D collating*

## Software

Software comprises the computer programs that operate and control the computer system for specific purposes. There are several categories of software as follows.

- **Application software** is used for specific commercial applications, e.g. payroll, accounts, stock control and order processing. These systems may be obtained 'off the shelf' as a package or may be 'made to measure' by carrying out a bespoke systems design and development where software is specially written.

- **Office software** is used for general purpose office activities, e.g. wordprocessing, spreadsheets, presentation systems and E-mail.

- **Operating system** software provides an environment for using the above categories of software. The operating system closely controls and monitors the systems hardware resources. Examples are MS-DOS, Windows '95, OS/2, Novell, UNIX and VMS. Associated with the operating system will be utility and accessory software that performs basic text editing, file management, file copying and conversion, file printing and file security.

- **Application development software** comprises the third generation programming languages and the more recent fourth generation software development environments, used to write bespoke and packaged application software. Popular programming languages are C and C++, COBOL, Pascal and Delphi, Visual Basic. Database development products include Access, Paradox, Oracle, Ingres and Informix, that provide a faster but slightly less flexible development environment to the earlier languages.

## Question 1.17

*Windows NT is an example of which type of software?*

*A application*

*B office*

*C operating system*

*D development*

# Question 1.18

*Access is an example of which type of software?*

*A application*

*B office*

*C operating system*

*D development*

# Question 1.19

*Quattro spreadsheet is an example of which type of software?*

*A application*

*B office*

*C operating system*

*D development*

# Question 1.20

*Sage accounts is an example of which type of software?*

*A application*

*B office*

*C operating system*

*D development*

# Task 1.5    PC 3

*For one of the commercial IT systems that you investigated in Tasks 1.1 or 1.2, or any other commercial IT system you have investigated, write a report that explains its principal features under the headings of purpose, data, hardware, people, processing, software and effectiveness. You should analyse its effectiveness by talking to and observing as many people connected with the system as possible.*

## 1.1.4 Features of industrial systems

An IT industrial system will have the same general features of data, hardware, people, processing activities and software as described for commercial systems. However, there are a number of differences, particularly in the hardware and people features. Industrial systems have often been referred to as real-time systems, because they interact directly with their environment and often need to respond quickly, in real-time, to events that occur. They also tend to operate continuously 24 hours a day, on every day of the year.

- **Data** tends to be input and output in smaller packages, from and to a variety of devices. Input is from sensor devices that monitor activities, while output to devices may be triggered by input or elapsed time. Data storage is in the form of log files that store values' input and output together with a date and time stamp.

- **Hardware** for input to an industrial system can consist of a variety of data capture devices or sensors that monitor processes and feedback measurements to the central system, output devices can alter process conditions on receipt of instructions from the system.

- **People** are dramatically reduced in numbers in a computerised industrial system. The reason for adopting the system is often to reduce the need for personnel to carry out certain tasks, some of which might be hazardous. The people involvement with industrial systems is in a control room monitoring capacity, where they observe system performance and condition through display devices, here they may be alerted to abnormal conditions that require their intervention.

- **Processing** within an industrial system tends to be continuous when it is operating. The input sensors are constantly monitoring the process being controlled and passing readings back to the main processing unit. The processing unit analyses the readings received and if necessary will trigger any corrective action or raise some warning or alarm. When a large variety of signals are being received the system must be able to give priority to the most important and usually most critical events, less important events may be delayed. For example, a home security system starts processing once it is 'armed' and will continue to monitor house 'movements', through sensors placed around the house, until disarmed. If movement is detected, the system will raise an alarm should an intruder not correctly disarm the system within a short set time.

- **Software** basically consists of two components, the operating system and the specialised applications software developed specifically for the industrial application. Such software must have the capability of simultaneously handling a number and variety of different devices and must be able to respond quickly enough to any one of them in order to have any effect on their activities.

### Question 1.21

*Using a dial to select a particular washing machine program is an example of which operation?*

*A  data capture*

*B  process monitoring*

*C  process control*

*D  hardware selection*

## Question 1.22

*Checking the state of the magnetic sensors placed on outside doors is an example of which type of operation?*

*A   data capture*

*B   process monitoring*

*C   process control*

*D   hardware selection*

## Question 1.23

*Ignoring a movement caused by post or newspapers dropping through a letter box and detected by a movement sensor is an example of which type of operation?*

*A   data capture*

*B   process monitoring*

*C   process control*

*D   hardware selection*

## Task 1.6    PC 4

*For one of the industrial IT systems that you investigated in Tasks 1.3 or 1.4, or any other industrial IT system you have investigated, write a report that explains its principal features under the headings of purpose, data, hardware, people, processing, software and effectiveness. You should analyse its effectiveness by talking to as many people connected with the system as possible.*

# Examine the components of a stand-alone system

At the centre of any IT application system will be a computer. A **computer** is a processing machine, an electronic device that is able to store instructions or commands and then execute those instructions to carry out some task. In order to function, the computer processing unit requires **data** that it **processes** and turns into **information**.

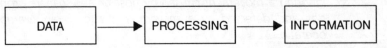

*Figure 1.3 Data input, processing, information output*

The physical computer system that we see or touch (the 'boxes') is called the computer **hardware**, the logical computer system that we can't 'see' is called the **software**. The computer's software controls its hardware.

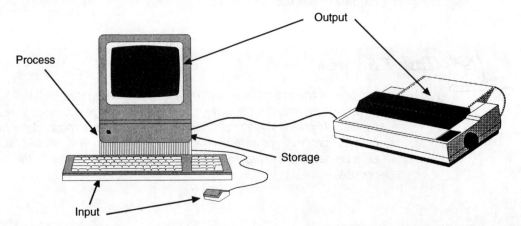

*Figure 1.4 The components of a micro-computer system*

Any computer system has four basic components for input, processing, storage and output, as figure 1.4 shows. The input component allows the 'user' to communicate with the processing component; the storage component is able to hold commands and data for use by the processing component; the output component allows the processing component to communicate with the 'user'.

Data flows between the components (as shown in figure 1.5), but there is no direct communication between the input and output components, or the input and storage components, or the storage and output components. Everything is routed through the processing component.

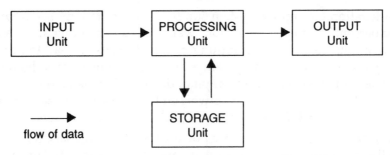

Figure 1.5 A computer system block diagram

## Question 1.24

*A human being is a living computer system. List its input, processing, storage and output components.*

## Computer system types

There are many different types of computer systems. They are classified by their power (which is related to their size, in terms of storage capacity) and their processing speed (how quickly they do things). The distinction between one type of computer system and the next may not be very clear – categorising computers in this way acts only as a guide and is no way definitive. The types in descending order of their processing capabilities are as follows.

- **Supercomputers** are very high performance systems capable of processing large amounts of data very quickly. They are very expensive and are used mainly in specialised scientific and mathematical applications such as weather forecasting, where there is a requirement to do many calculations in the shortest possible time.

- **Mainframes** are large centralised computer systems that are able to support hundreds of users simultaneously. They are able to handle a variety of processing applications as required by their users. These systems were expensive to purchase initially, have an expensive annual maintenance charge, require specialist operator support and often require an air-conditioned room to operate in. Today such systems are being phased out and replaced by networks of smaller systems, often using a client server architecture for a fraction of the mainframe costs.

- **Minicomputers** are smaller and cheaper, but less powerful, offering less capability than a mainframe. Originally such systems would usually support less than a hundred users simultaneously and would have less variety in the processing supported. As computer power has increased, so the distinction between superminis and mainframes has become blurred.

- **Microcomputers** or **personal computers (PCs)** are low cost, small stand-alone computer systems based on the microprocessor on a single silicon chip. Originally developed for the personal computer market for hobbyists by companies such as Apple, they were given a stamp of approval by IBM in the early eighties. Today the micro is now found in most offices from the largest to the smallest of organisations and in millions of homes. They now come in many forms: pocket PC, laptop PC, desktop PC and tower PC, and can be linked together to form powerful processing networks. The latest micros can now provide processing power that previously was only available in minis and micros, and provide it at a cheaper price.

25

- **Workstation** a computer system similar in power to a minicomputer that was used by one person. The main applications were in CAD and other applications, using graphics or requiring substantial computing power. The system had to provide a fast powerful processor, large amounts of main and secondary memory, a high resolution VDU and maybe support of additional graphics devices. They tended to use an operating system such as UNIX and were often networked to share software and printing. The more powerful PCs now available have began to challenge such systems.

- **Fileservers** are specialised more powerful PCs that manage a PC network and provide additional services, such as software and data sharing. Today, many organisations are installing client server systems that are a development from the original fileserver concept.

The topics that follow apply to all types of computer system, but make reference to typical stand-alone microcomputer systems.

## 1.2.1 Hardware components

The central component of the hardware of a computer system is the **main processor unit**. It is served by the other hardware components of input, output and data storage devices, often called **peripheral** devices.

## Bits and binary

The **digital** computer stores and manipulates data using the **binary** (base 2) number system. Binary has just two digits, 0 and 1. These digits can easily be represented electronically by switching something 'off' or 'on'. Some binary numbers with their equivalent decimal, base 10, values are:

$$0001_2 = 1_{10} \qquad 0010_2 = 2_{10} \qquad 0011_2 = 3_{10} \qquad 1111_2 = 15_{10} \qquad 1000000000_2 = 1024_{10}$$

**Bits** (**b**inary dig**its**) are used to store items in the computer's memory. Each bit has one of only two possible values '0' or '1'.

A **byte** is a group of **eight** bits. A byte is the basic identifiable or addressable unit of storage of computer memory, it is also used to state the capacity and speed of the different types of storage and other hardware components. A memory location of one byte can represent one character of data, a single letter ('A', 'a', 'B', 'b', 'C', etc) or single **digit** ('1', '2', '3', etc) or single **symbol** ('%', '+', '-', etc). Examples of byte bit patterns are:

| | | | |
|---|---|---|---|
| A = 01000001 | a = 01100001 | 1 = 00110001 | + = 00101011 |
| B = 01000010 | b = 01100010 | 2 = 00110010 | { = 01111011 |

## Question 1.25

*Which character or symbol does the following byte bit pattern '00110011' represent?*

*A  C*

*B  3*

*C  c*

*D  }*

# Input component

Data needed by a computer system for processing originates in many places and in many forms. Before that data can be processed by and stored in a computer system, it must be converted into a form that the computer can interpret. Input devices perform this activity: they allow data to be input or captured, converted to a form that the computer understands, and then passed on to the main processing unit for processing.

In commercial systems, the input device allows the user to communicate with the system. In industrial systems, the input device passes data readings from some process back to the central control system. The trend in data entry has been to enter data as close to its originating source as possible by reducing the need to transcribe data manually from one form to another. There are many types of input device that provide a variety of **interfaces** for using the computer system. These are explained as follows>

- **Keyboard** – most computers use the standard QWERTY keyboard of 102 keys. These keys include: the letters of the alphabet ('A' to 'Z', 'a' to 'z'), the numbers ('0' to '9'), punctuation and other text symbols (, . ; : ? + * / – ( )). There are also additional keys that perform functions for use with the screen and software. Where the range of input is narrow (such as in the retail trade), the typing keyboard may be replaced with a set of keys that relate to each product or service available (fast-food restaurants are often users of such an interface on their computerised tills).

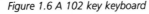

*Figure 1.6 A 102 key keyboard*

*Figure 1.7 A two button mouse*

- **Mouse** – this is a point and press device that is used with **graphical user interface (GUI)** with Windows-based software and also with graphics software. It is a hand-held device that controls the position of the screen cursor. Mouse buttons are single or double clicked to make a screen selection or initiate some activity. Some systems provide mouse-like support through having **touch-screens**, where the user points to selections by pressing the screen with a finger (information kiosks often use this type of interface).

- **Joystick, tracker ball, digitiser tablet and pen**, and **light pen** – these are other point-and-draw input devices used to move the graphics cursor. The joystick and tracker ball are popular devices in video arcade games, but, like the other devices, have a more serious use in CAD and other graphics systems.

- **Scanners** – these are optical light sensitive or magnetic devices that can 'read' printed characters, different types of codes (such as a barcode) and magnetic swipe cards.

  - **Barcode laser scanning device** reads barcodes attached to items. The device may either be fixed, where the items to be read are passed over it, or portable, where a hand held 'wand' is waved over the item to be read.

  - **Magnetic ink character readers (MICR)** require the use a special text font and are used extensively by banks to scan cheques.

  - **Optical mark readers (OMR)** scan marks placed on a defined grid or dial within a document. They are used to enter meter readings, play the national lottery and computer mark multichoice examination questions.

  - **Optical character or text (OCR)** scanners can read documents such as order forms and pages of text. Some scanners are portable and are dragged over the document, others are of the flat bed type similar to a photocopier.

  - **Image scanners** can read drawings and photographs to produce a computerised digitised image.

  - **Badge or magnetic swipe card** and **smart card scanners** are common place in banking and retail stores. They also control the use of facilities such as entry to car parks, computer laboratories or identification of staff when using tills in bars and restaurants. They can also be used as localised payment cards for use by members of a club, the card is encoded with an initial spending amount which is reduced each time the card is used.

- **Sensors** use a variety of technologies to capture data from the environment. Sensor devices can be used to measure temperature, liquid or gas flows, light, vibration, sound and even taste. Light sensors can detect movement events and log usage of a facility, when used in vision-inspection systems they can detect defective parts.

- **Voice speech input systems** are used in two ways:

  - The user speaks, the system records the user's voice (it does not try to interpret what has been spoken) and it stores the recording which can be played back later, possibly by another user and on another system.

  - The second method involves speech recognition which works with a defined limited vocabulary of spoken commands. The systems are speaker dependent and need training to the users voice patterns in order for the system to interpret what command has been spoken.

## Question 1.26

*Which of the following is **not** an input device?*

*A   screen*

*B   mouse*

*C   keyboard*

*D   microphone*

## Question 1.27

*The National Lottery uses which method to scan tickets?*

*A   magnetic ink character recognition*

*B   optical mark sensing*

*C   text reading*

*D   keyboard typing*

## Processor component

The **main processor unit** comprises the electronic hardware components that are 'boxed' to form the central part of the computer system. The pieces that make up the box are the central processing unit (CPU), the motherboard, device controller boards, input-output ports and storage memory.

- **Central processing unit (CPU)** or 'chip' is the computer's brain. It has two main parts, the **control unit** and the **arithmetic/logic unit (ALU)**. It processes instructions and data while interacting with all the other components, particularly memory. The control unit receives program instructions from the memory one at a time, and supervises their execution by sending out signals to other components.
  - The speed at which the control unit carries out its operations is measured in millions of cycles or pulses per second, **Megahertz (MHz)**. The higher the MHz, the faster the computer can work. Today many Pentium PCs operate at 100MHz and a fast processor will operate in excess of 150MHz.
  - The ALU carries out the basic arithmetic operations of addition, subtraction, multiplication and division, and the logical operations that can manipulate data and determine if something is true or false.

*Figure 1.8 A chip with ant for size comparison*

- The chip or processor type is continually being developed with new versions or models emerging each year. The latest model found in most new IBM PC compatible micro-computers is the Pentium or 586 chip, it is the latest from the 80xxx family from the Intel company. Apple Macs use the Motorola 68xxx chip family. Each new version provides additional speed and increased processing capability enabling the micro-computer to become more and more powerful.

- **Motherboard** is the main system board. It is an electronic circuit board that holds and connects together the CPU, primary memory, controller boards and input/output ports. The CPU chip, memory chips and controller boards 'plug into' the motherboard and are connected together by its circuitry.

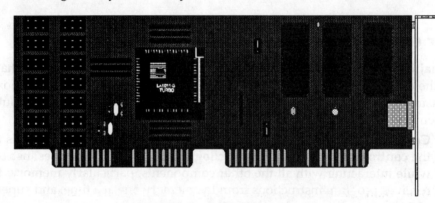

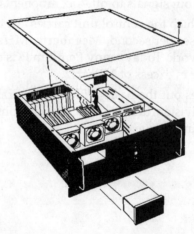

*Figure 1.9 A controller board*

- **Controller boards** or adapter cards are specialised pieces of electronic circuitry that are used to connect and control particular peripheral devices (such as disks, CD-ROM and sound devices), and to connect them to a network. Some boards enhance existing facilities such as extending and improving the screens graphics capabilities.

- **Input-output ports (I/O ports)** are connections that allow external peripheral devices to be connected to the processor board. A port allows either serial or parallel transmission of data between the primary memory and peripheral devices. Serial ports transfers data one bit at a time. A parallel port may transfer a group of bits at a time (e.g. one byte).

- **Co-processor** – this may be an additional processor chip that helps the CPU carry out some tasks. A Maths co-processor is used on computer systems that are likely to be used for 'number-crunching' applications. Using a co-processor will help increase system performance;

- **Buses** are internal electronic pathways that are used to transfer data and instructions between the CPU, memory and peripherals. Buses have a capacity that states how many bits can be moved in one go. An 8 bit bus moves 1 byte at a time, a 16 bit bus moves 2 bytes, and a 32 bit bus moves 4 bytes. The bus capacities influence how fast the computer works.

# Output component

The information that results from the processing of data within a computer system must be converted back into a form that the user understands. **Output** devices perform this activity. They allow results to be output from the main processor unit and for the system to communicate with the user or a device that it is controlling. In commercial systems, the screen and printer are the principal output devices. In industrial systems, display screens, panel displays with lights and other gauges, and process controllers and actuators receive the output. Some output devices are explained below.

### Visual Display Unit (VDU)

The **Visual Display Unit (VDU)** is the computer screen or monitor that displays text, graphics or pictures. Today's technology of the VDU may be the cathode ray tube (similar to that used in TVs) or liquid crystal, or gas plasma displays (used in flat screens). Most screens today provide full colour displays, can support 256 colours, and are capable of running video clips; however, some systems still rely on the use of monochrome 80 character by 25 line text displays.

A screen's resolution defines the quality of its picture and is measured in **pixels** (a pictorial element, a very small area or 'dot' on the screen). Most PC screens today support the VGA standard of 640 (horizontal) by 480 (vertical) pixels and 16 colours. Newer machines offering the higher resolution standard, Super VGA or SVGA of 1024 by 768 pixels and 256 colours. In industrial systems and some specialised commercial systems the screen may be smaller.

In many applications, the screen provides a view or 'window' of a much larger piece of text or diagram and allows the user to scroll up and down, or pan left and right. Normally anything typed at the keyboard is displayed on the screen at the appropriate place. Position on the screen is indicated by the screen cursor that may be a flashing block, a hairline or an arrow. GUIs and Windows increase the versatility of the screen.

## Printers

**Printers** are hard copy devices that print text and/or graphics. There are a variety of types of printer, but they can be broadly classified as being either impact or non-impact. The speed and quality of output is directly associated with their price. Draft text will be printed very quickly, whereas complex pages that are a mix of text, graphics and pictures will take longer to format and print.

- **Non-impact** printers use laser or ink-jet technology to print on loose leaf paper a page at a time. Such printers are quiet, so they are very suitable for office use and versatile in their support for text fonts and sizes. The two main types are the **laser printer** and **ink-jet printer**, the latter being a popular type for home use. Non-impact printers deliver their output a page at a time, their speed being a **number of pages per minute (ppm)**. PC laser printers are available that operate at up to 20 ppm with up to 6 ppm being common for home use.

- **Impact printers** are older technology and rely on print heads banging on a ribbon to print on continuous plain or pre-printed stationery. They are suitable for high volume and multiple copy printing. They can be noisy, may have a fixed set of text fonts and size so are less versatile. **Dot matrix printers**, (9 pin or 18 pin), are the workhorses of many systems and are able to produce print of acceptable quality and handle a variety of printing requirements. Many retail systems use small printers that print onto a narrow continuous till roll. Impact printers either deliver their output a character or a line at a time, their speed being **characters per second (cps)**, or **lines per minute (lpm)**. A low cost dot-matrix printer would operate at up to 300 cps in draft mode.

- **Plotters** are specialised devices for producing high-quality graphical output such as technical drawings. Plotters are either flat-bed or drum, can support more than one plotter-pen and paper of non-standard size.

## Sound

In the age of multi-media many computer systems have a sound capability. In a simple form this might be an integral speaker that has a limited capability. External speakers coupled with a sound card are able to produce high quality sound reproduction for music and text-speech.

## Actuators

**Actuators** are output devices. On receipt of a signal from the processor they produce movement, or start or stop a motor, that in turn will affect the environment in which the system operates. They are usually closely coupled to the sensor input devices that provided the readings that triggered the response.

## Question 1.28

*What is the main purpose of the screen?*

*A   enter data*

*B   store data*

*C   display data*

*D   process data*

## Question 1.29

*What is the main purpose of a printer?*

*A   produce hard copy*

*B   store information*

*C   display input data*

*D   correct text*

## Question 1.30

*What of the following cannot be used for output?*

*A   mouse*

*B   plotter*

*C   printer*

*D   speaker*

## Storage component

The computer's memory for storing data and program instructions is usually at two of the following levels.

- **Primary** or **main memory** holds the current program instructions and data that is directly and immediately accessible to the CPU. Several different software modules may be loaded into and become resident in the main memory at the same time; but only one is currently in control of the system.

- **Secondary memory** holds additional software programs and data files. Any software and data can only be used or processed by first being loaded from secondary into primary memory for access by the CPU.

Most of primary memory is volatile and its contents are lost when the computer is switched off. Secondary memory is permanent, with the contents being retained when power is removed. Application software require users to **save** their work or data that is currently in primary memory as a **file** on a secondary storage device (such as a floppy or hard disk). To subsequently use the saved work the disk must be accessed, the file **opened,** which **loads** it (or part of it) into the computer's primary memory from the disk.

Storage capacities for devices are given in:

- **Kilo**bytes or Kbytes or Kb  = 1 thousand bytes  = 1024 bytes
- **Mega**bytes or Mbytes or Mb  = 1 million bytes  = 1024 Kbytes
- **Giga**bytes or Gbytes or Gb  = 1000 million bytes  = 1024 Mbytes

A computer system described as having 64Kb ROM, 8Mb of RAM memory, 0.5 Mb of cache and a 512Mb or 0.5Gb hard disk has a byte capacities of:

| | | |
|---|---|---|
| ROM memory: | 64 × 1024 bytes | = 65,536 bytes |
| RAM memory: | 8 × 1024 × 1024 bytes | = 8,388,608 bytes |
| Cache memory: | 512 × 1024 bytes | = 524,288 bytes |
| Hard disk: | 512 × 1024 × 1024 bytes | = 536,870,912 bytes |

## Question 1.31

*Which is the largest capacity?*

*A   640 Kbytes*

*B   8 Mbytes*

*C   500 Mbytes*

*D   1 Gbyte*

The components of computer storage are as follows.

- **Random access memory (RAM)** is the main component of primary storage. It has no moving parts and thus provides the CPU with fast access temporary storage for program instructions and data. The CPU can read data from and write data to RAM, input/output devices can also communicate with RAM. RAM is volatile and loses its contents when the power is switched off. The size of RAM is generally specified for a computer system, PCs today are typically sold with 8 Mbytes of RAM and can be extended by adding additional memory usually in increments of 1 Mbyte. Increasing RAM provides more main memory space for use by software and can improve system performance.

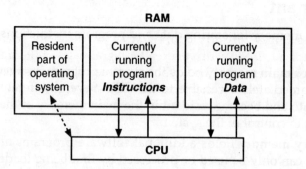

*Figure 1.11 Contents of RAM*

- **Read only memory (ROM)** is a smaller component of primary storage than RAM. It contains important instructions and data, that are stored in it at the time of manufacture. It is non-volatile and its contents remain intact when the power is switched off. ROM cannot be written to, its contents are permanent and cannot be changed. The resident software that is used when the system is powered up (its 'bootstrap' program) resides in ROM. A typical size for ROM would be up to 64 Kbytes.

- **Cache memory** is additional memory that provides a high-speed buffer storage area for data and instructions likely to be needed next by the CPU. It is similar to RAM, but uses technology that may be ten times faster than RAM; it is also 100 times as expensive and so will have a much smaller capacity (256Kb being a typical cache capacity). Use of cache will improve system performance.

- **Disk drives** are the most common form of high capacity secondary storage used on PCs today. They support **magnetic** disks that are used in **read or write mode**, provide a permanent storage facility for use by the CPU and store their contents in **files**, that can be accessed independently of each other.

  - A typical PC will have two internally-mounted drives, one for a **fixed hard disk** (having a capacity from 250 Mb up to 1 Gb) and a second for an **exchangeable floppy disk** (with a capacity of 1.4 Mb). Lately, new 'Zip' disks have become available that provide an exchangeable disk capacity in excess of 100Mb; currently these are loaded onto the system via an additional special external drive. Extra disk drives can be attached to PCs and drives can also be replaced with ones of higher specification. With greater disk capacity more data and software can be stored. Disk speed (the rate at which it can transfer data to or from main memory) is also important. Hard disks are much faster than floppies, but they work more than a thousand times slower than the CPU.

  - Data and instructions stored on disk are non-volatile and are retained when power is switched off (or in the case of a floppy or Zip disk, when it is removed from the machine). New technology will continue to increase the capacities of both the fixed hard disks and the exchangeable 'floppy' disk.

- **Tape drives** are magnetic tape media in the form of large spools or smaller cassettes, having a high data capacity. They provide permanent storage and can be used in read or write mode. Tape storage was very common, but it is used less and less today – the principal use is as a disk backup medium to keep security copies of disk files. Access to data on tape is much slower than using disk storage.

- **Compact disk-read only memory (CD-ROM)** are optical disks that have a huge storage capacity and are used in **read-only** mode. CD-ROMs are available with all sorts of goodies, including software, text, pictures, graphics and video. They are the principal component of multimedia PCs. A PC with a suitable sound card and CD-ROM drive can play audio CDs giving good sound reproduction. Again, new technology will continue to extend the capacity and use of optical devices.

- **Cables and connectors**, the chip, ROM and RAM memory, the hard disks, floppy drive and perhaps a CD-ROM drive are all integral parts of the main processor unit box and are connected internally. The keyboard, mouse, display screen and printer are connected externally to the rear of the processor box (see figure 1.12). Each device has a unique plug and socket. The power source cable and a power link to the VDU will also be connected.

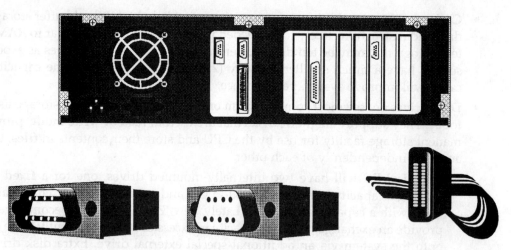

Figure 1.12 The rear of a processor box, with plugs for attachment

## Question 1.32

Which of the following is a read-only device?

A   floppy disk

B   hard disk

C   tape cassette

D   CD-ROM

## Question 1.33

Which is the main purpose of a floppy disk?

A   storing data for future use

B   processing data

C   displaying data

D   storing data that can never be altered

## Question 1.34

Which of the following would be used to store a database of library books?

A   random access memory (RAM)

B   read only memory (ROM)

C   a magnetic hard disk

D   a magnetic floppy disk

### Question 1.35

Which would most likely make a slow chess program run faster?

A   change to a faster VDU

B   increase main memory

C   add a CD-ROM drive

D   increase the hard disk size

### Question 1.36

Which advantage would a model of computer with cache memory have over an identical model without cache memory?

A   it can access more disks

B   it has extra instructions

C   it has greater capacity

D   it runs programs more quickly

### Question 1.37

Which could be used to speed up a slow screen display?

A   install a faster graphics card

B   install a bigger VDU

C   use less colours

D   reduce the number of disk drives

### Task 1.7   PC 1

Prepare a small presentation (with pictorial examples) to illustrate the hardware components of a commercial computer system and their characteristics. You should have access to the system or have researched it in the library or computer press.

### Task 1.8   PC 1

Write a short report to describe the hardware components of a typical games machine.

## 1.2.2. Purposes of hardware components

## Purpose of the input component

The main purpose of the input component is to capture data, convert it to an acceptable computer format, and transfer it to the processor unit for processing or storage. The keyboard and mouse coupled to the screen are the main forms of input device for users. Other methods can be used to speed up or improve the accuracy of the data capture activity. User input involves typing (or selecting) commands to activate a task or application and typing (or entering) data into the computer system under the control of some program.

- **Form filling** – sometimes the user will have to fill in a screen form (or template) that mimics manual form filling, using a pencil or pen to fill in the boxes. Such systems try to keep data entry to a minimum – the users key in data from source documents similar to the screen. Sales order entry systems will often require extensive text entry onto screen forms – the data source may be a completed paper order document or direct from information to the operator over the telephone.

- **Automated methods** – form filling is time consuming and subject to error, and so for high volume data entry automated methods are often used to speed things up and reduce errors. Use of scanners to read barcodes is common in supermarket checkouts and avoids the need for the operator to type the code of each item purchased. In DIY stores a similar system is used, but because of the variation in size and weight of items, a portable wand is waved over the barcode on the item. In bars and fast-food restaurants, staff use special keys to identify themselves at a till and use special keyboard pads to enter details of purchases.

- **Text scanning** – text and document scanners can also improve the data capture process. **Magnetic ink character recognition (MICR)**, **optical character recognition (OCR)** and **optical mark reading (OMR)** are used extensively in industry to handle high volume input transactions.

Banks are the biggest users of MICR: they have used magnetic ink characters on cheques for many years now. Blank cheques come encoded with the bank sort code, the account number and cheque number; prior to being read into the computer, the cheque amount must be encoded as an additional field onto the cheque.

The gas, electricity and water companies have billing systems that use OCR turnround documents. The document is produced by the computer and sent to the customer, who pays; the form or part of it is the returned for subsequent input to the computer. These same companies use OMR in their meter reading activities. A pre-printed card is sent out to the consumer who marks positions of dials, or crosses out numbers on a grid to represent the current meter reading. A popular application today that uses OMR to automate data capture is the National Lottery. It records selections by crossing out numbers in a grid from 1 to 49. Imagine the queues if each of your selections had to be typed in and how many errors would be made?

A simple system requiring a minimum of user typing is the banks 'hole in the wall' automated teller machines. These systems use a combination of input devices for the user interface. Having inserted a magnetic swipe card into the machine, the user partakes in a simple dialogue using a small numeric keypad and a small VDU screen. The system enables the user to identify themselves via their PIN code, choose a particular service via the keypad, and then the amount of money required is keyed in. Details on the swipe card confirm the users identity and also contain a limit on the amount of money that can be withdrawn.

The music and video store uses barcodes both to identify its members and on the products it sells. The staff serving identify themselves to the system via a keyboard, and then a customer's membership barcode is scanned, followed by the barcode on each product being purchased. The members receive a discount on each purchase and receive a personalised itemised bill. The company accumulates valuable marketing information about its customers.

A college library uses a number of different devices to process its transactions. It places barcodes in all its books and issues its members with personal smart cards. To borrow books, the issues counter clerk uses a keyboard and screen to initiate the operation. The member presents their smart card for swiping and the screen displays the member's details. The counter clerk then issues each book by scanning its barcode with a laser wand. Return of the books is handled similarly.

## *Task 1.9*  PC 2

*Prepare a small presentation (with pictorial examples) that illustrates at least six different formats or methods for interfacing with a computer system. For each format or method, give an example of an application that uses it.*

## Purpose of the processor component

The **processor** is the nucleus of the computer system. It is responsible for the execution of machine instructions (stored as programs) that tell the computer what to do. The program currently in control of the system will be held in primary memory, its instructions will be written in a language that the CPU understands (machine language based on binary). Each program instruction will be read from memory into the CPU, understood by the CPU and then executed by the CPU.

- **Instructions** – these will usually require the CPU to process data also held in the main memory. Data will be read from the memory into the CPU, processed by the CPU and the data results written back into the main memory. Some instructions will require action from the input, output or storage devices and the CPU will initiate that activity. This will either cause data to be input (or read) into primary memory from an input (or storage) device, or data to output (or written) from primary memory to an output (or storage) device.

- **Calculations** – many instructions require the CPU to perform calculations on data. To do this the CPU operates in a similar manner to an electronic calculator, using the basic arithmetic operations (+ − * /). However, the computer takes its instructions from its own memory, whereas the calculator takes its instructions from you, the user.

- **Input-Output** – some instructions will perform I/O operations by communicating with a particular I/O device. An input (or read) instruction will transfer data from the input device (or secondary storage) into primary memory; an output (or write) instruction will transfer data from primary memory to the output or secondary storage device.

- **Selections** – some instructions require the CPU to take a logic decision, make a selection based on the value (or condition) of an item of data. This enables the CPU to carry out different sets of instructions based on the outcome of the selection. In computer logic things are either 'true' or 'false', the answer to a question is either 'yes' or 'no', there is no 'maybe'. For example, a stock item is either subject to VAT in which case the computer program must calculate the VAT amount due, or not subject to VAT and no VAT calculation is necessary.

- **Repetition** – often the CPU must repeat the same set of instructions over and over again. On completion of a set of instructions, it can loop around to the start and go through the same instructions again, but processing a different set of data values. This feature enables the computer to process all the items in the supermarket trolley. The looping terminates when the CPU determines (or is told) that there is no more data to process.

The flowchart in figure 1.13 outlines the high level logic flow for processing customer purchases at a supermarket checkout. Each checkout is connected to the store computer where the master product file is located. The customer payment box can be expanded to handle the various forms of payment and store card activities.

## Task 1.10  PC 2

*Investigate a computer system that you have access to or have read about, such as a library system. Make a list of the calculations, input/output, selections and repetition that the system must undertake. This should not be a very detailed list, for example, one similar to those in Figure 1.13 will do.*

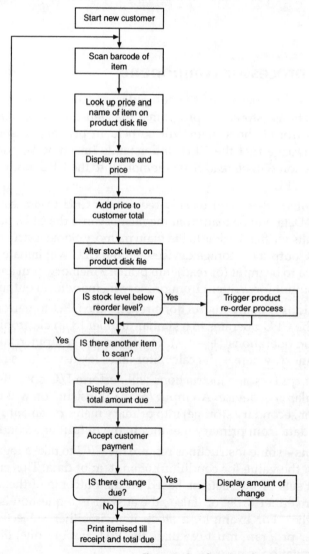

*Figure 1.13 A flowchart for processing of a supermarket checkout*

# Purpose of the output component

The main output media for the human user is the screen and hard copy print-out, although use of sound is also gaining in popularity (particularly in CD-ROM based multimedia applications).

### Display screen

The display screen provides on-line immediate feedback of results (or commands) to the user. The amount of information that can be displayed on a screen is limited: it should be used for low volume output, or for selectively browsing larger volumes of output. From once being a just basic text and graphics device, some screens can now display high quality picture images and run video clips (such applications require special graphic display controller cards and screens of high resolution). Such screen display allows the users to browse on-line stored data banks and other applications (such as encyclopaedias on CD-ROM). They can also access the Internet and experience the full effects of multimedia.

In some applications the screen is small and has a limited capability (e.g. 'hole in the wall' screens at banks or in a supermarket checkout display). Other commercial applications use full-screens (e.g. in many DIY stores or with office applications). Industrial applications can have special screens that display many readings from different devices; they may be very large, covering part or the whole of a wall. For example, gas, electricity and water companies often have huge electronic maps that show important locations or devices, and railway systems use large electronic displays to show locations of rail traffic.

### Printing

The printer is a high volume output device and provides a permanent hard-copy that can be read or browsed away from the computer. Many PC printers use cut-sheet paper printing on standard A4 size (in portrait or landscape format). Some impact printers can use continuous computer stationery with a number of different widths (80mm, 120mm and 132mm columns), they can also print on multi-part stationery to provide several copies for filing. Some documents requiring a high quality of print will need the use of a laser printer, other documents to be used in draft form can use a dot-matrix printer.

The computer has revolutionised document preparation through the use of word-processing systems. Amendments and insertions to documents can be easily accommodated. In business applications, a printer may be loaded with special stationery that is pre-printed, sales invoices, payslips with field headings and blank contents, and company cheques complete with signature. In each case the paper must be properly loaded if the output from the computer is to be printed in the correct position. Most application systems allow the user to do a test print out with dummy data to check alignment, and any adjustments can be made prior to the proper print run. Office systems use headed notepaper for letter printing and label printing software to print address labels to stick on envelopes. BT itemised telephone bills show how it is possible to achieve high quality volume printing.

### Sound

**External speakers** connected to a special sound controller card can provide quality sound reproduction. Text-to-speech software can read and speak text documents, which is a great help to sight-disabled people. Sound can be digitised and stored in files that can subsequently be edited and changed, however sound files require a lot of storage space. Sound can be an integral part of many multimedia applications supplied for use with CD-ROM.

### Control

In dedicated industrial systems there is less reliance on the printed output, although this might be used to print event logs. The forms of output used depends on the application and there are a variety of devices. For example, levels or values may be shown graphically using gauges and warning colours. An actuator can control a device, for example, it could move a robot arm, start or stop a motor and open or close a valve.

### *Task 1.11* PC 2

*Prepare a catalogue showing the price and characteristics of different types of printer, suitable for use with a micro-computer at home or in a small office. Use local computer retail stores and computer magazines as your sources of information.*

## Purpose of the storage component

Programs and data are stored **permanently** in secondary storage to be retrieved as required, and stored **temporarily** in primary storage.

### Primary storage

**Primary storage** holds the software program instructions that currently control the computer system and any data that those instructions need immediately. It has a capacity measured in megabytes. The contents of primary storage can be changed by loading into it new software programs to perform different tasks, for example, a sales clerk entering customer sales invoice details will be interacting with a program from the Sales Ledger Accounting package that has been loaded into the main memory and is now in control. A part of the operating system is always resident in primary storage ready to take over when the application program terminates.

### Secondary or auxiliary storage

The main devices used on computers today for secondary or auxiliary storage are magnetic disks which have a capacity measured in hundreds of megabytes and gigabytes; CD-ROM also provide a high capacity exchangeable secondary storage medium.

Secondary storage is used to hold any type of additional software (such as application packages or office processing suites), that can be run on the computer system. It also holds the data files produced and used by the different software applications. Data and software stored on secondary storage can be created, deleted and copied.

To help organise this vast storage area the operating system will use an organised filing system of directories, and sub-directories and provide special utility software to help the user manage and control it. Figure 1.14 shows the directory structure on the D: hard drive, where there are a number of application directories at the top level. Microsoft Office has a number of application sub-directories that in turn have more sub-directories. In the

D:\MSOFFICE\ACCESS\SAMPAPPS directory there are application files of data and software.

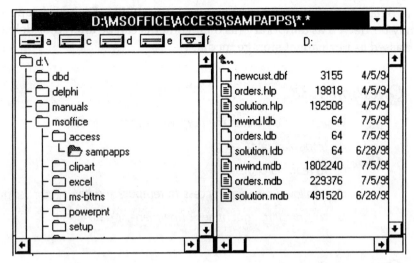

*Figure 1.14 Directory structure on a hard disk drive*

CD-ROM devices provide even greater storage capacity and are used to supply new software products plus on-line documentation (or reference data material), text, pictures, sound and video (as used with multimedia). A software product (such as Microsoft Office) can be distributed on one CD-ROM or on as many as thirty floppy disks. To date, most CD-ROMs operate in read-only mode and cannot be written to, so they could be regarded as permanent storage devices.

### Permanent storage

ROM provides low capacity (kilobytes) permanent non-volatile storage; and disk, tape or CD-ROM provide high capacity permanent storage.

In ROM, the data or instructions stored can never be altered or deleted and perform specific functions. The purpose on a typical desk-top microcomputer system will be to hold enough instructions and data (the **bootstrap**) to cold-start the machine, and to begin loading additional software from other storage devices to complete the start-up process and hand control over to the operating system. In small industrial systems (such as a washing machine in the home), the ROM device contains all the necessary instructions to control the appliance's wash programs.

Disks, tape and CD-ROM provide high capacity storage for holding files of data or suites of software programs for particular applications. On disk and tape, new files can be created, file contents can be accessed and changed or updated. Until physically deleted, data or software held on disk or tape is permanent. For example:

- a payroll package would keep its pay records in a payroll master file stored on disk. A student examinations system would keep a data base of subjects and student assignment and examination performances on disk,
- a word processing package would store documents on disk,
- a programming language compiler would store the source code and translated object code on disk,
- a drawing package would store its clip-art on CD-ROM,
- a software development tool would be stored on disk.

## Temporary storage

Temporary storage is mainly volatile RAM primary storage or main memory that temporarily holds the data and software for current use by the CPU. Disk and tape secondary storage media may be viewed as temporary (as their contents can be altered or deleted), however, they tend to classed as permanent storage media.

### Question 1.38

Which best describes the purpose of magnetic tape?

A to display text

B to read barcodes

C to allow immediate access to temporary data

D to store large quantities of permanent data

### Question 1.39

When running an application program in which part of the computer is each instruction executed?

A the main processor unit

B the magnetic disk drive

C the CD-ROM unit

D the user interface

### Question 1.40

What difference will installing a more powerful processor chip in a computer make?

A the computer will need less maintenance

B mathematical programs will run faster

C the software can use coloured icons

D the computer can store more data

### Question 1.41

Where in the system would the records of payments made to sales staff during the year be stored?

A on magnetic disk

B on CD-ROM

C in RAM

D in ROM

*Task 1.12* PC 2

Prepare a table that shows the capacity, price and price per byte for the different forms of secondary storage. Use as your sources local computer retail stores and computer magazines.

## 1.2.3  Software components

Software represents the programs of sets of instructions that control the computer's operations (that tell it what to do). The operation of the computer when performing a specific task will be under the control of the software program currently resident in the computer's primary memory and 'in charge'. The software products available on a system are stored on the hard disk and can be loaded into the main memory via the operating system interface. Once loaded, a particular piece of software takes control of the system. There are a number of categories of software.

## Operating systems software component

The operating system (o/s) is the 'boss' and manages the computer system. When a computer is switched on or powered up, it is the first piece of software to take control of the system. Once up and running, the o/s is the centre of all software activity by providing an environment in which all other software operates. The o/s is a collection of program modules that directly control and manage all the hardware components of the computer system, other software may only communicate with those components via the o/s. Common operating systems are MS-DOS, Windows 95, OS/2 and UNIX.

```
C:\WINDOWS>mem/c|more
Modules using memory below 1 MB:

   Name            Total
  --------      ----------------
   MSDOS          37,421    (37K)
   HIMEM           1,168  , (1K)
   EMM386          8,368     (8K)
   CTSB16         26,816    (26K)
   CTMMSYS        10,544    (10K)
   QD6580          3,296     (3K)
   SETVER            480     (0K)
   DISPLAY         8,304     (8K)
   CDMKE          11,440    (11K)

--More--
```

*Figure 1.15 A section of a memory map showing some o/s modules resident in memory*

The operating system family of programs carry out a variety of tasks necessary to use the system resources effectively, for example:

- bootstrap the computer when it is first switched on – a small piece of software resident in ROM will initialise the system and load additional o/s software from secondary storage into RAM;
- check out the hardware configuration of the system, to see that all is functioning correctly;
- provide the user interface, to enable the user to interact with the system;
- load application software and hand control of the system to RAM, and take control back when the software terminates successfully or otherwise;
- monitor and control data input/output, and manage the transfer of data between RAM and peripheral devices;
- organise and manage the storage of data and software on secondary storage by keeping track of where items are physically located (via directories, files, file names, file types), perform other housekeeping operations (like file renaming, saving, loading, copying, deleting, moving, searching, file display and printing, formatting of new disks);
- provide a basic text file editing facility to create and modify necessary o/s files;
- provide data security facilities to enable file backup and recovery;
- provide system security facilities for registering authorised users and password protection;
- enable and manage sharing of system resources by more than one program through multitasking or multiprogramming.

## The operating system user interface

The operating system user interface allows the user to communicate with an operating system once the computer system has been powered up. Until recently, most IBM compatible PC systems would initially power up and hand control to the MS-DOS operating system; very many still do, but new systems may power up directly into Windows. (Apple Macs have for many years powered up into a Graphical User Interface (GUI) of application windows.)

- **MS-DOS** uses a command line user interface that requires the user to type o/s commands. This requires that the user be familiar with at least a basic set of commands in order for them to make use of the machine. The command instructs the operating system to carry out a specific task (e.g. display the files of a disk directory, copy a file from one directory to another), and in doing so the o/s may display messages back to the user. Some users will have extensive MS-DOS knowledge while others will know enough to get by. For the novice user MS-DOS can be quite a hurdle to overcome.

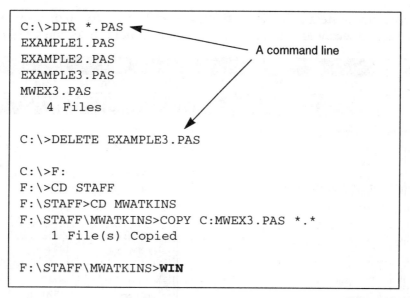

```
C:\>DIR *.PAS
EXAMPLE1.PAS
EXAMPLE2.PAS
EXAMPLE3.PAS
MWEX3.PAS
   4 Files


C:\>DELETE EXAMPLE3.PAS


C:\>F:
F:\>CD STAFF
F:\STAFF>CD MWATKINS
F:\STAFF\MWATKINS>COPY C:MWEX3.PAS *.*
   1 File(s) Copied


F:\STAFF\MWATKINS>WIN
```

A command line

*Figure 1.16 MS-DOS commands*

- **Graphical user interfaces (GUI)** were pioneered by Apple and are now available on all PCs today. The original PC Windows provided a GUI to front-end MS-DOS but more recent versions (Windows NT and Windows '95) are operating systems in their own right. GUIs provide a more user-friendly environment for the user who is able to select tasks from displayed **icons** using the mouse actions of point and click.

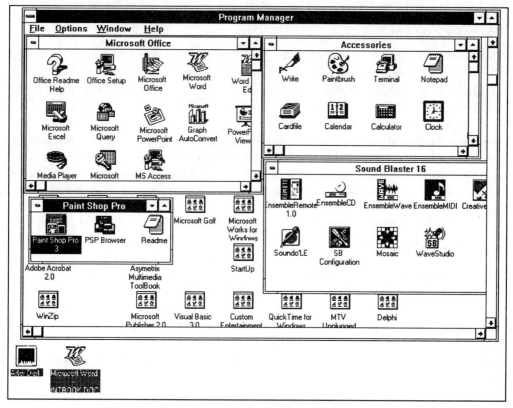

*Figure 1.17 A Windows graphical user interface (GUI) showing application panes and icons*

Having selected application or task icon the user performs many tasks through mouse controlled menu option selection and drag and drop operations. A frequently used

47

operating system utility is the file manager. This is used to organise and manipulate files stored in secondary storage, the floppy disks, hard disks and CD-ROM.

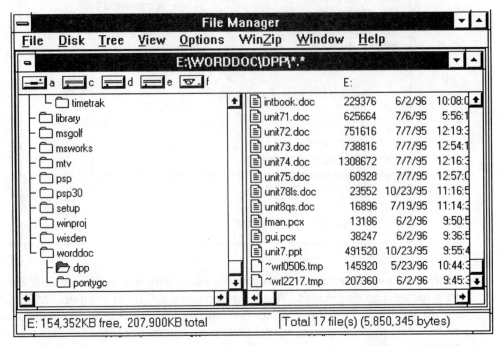

*Figure 1.18 The File manager Window*

## File management

The secondary storage media of disks or CD-ROM store their contents in files. An individual file may hold data to be processed by an application, hold the outcome of some user activity and hold program instructions of an application that can be loaded into primary memory. Files are identified with a name and a type code, used to give the user some indication of their contents. Applications will create files with a particular type code, such as **.doc** for Microsoft Word files, **.pas** for Pascal program files. Additional data stored about the file include its size and the date and time it was created or amended. To help locate files, the file storage space will usually be split into directories or folders as with manual filing cabinets. Files are normally created and amended by application software, the file manager is used to locate, copy, move, rename and delete files.

## System control

All hardware and software components of the computer system are managed by the operating system that monitors and controls their activities. All interaction with input-output and file storage devices is controlled by the operating system. The o/s will buffer data transfer to handle the difference in operating speeds between primary storage executing in time frames measured in millionths of a second, and say a disk working in thousands of a second, a thousand times slower! The o/s will control system security through the use of passwords to prevent unauthorised access.

# Utility software component

In addition to the software components of the operating system, a computer system will have additional software programs to carry out common tasks.

- A **sort utility program** is used to arrange files of data records in a particular sequence prior to further processing or for printing a particular report. A file of student marks in a subject could be sorted to descending mark order to view the class performance. The file could be sorted again to student name order for entry onto the student's record.

- A **backup/restore utility program** is used to take security copies of data stored on disk onto another disk or tape. The program must also allow for the data to be restored onto the disk if necessary. Most commercial systems take daily copies of their data files in case of system failure.

- **Accessory utility programs** provide additional facilities such as basic text editing, calculator and so on.

# Application software component

Application software consists of ready-made programs purchased as a package (or specially developed) that carry out the processing required by a particular application (commercial or industrial).

General purpose office application software systems (such as Microsoft Office) have a suite of software components that enable the user to process:

- textual documents using a word processor package (Word);
- numerical data using a spread sheet package (Excel);
- graphical data using a presentation package (PowerPoint);
- structured data using a database package (Access).

Other general purpose applications include: **Desk-top publishing (DTP)** that computerises typesetting and text compositions, computer graphics software that enables 2D or 3D drawings to be manipulated, and statistical packages that perform data analysis. Additional packages support office automation through **E-mail**, computer and video conferencing, and **electronic funds transfer (EFT)**.

More specific application software perform particular functions within, say, a commercial enterprise. Such software packages are used to computerise the accounts function, the payroll and personnel function, the sales and marketing activity, stores and stock control and production function. These software packages support the operational activities within an organisation. Other software applications will be used to support the management activities through **management information systems (MIS)**, and **decision support systems (DSS)**.

Industrial application software is usually **dedicated** to the application being monitored or controlled. CAD software is adaptable and provides similar facilities for users as general purpose office software.

## Application development software component

Application development software includes the **programming languages** that are used to develop new application software. The majority of software products today are programmed (or written by programmers) using a high-level language that is:

- a **third generation language (3GL)** such as C, C++, Pascal, COBOL or BASIC;
- a **fourth generation language environment (4GL or 4GLE)** such as Access, Paradox, Visual Basic, Delphi, Oracle or Informix.

Most 4GL products are associated with a database that provides powerful facilities for defining, managing and manipulating (large) quantities of associated data, often using the database language **SQL**.

There are in fact many hundreds of 3GLs that have been invented over the years, but only a small few have gained widespread acceptance amongst the programming community. The 4GLs provide additional facilities that help improve programmer productivity and shorten the time needed to develop new products, however, they are not as flexible as the 3GLs and may not perform some tasks efficiently.

Development of a new program involves: taking a requirements specification, designing the program and writing a source program (that is, a set of commands required to perform a specific task). To do this most languages provide a development environment that manages the programming activity. Before a program can be used it must be translated from a high-level language form to a machine language form (that the computer can then execute). This process is called **compilation** and the program that carries it out is a **programming language compiler**.

### Question 1.42

*Which one of the following is carried out by applications software?*

*A   formatting a disk*

*B   drawing a picture*

*C   renaming a file*

*D   compiling a program*

### Question 1.43

*Which one of the following is carried out by operating system software?*

*A   changing the text font in a document*

*B   compiling a program*

*C   copying a file*

*D   executing a database query*

## Question 1.44

Which type of software controls the running of a computer?

A   an application

B   a utility

C   a programming language

D   an operating system

## Question 1.45

Which one of the following is an example of application software?

A   a language compiler

B   a network manager

C   an operating system

D   an accounts package

## Question 1.46

Which one of the following is an example of utility software?

A   a file back-up and recovery program

B   a GUI

C   a network manager

D   a stock control package

## Task 1.13   PC 3, PC 4

Prepare a short report that lists and classifies the main pieces of software found on a computer system you have access to or have studied. For each item of software, give its name, supplier, purpose, hardware requirements and, if possible, cost.

# Set up a stand-alone computer to meet user requirements

A stand-alone computer system is a typical desk-top microcomputer system that comprises the hardware and software components. The particular components that make up a system are dependent on the processing tasks it will be required to carry out. A description of such processing activities are usually specified in a specification document that lists the users' requirements.

## 1.3.1 User requirements specification

Before purchasing any hardware or software a requirements specification is usually written. This lists the user's requirements – describing what the computer system is to be used for. If purchasing a computer for home use, the activities that it will be used for need to be listed. For example, will it just be a games machine for the family or is there a requirement for it to be used to help mam or dad in their work, or to help children in their education?

For a small commercial business, such requirements might indicate the need to support word-processing, spreadsheet and accounts processing. A bakery or pharmacy business might include the requirement to print small labels for its products, while a packaging company might have a requirement for very large labels for its products packaging; both activities may require specialised printers or printer support.

A vehicle-leasing company may require a new system to handle its leasing business, and this may need to be compatible with other computer systems that its dealership operation uses.

A local authority directs its road inspectors to use portable pocket computers, to record where road repairs are required. After a day inspecting, the data entered onto the pocket computers by the inspectors can be uploaded into a larger system for processing.

In order to prepare a requirements specification an initial **analysis** needs to be undertaken that **interviews** the potential users of the system. Having produced a requirements specification, the first step would be to choose the software that best meets those requirements, and then choose the hardware that will best support the software! An IT 'information kiosk' system might well require touch-sensitive screen hardware. There should be enough detail in the specification to enable an advisor (or supplier) to propose a suitable IT solution to meet the requirements.

For all but the very specialised applications, choosing a software package should not be too difficult if a checklist of requirements has been well prepared. However, before actually purchasing any software the operating system and hardware requirements for it should be checked out. Some application software only operates under a particular version of an operating system, this would then tie the system into it, and may prevent expansion (or not provide an ability to take advantage of new developments). There are other operating systems in addition to MS-DOS and Windows. Today many users are agonising over whether to commit themselves to Windows '95 or Windows NT products – unlike the micro 'butterflies' who flit from one latest product to the next, a business needs a certain stability in its IT operations.

The specification should identify the following aspects of the proposed system.

- The purpose for which the system and its software will be used. It will be a list of the functions that the system is expected to support and who the users are. An architect's practice might require a system to support its accounting functions of sales, purchase and nominal ledger, and require a system to manage its projects and employee time sheets.

- The type of processing activity – what processing the computer will perform, and what processing will be performed manually. Manual activities are performed **off-line** (and are usually concerned with preparation of data or documents) for future **on-line** processing using the computer. On-line processing will be concerned with transaction processing, data manipulation of files and records, reporting, sorting and searching, provide user access to support enquiries.

- The methods of processing – the different ways in which data transactions are processed using the computer. **Batch processing** lets a group of transactions accumulate prior to processing them in one lot. The batch accumulation of transactions usually takes place off-line, the control data is calculated manually and associated with the batch. The batch of transactions are subsequently input to the computer where they may be subsequently stored on disk for later processing (such as sorting) or processed immediately. **Interactive processing** handles transactions as they arise, they may be immediately processed or held in a 'batch' for later processing. On-line enquiry systems need immediate access to the 'database' of stored files and records, with the requirement to produce screen displays and printed hard-copy. What are the input (or data capture) and output (or report) requirements?

## Question 1.47

*Preparing a batch of documents for data entry into a computer system is an example of which activity?*

*A   off-line*

*B   on-line*

*C   interactive*

*D   dedicated*

## 1.3.2   Software and hardware

Detailed analysis of the user requirements should enable software to be selected to meet them. There are two possible software solutions as follows.

- **Packaged** – where an 'off-the-peg' software package is available to meet the system requirements. Users need to beware of obtaining packages that need slight tailoring to meet their requirements: this can often lead to trouble between the supplier and user. Packaged solutions are common for accounts systems, payroll and stock control systems.

53

- **Bespoke** – where a 'made-to-measure' software development is undertaken to provide a system that meets the 'exact' user requirements. This is a far more expensive solution than the packaged one and requires a commitment by the user and the developer.

Some systems may require a mix of packaged and bespoke software development. However the software is supplied, it must operate under a particular operating system with which it is compatible. When choosing an operating system, there is a need to be aware of developments in the field, what has happened in the recent past and what is likely to occur in the future. There are many examples of users purchasing software products only for them to become virtually obsolete overnight.

Having decided on the software components, hardware should be specified that is able to support the software and data processing requirements, and meet any particular user requirements for data capture, data storage and results output (or responses). Component specification will define the following components.

- **Main processor unit** – this will include the micro-processor type and speed (486 DX2 66MHz).
- **Primary storage** or main memory – the amount of RAM in megabytes – 8 Mbytes, plus an amount of cache memory in kilobytes – 256 Kbytes.
- **Keyboard** – must be compatible with the main processor unit, although the 102 keypad is fairly standard, specialised ones are available (such as those used in the retail trade).
- **Mouse** – these too are fairly standard, but there are variations and again compatibility with the main processing unit must be assured. Special mouse driver software may require loading into the operating system.
- **VDU screen or monitor** – the standard screen size is 13 inches, but 15 inch are common, and 17 inch are available but expensive. In addition, its display capabilities need specifying, particularly where there is a need for high resolution and colour ($800 \times 600$ and 256 colours). A special additional hardware card attached inside the main processor unit may be necessary to meet the display requirements in terms of resolution and speed.
- **Other I/O devices** – additional special purpose data capture or output devices to be supported.
- **Printer** – there are a vast number of printers available, the main factor determining which one to use will be: the environment, some printers are very noisy, the quantity of usage, the quality of print resolution. Printers are connected to the main processor unit in either serial or parallel modes.
- **Hard disk capacity** – in hundreds of megabytes up to several gigabytes, plus floppy disk.
- **Input output ports** – serial and parallel, device connection standards.
- **Controller boards** – for quality graphics or sound support.
- **Upgrade path** – availability of expansion slots for say multimedia support.
- **Cables and connectors** – the external devices can be connected to the main processor unit using specialised cables compatible with the ports on the back of the main processor unit. Serial devices tend to use 7 pin circular connectors, whereas as parallel devices may use 25 pin rectangular connectors.

### Question 1.48

*Which activity should be done first?*

*A install software*

*B choose software*

*C choose hardware*

*D configure hardware*

### Task 1.14 PC 1, PC 2

*Investigate the possible uses of smart cards in your school and college. Identify potential new applications of smart cards for both staff and students. For each application specify the purpose and requirements of the system and the likely benefits of using the smart card. For one application identify and specify the software and hardware requirements. This could be undertaken as a group activity.*

## 1.3.3 Connect hardware together

Connection of the hardware components basically requires attaching the external devices of keyboard, mouse, screen and printer to the main processor unit. If a system has multimedia facilities, then connection of the external speakers may also be required. The keyboard, mouse and screen should pose few problems (as their connectors are unique). Printers can pose a few problems where more than one port is available but should be easily sorted out using the documentation supplied with any product.

Having connected the hardware, the system may need to be configured through setting or adjusting internal settings of the main processor unit (or operating system). Appropriate screen and printer drivers should be selected and activated through set-up, control or manager software. Many of the necessary hardware settings are standard, or the devices are intelligent enough to establish the configuration of resident hardware and adjust their own settings accordingly (for example, to allow for the amount of memory available).

Having installed the operating system, it is usually necessary to set the correct system date and time that it then uses when managing stored files.

```
C:\WINDOWS>Date
Current date is Mon 03/06/1996
Enter new date (dd-mm-yy):

C:\WINDOWS>time
Current time is  22:14:39.39
Enter new time:

C:\WINDOWS>
```

*Figure 1.19 Setting date and time under MS-DOS*

**Task 1.15** PC 1.3.3

*You are given the hardware pieces of a microcomputer system together with their connecting cables and support documentation. Make sure that nothing is connected to any electrical power source. Assemble the computer system by connecting the components together, if in doubt consult the support documentation. Do not force any plugs onto connectors. Do not attempt to power up the system.*

## 1.3.4 Install software

Software applications are usually supplied on multiple floppy disks or the far more convenient CD-ROM. As with hardware assembly and configuring, the installation of application software under the operating system is normally fully automated. An associated **setup** or **install** program is run to load the software automatically from the floppy disk or CD-ROM.

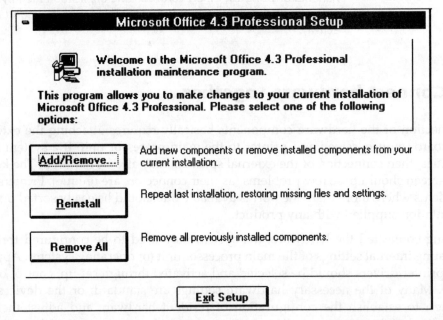

Figure 1.20 A set-up dialogue screen

The set-up program performs all the necessary checks on system components and system settings.

The steps necessary to load an application software product are as follows.

- Create directories to hold the software products programs and associated files.
- Create data directories necessary for holding the product's data files.
- Install or load the software into the appropriate directories from the floppies or CD-ROM.
- Load any necessary new device drivers. A **driver** is a program that enables the use of a specific hardware device (such as the VDU screen or printer or a CD-ROM drive). If a new device is added to a system then a driver must be added to the system for it. To add or change a driver for a mouse, keyboard or screen, click the Windows Setup icon (see

figure 1.21). To add or change a CD-ROM or sound driver click the Control Panel icon (see figure 1.22). Printers can be configured either using the Printers option of the Control Panel or the Printer Setup command in the Print Manager.

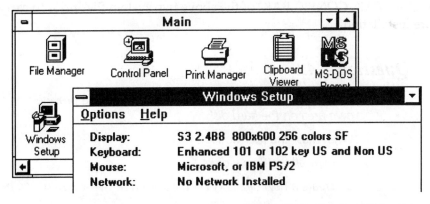

*Figure 1.21 Windows Setup Dialogue box to access drivers*

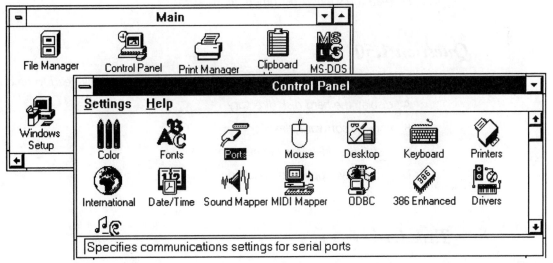

*Figure 1.22 Windows control panel to change settings*

- Update the relevant operating system files (AUTOEXEC.BAT and CONFIG.SYS) so that it knows about the new software on the system.

```
C:\>type autoexec.bat
  c:\windows\AD_WRAP.COM
SET SOUND=C:\SB16
LH C:\DOS\SHARE.EXE /L:100
SET BLASTER=A220 I5 D1 H5 P330 T6
SET MIDI=SYNTH:1 MAP:E
LH C:\SB16\DIAGNOSE /S
LH C:\SB16\SB16SET /P /Q
C:\DOS\SMARTDRV.EXE /X
@ECHO OFF
PROMPT $p$g
PATH
C:\WINDOWS;C:\DOS;D:\TB30;D:\MTB30;
  PATH=C:\IBLOCAL\BIN;C:\IDAPI;%PATH%
```

```
C:\>type config.sys
  DEVICE=C:\DOS\HIMEM.SYS
  rem DEVICE=C:\DOS\EMM386.EXE NOEMS
/Y=C:\DOS\EMM386.EXE
  DEVICE=C:\DOS\EMM386.EXE
  DOS=HIGH, UMB
  LASTDRIVE=H
  BREAK=on
  DEVICEHIGH=C:\SB16\DRV\CTSB16.SYS
/UNIT=0 /BLASTER=A:220 I:5 D:1 H:5
  DEVICEHIGH=C:\SB16\DRV\CTMMSYS.SYS
  BUFFERS=40
  FILES=40
```

*Figure 1.23 Contents of typical AUTOEXEC.BAT and CONFIG.SYS files*

If this is to be done manually, then you will need to refer to the support documentation that should accompany the software product. The automatic set-up software will take all the necessary actions, prompting you for any information that it needs. Always take copies (AUTOEXEC.BAK, CONFIG.BAK) of the above two system files prior to carrying out any new software installation.

## Question 1.49

*A user wishes to install a new piece of software provided on floppy disks in its own area on the hard disk.*

*What must the user do first?*

*A   copy all the floppy disks*

*B   create a new directory on the hard disk*

*C   remove unwanted disk files*

*D   read the support documentation*

## Question 1.50

*A user wishes to set up a new printer. Which operation will need to be done?*

*A   display the hard disk directory*

*B   copy all software files*

*C   install the driver for the new printer*

*D   test a new application package*

## Task 1.16   PC 4, PC 5

*You are given a software product on floppy disk or CD-ROM (together with any support documentation) to install on a configured system having an operating system installed. Read the installation documentation and check that your system has the capacity to hold it. Make a list of things to do in order to install the software prior to starting the installation. Make any necessary backup copies. Install the software in an appropriate manner and tick off items from your prepared list. Carry out any additional software configuration activities. Activate and test the software, carry out any necessary amendments, and retest.*

# *Produce an applications software macro to meet user requirements*

Office applications software packages like wordprocessors, spreadsheets and databases for micro computers provide support for a handy feature called a 'macro'. A **macro** is a sequence of operations (e.g. save a file, print a file, close a file) that can be activated or invoked, as needed, by:

- using a simple unique keystroke combination (e.g. CTRL + ALT + D);
- pointing and clicking the mouse at a toolbar icon;
- selecting from a macro drop-down menu.

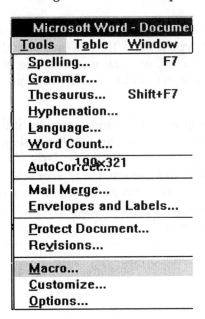 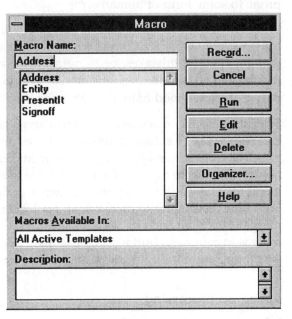

*Figure 1.24 Microsoft Word Macro menu selection*

A macro is created by:

- recording the execution of a sequence of operations within the applications package;
- storing the sequence of operations on disk under the macro name.

Figure 1.24 shows four macros available to a wordprocessing application. Recording a macro puts the application package into 'remember' mode. While recording, any actions taken are stored in the macro. Once recorded and stored as a macro the actions can be 'played back' when needed, by invoking them using a keystroke, the mouse or selecting from the menu, saving all that work necessary to create it. For example, the 'address' macro of figure 1.24 will insert an address (right justified) and will be invoked when starting a letter (see figure 1.26.)

Macros are in-built to most office application software, to provide commonly needed functions. Examples are: spell-checking in a wordprocessor; default text size and font in a new document; a document template; spreadsheet summation and averaging. These supplied macros (and any new ones created by the user) save time, make things easier, and generally make the applications package more convenient and effective to use.

## 1.4.1 Purposes of macros

Using a macro to carry out a specific set of operations for a frequently required task can reduce the possibility of making an input error, speed up processing and standardise procedures. The macro makes things more convenient for the user by automating the many actions that must be taken to accomplish some task.

### Reduce input error

Any manual entering of text (or manually carrying out a sequence of processing operations) is prone to some form of human error.

When entering text that must be retyped within the same or different documents, not only must we remember the correct text, but we must type it correctly. Leaving something out' or making spelling mistakes, or using an incorrect format will cause errors. Use of **paragraph macros** can enable the customisation of standard letters to meet a variety of requirements and reduce the likelihood of making an error.

Selecting a series of actions to perform some task must also be done correctly, if the expected end result is to be achieved. Many activities involve a series of steps and may require the user to select from a number of choices – mistakes are easily made, particularly if the user is a novice. The macro replaces the need for the user to remember what to type or select. For example, it may be lengthy text plus a sequence of operations to carry out some task, which may be both time consuming to carry out and subject to error – returning text to a standard default of margins, text font and size requires several actions and selections. Database systems can attach macros to command buttons, and use them to automate and coordinate actions when someone is entering and modifying data, or opening and closing forms.

### Speed up processing

Where an activity using office application software involves repeating some specific task, then using macros will complete that activity faster. For example, using a macro to place your address at the top right of each letter, saves having to type and position that text. A macro can be used to select and position company logos on each document of a report. Letters and documents can be composed from sets of standard paragraphs, each having its own macro. Using a macro to automate a drawing activity that usually involves a sequence of steps and selections, will save the user time by not having to repeat those steps each time. Form templates and macros make it easier for the user to fill out standard forms.

### Standardise procedures

The macros supplied with application software have been designed and implemented by IT professionals to provide users with a set of standardised procedures and formats. For example, an organisation may set up procedures, the format and functionality of which follow an agreed standard. Irrespective of the originator of a procedure, any user will be able to interpret, follow and use it to complete a task correctly. For example, template macros for documents ensure that a particular house-style is used, and template macros for forms ensure that the correct data or information is obtained.

### Convenience

To summarise, a macro is a single command that, when activated, is replaced by a sequence of operations. By using macros the user's life is made easier and the applications software is more convenient to use for both the user and the organisation, because the macro has automated the many operations that must take place to accomplish a particular task. Once designed and implemented, a macro that performs a specific task can be made available to all users within the organisation.

## 1.4.2 Uses of macros

Office application software packages for wordprocessing, spreadsheets and database development come supplied with macros and provide facilities to create new ones. A macro is used to replace repetitive key strokes and mouse actions, to set up document templates, to set defaults to commence an activity and to make calculations.

### Repetitive key stroke sequences

A basic macro will be a single command that is replaced by (or triggers) a series of key strokes and mouse actions. The activities the macro replaces will be ones that are used over and over again within the application software and so creating a macro to do the same thing will be beneficial to the users. When a macro is created it is assigned to a keystroke combination or a toolbar button or a menu item, and using or selecting this will invoke the macro (see figure 1.25).

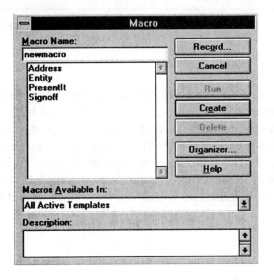
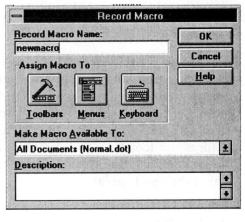

*Figure 1.25 Microsoft word new macro assignment*

For example, letters that a lecturer sends would have an address and other contact information at the top of the first page (as shown in figure 1.26).

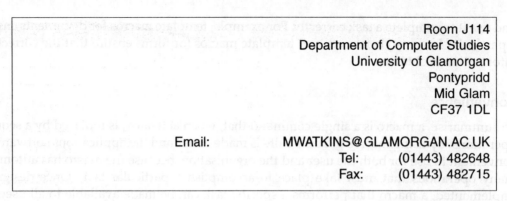

Room J114
Department of Computer Studies
University of Glamorgan
Pontypridd
Mid Glam
CF37 1DL

Email:        MWATKINS@GLAMORGAN.AC.UK
Tel:         (01443) 482648
Fax:        (01443) 482715

*Figure 1.26 Address and contact text for a macro*

The text in figure 1.26 is over a hundred characters and from a macro named 'Address,' which is invoked by the keystroke combination (Alt+Ctrl+D). User macros like 'Address' are easily created in application software packages using the macro record function. The sequence to do this in Microsoft Word is given in figure 1.27 (some of the windows are shown earlier in figures 1.24 to 1.25). When recording a record control button is displayed that can be used to stop the macro create process if necessary.

1.     Select Tools pull-down menu
2.     Select Macro.. option to open a dialogue box
3.     Type a name and give a brief description of the macro's purpose
4.     Press Record button to create macro
5.     Assign macro invoke method, keyboard or toolbar or menu.
6.     Start recording process
7.     Carry out typing and actions to be included in the macro
8.     Stop the recording process

*Figure 1.27 Steps to create a macro in Microsoft Word*

## Templates

A **template** is a standardised layout (or format) for a pro forma document that usually has a specific purpose, for example, an assignment front sheet, a fax cover sheet, an Intermediate IT unit definition sheet or an invoice. The template image is created and saved, and when the template is invoked, a sequence of commands is executed to produce the required pro forma image – the user then adds their particular data. The template can position text; set styles for text, headers and footers; include graphics and logos. When creating a new template it is usual to base it initially on an existing document (or template) which can then be modified to the format of the new template.

## Set defaults

When starting an office application software package, it sets itself up using a set of default characteristics. But a user can change the default settings to meet their own individual needs, and once changed, all new applications will initially take on the new default values. For example, in wordprocessing a user may choose Times New Roman font and a font size of 12 to be the default text style (see figure 1.28). In a database application, a macro can define default colours and borders for a data entry screen.

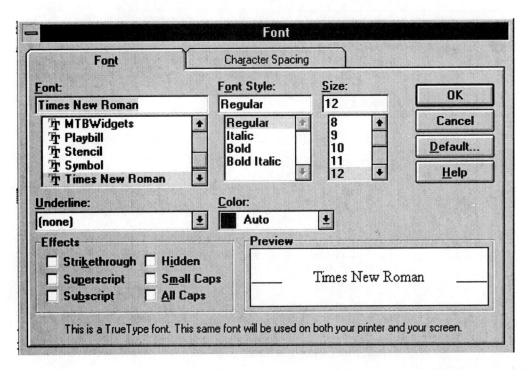

*Figure 1.28 Font dialogue box of Word 6*

## Calculations

In spreadsheet applications, users must understand and remember the details of calculations to be applied to the spreadsheet data; this can be difficult if the activity is not a frequent one, and as such can be exceedingly prone to errors. Many other spreadsheet activities also require a great deal of mouse activity in carrying out a number of operations in a particular sequence. Using a calculation macro can make life easier for the user: having recorded and tested the macro to ensure that it does things correctly, the calculation is instantly available through invoking the macro.

## Question 1.51

*A macro allows different keystroke combinations to select fonts for a report. Why is the macro used?*

*A  to standardise the report layout*

*B  to increase the number of fonts*

*C  to make it easier to change font*

*D  to avoid making spelling mistakes*

## Question 1.52

A macro is used to insert an organisation's address automatically on all its correspondence. Why is the macro used?

A  to reduce disk space

B  to speed up letter production

C  to improve validation checking

D  to use less paper

## Question 1.53

A secretary uses a macro to speed up the production of several similar letters. What is done by the macro?

A  inserting standard paragraphs

B  copying the manager's signature

C  proofreading of the letters

D  correcting spelling mistakes

## Task 1.16  PC 1, PC 2

You have been asked to explain to some new users of a wordprocessing package, the purpose and uses of macros. Prepare and give a brief presentation that explains what a wordprocessing macro is, and describe with examples the purpose and uses of at least two wordprocessing macros, showing the different ways in which they can be invoked.

### 1.4.3  User macro specification

Creation of many macros is a relatively simple task. Most experienced application software package users are capable of doing this to meet their own requirements. However, a macro is a piece of software, and as such should be subject to software design and implementation methods. This is particularly true for macros which will be used across an organisation by many different users, and for the more powerful and complicated macros.

The process starts by recognising the needs for and the requirements of a new macro – this will result in a **specification** for the macro. The specification is then used to design the macro to meet the requirements. The design is used to implement the macro, and it is then tested against the specification before finally releasing it to the users.

The macro specification is a result of meeting with the user(s) and analysing their requirements. The user(s) will be able to explain their use of the application software and what their needs are. The macro developer must be experienced in the same application software and should possess an in-depth knowledge of its facilities and functionality. The specification will then be structured around the following sections.

- **Applications software to be used** – this describes the application software title and version number that the user has access to. The product may have supplied macros itself that meet all or most of the user requirements and the user is unaware of them. The macro developer must be sure to be familiar with the macro development facilities of a particular version.

- **Purposes of using the macro** – this is a clear description of what the user wants the macro to do. This is obtained by interviewing the user, assessing what they are trying to do (possibly with a demonstration that may highlight a problem), and why the macro is required. It will identify the benefits that the new macro will provide to the user.

- **Uses of the macro** – this describes the specific uses that will be made of the macro. It describes the type of macro (as classified in Section 1.4.2) by outlining what it produces, and when and where it should be used.

- **Method of executing the macro** – the user and developer must agree on how the macro is to be invoked. The developer should explain the different methods, and help the user decide which method would be most convenient to their method of working. This section should detail how the macro will be invoked.

- **Data to be embedded in the macro** – having assessed the needs of the macro, this section details data (such as graphics and text) that is to be embedded in the macro. The data must be supplied by the user, but it may require several tests and reviews in order to get it complete.

- **Layout styles** – this section applies to how the output from the macro will appear, and is particularly necessary for templates. Template design often requires form design skills, the user and developer should initially sketch out an outline and then add the details – getting things right will require several attempts.

- **Tests to be applied** – once created, the macro should be tested initially by the developer to iron out any problems. Once satisfied, the developer should allow the user to test it in its working environment. Testing will reveal logic and operational problems that will require amendment of the macro to get things right. The testing should check that the macro meets each of the purposes, uses and method of execution specified earlier. If test criteria are not clearly specified then you can never be sure if the macro works correctly.

### Task 1.17  PC 3

*Develop a user specification for a macro to do the following activity. A template is required that is suitable for staff to use as a front sheet for any assignments given in delivering the Intermediate IT course. You will need to discuss with staff their particular requirements. Here are some typical characteristics to get started with: unit title, staff name, assignment title, assignment date set, assignment date due in, performance criteria assessed, assignment requirements.*

### Task 1.18  PC 4, PC 5

*Implement the macro from the specification in Task 1.17. Get a member of staff or a classmate to test your macro and review its use. List at least two other activities in the administration and delivery of the Intermediate IT course where macros may be useful, such as recording and ranking student performances in individual units.*

# Answers to questions in Unit 1

| | | | | |
|---|---|---|---|---|
| **Answer 1.1** | C | | **Answer 1.26** | A |
| **Answer 1.2** | A | | **Answer 1.27** | B |
| **Answer 1.3** | B | | **Answer 1.28** | C |
| **Answer 1.4** | A | | **Answer 1.29** | A |
| **Answer 1.5** | C | | **Answer 1.30** | A |
| **Answer 1.6** | B | | **Answer 1.31** | D |
| **Answer 1.7** | B | | **Answer 1.32** | D |
| **Answer 1.8** | C | | **Answer 1.33** | A |
| **Answer 1.9** | C | | **Answer 1.34** | C |
| **Answer 1.10** | A | | **Answer 1.35** | B |
| **Answer 1.11** | B | | **Answer 1.36** | D |
| **Answer 1.12** | C | | **Answer 1.37** | A |
| **Answer 1.13** | A | | **Answer 1.38** | D |
| **Answer 1.14** | D | | **Answer 1.39** | A |
| **Answer 1.15** | A | | **Answer 1.40** | B |
| **Answer 1.16** | B | | **Answer 1.41** | A |
| **Answer 1.17** | C | | **Answer 1.42** | B |
| **Answer 1.18** | D | | **Answer 1.43** | C |
| **Answer 1.19** | B | | **Answer 1.44** | D |
| **Answer 1.20** | A | | **Answer 1.45** | D |
| **Answer 1.21** | C | | **Answer 1.46** | A |
| **Answer 1.22** | B | | **Answer 1.47** | A |
| **Answer 1.23** | C | | **Answer 1.48** | B |

**Answer 1.24**
Input – five senses
Processing – brain
Storage – brain memory
      – books and paper
Output – speech
      – writing
      – actions

| **Answer 1.49** | D |
|---|---|
| **Answer 1.50** | C |
| **Answer 1.51** | C |
| **Answer 1.52** | B |
| **Answer 1.53** | A |

**Answer 1.25** B

# Unit 1 Sample Test Paper

**Commercial and industrial IT systems**

A modern DIY store uses an electronic point-of-sale (EPOS) system, with laser operated check-outs that scan barcodes on products.

1   How does the system benefit the DIY store?

    A   less shelf space needed
    B   store has longer opening hours
    C   stock levels are accurately maintained
    D   staff enjoy using computers

2   How does the system benefit the customers?

    A   there are fewer pricing errors
    B   there is more choice of items
    C   more checkouts are available
    D   the DIY items are cheaper

3   DIY items purchased can be paid for with a payment card. Which IT development has made this possible?

    A   stock control systems
    B   electronic funds transfer (EFT)
    C   order processing
    D   booking systems

4   The DIY company employs a large number of staff. Which of the following is a benefit of computerising the staff payroll?

    A   less time is spent calculating staff pay
    B   staff can be paid whenever they like
    C   staff wage details are more confidential
    D   more part-time staff can be employed

5   The DIY company is deciding whether to computerise its warehousing with robotics and automated shelving. Which of the following will be a major limitation?

    A   efficiency
    B   cost
    C   accuracy
    D   security

6   Some of the DIY store suppliers use CAD systems to design their products and computer controlled robots to manufacture them. What is the main advantage to the manufacturer of using robots?

    A   robots can do any job
    B   robots use the latest computer technology
    C   production requires less space
    D   robots perform repetitive tasks accurately

7   Which of the following is a problem with robot automated production?

    A   there are fewer jobs for the workforce
    B   the supplier makes lower profits
    C   there are more manufacturing injuries
    D   industrial pollution levels are higher

8   Why use a CAD system to design products?

    A   designs do not need testing
    B   CAD systems are cheap to buy
    C   designs can be easily changed
    D   designers require no training

**Components of a stand-alone computer system**

Questions 9 to 21 refer to the following application system.

An estate agents has purchased a computer system to store client/property data and produce leaflets. The system was supplied with a main processor unit, VDU screen, keyboard, mouse, floppy and hard disk drives.

9   Which additional hardware component is needed?

    A   a CD-ROM drive
    B   a document scanner
    C   a laser printer
    D   a pair of speakers

10   Which component of a computer system is used for input of client/property data?

    A   keyboard
    B   main processor unit
    C   VDU screen
    D   printer

11  Which component performs client mortgage calculations?

A   a VDU screen
B   a keyboard
C   a hard disk
D   the main processor unit

12  The system has graphical user interface (GUI) software to help users. Which component is used to select actions with GUI software?

A   a hard-disk drive
B   a VDU screen
C   a mouse
D   a keyboard

13  Which of the following is the main function of a floppy disk?

A   to display customer/property data
B   to process customer/property data
C   to store customer/property data for future use
D   to input customer/property data

14  A user lost new customer/property data when the computer was switched off. Which type of storage was being used for the customer /property data?

A   RAM
B   floppy disk
C   ROM
D   hard disk

15  The agency needs to include photographs in the property database. Which component is needed to input the photographs into the computer?

A   a scanner
B   a light pen
C   a CD-ROM drive
D   a VDU screen

16  The property database application displays colourful data entry forms and pictures. Which is the best device for displaying the forms?

A   a CD-ROM drive
B   a VDU screen
C   a laser printer
D   a document scanner

17  Which of the following best describes the purpose of adding a magnetic tape drive to the system?

A   to display documents in a user-friendly manner
B   to read barcodes from documents
C   to provide immediate access to stored documents
D   to provide backup data storage

18  Which advantage does the addition of cache memory provide to the computer system?

A   it can access more disks
B   it has extra instructions
C   it has greater accuracy
D   it runs programs more quickly

19  Which of the following is carried out by applications software?

A   formatting a disk
B   drawing a property plan
C   renaming a file
D   compiling a mortgage loan program

20  Which of the following is carried out by operating system software?

A   adding a new property record to a database
B   drawing a property plan
C   copying a file
D   compiling a mortgage loan program

21  Which type of software is used to send a letter to all the agency's clients?

A   database
B   spreadsheet
C   word-processing
D   graphics

**Set up of a stand-alone computer system**

Questions 22 to 27 refer to the following event.

The estate agency has purchased a new desktop publishing package (DTP) on floppy disks.

22  A user wants to install the DTP software on the systems hard drive. Which of the following should be done first?

A   tidy up the hard disk
B   take security copies of the floppy disks
C   create a directory on the hard disk
D   run the DTP setup

23 Each user will keep all DTP documents in a special disk area. How is the area set up?

   A   by using a special type of disk
   B   by giving documents the same file type
   C   by creating a data directory on the hard disk
   D   by making a backup copy of the DTP software

24 The control panel window of the GUI has a printer icon that is used to set up a laser printer for use with the DTP package.
   Why is this necessary?

   A   to install the driver for the laser printer
   B   to print the DTP hard disk directory
   C   to copy software files
   D   to test the new DTP package

25 Having installed the DTP system it must be tested. Which of the following operations comes first?

   A   retrieve an example DTP file
   B   print a page on the laser printer
   C   load the DTP package
   D   save a new DTP file

26 Which operation will test that the current document has been saved to disk successfully?

   A   printing the current document
   B   retrieving the saved document
   C   saving a similar document
   D   entering more text into the document

27 Which operation tests that the new printer driver is working correctly?

   A   switch off and power up the system
   B   load a saved document
   C   save a current document
   D   print the current page

**Application software macros**

28 Which of the following best describes a macro?

   A   a way to set up a printer
   B   a way of utilising computer memory
   C   a way of automating computer tasks
   D   a way of using a GUI

29 Why might a macro be used?

   A   to reduce the number of users
   B   to reduce the number of computers
   C   to reduce the number of operating system tasks
   D   to reduce the amount of time taken to perform a task

30 What is not required before creating a macro?

   A   the users' passwords
   B   which software package is being used
   C   the use of the macro
   D   the purpose of the macro

31 How would you check if the macro works?

   A   display the macro commands
   B   get users to execute the macro
   C   create a shortcut key
   D   embed the macro in an application file

Questions 32 to 34 share answers A to D

Here is a list of some common computer tasks that could be carried out using a macro.

   A   calculating mortgage loan repayments
   B   filling in a property for sale header sheet
   C   drawing lines and shapes
   D   input transaction processing

32 Which will use a wordprocessing macro?

33 Which will use a spreadsheet macro?

34 Which will use a database macro?

by **Peter Hodson**

*Unit 2*

# *Using information technology*

## Introduction

This unit examines the impact that information technology has had on processing commercial documents and looks at the extended facilities that we now have in presenting this information. Such facilities allow us to create graphics and technical drawings and images. Of course with this ability comes a requirement to follow some standard structures and conventions in layout and presentation style. These issues will be covered in the first two elements of this unit.

The last two elements of this unit look at how we can store data, model systems and develop control systems. Element 2.3 provides an opportunity for us to explore and use the commonly available software that is used to store data. Typically the application software to store data and run predictive models is known as a spreadsheet. Setting up a spreadsheet will be taken as a task in this unit. This task models the way in which the financial income on a hotel room occupancy could work.

Having created a base of information we can then quiz the model to predict the way in which changes alter this system. This allows us to predict the impact of any changes. Take an easy example of a pub. Assume we set up a spreadsheet which details the cost of buying in the beer, the cost of labour and the income from sales. This will allow us to calculate the profits of the pub. If we decide to pay the bar staff more per hour the change in profit will be shown immediately.

Computers can also be used to keep control of systems. Frequent inputs of information to a computer (such as the temperature now in a heating system) can be quickly processed. For repetitive processing of data read from sensors, computers are much more effective than people.

# *Process commercial documents*

## Introduction

This element looks at the ways in which computer systems have helped us to manage to process documents. To do this well, commercial organisations and businesses have several different formats for information. Each are used by convention in particular situations. For example, documents used within a business will have a different format to those sent outside to other organisations.

For most businesses, their image to the public or their trading partners is influenced by the way in which the business communicates. The quality and appearance of letters and documents plays a big part in creating that image. Companies will often try to create a logo which represents and easily identifies them. If you see a big yellow 'M', you are probably thinking burgers! If we can capture such benefits and include them in the communication, then we give an advantage to the business.

Hence we need to identify the different communication formats used in business and look at how the computer systems can help us create and maintain such quality.

## 2.1.1 Commercial documents

### Agenda

An **agenda** is a document, normally on a single page, which outlines the topics that will be discussed at a meeting. The order in which the topics will be taken is implied by the relative position of the topic in the overall list. An agenda should cover several key points which tell the reader that:

- a meeting is taking place;
- the issues being discussed.

The key points covered are:

- the title of the meeting;
- the location of the meeting;
- the date and time of the meeting;
- a list of the topics being covered;
- any other reports or paperwork needed for the meeting.

Here is a typical example:

The second meeting of the
Newtown Scout Leaders to be
held at the Scout Hut on 6th July
1995 at 7.00 pm

Agenda

1. Minutes of last meeting
   (please bring these)
2. Matters arising
3. Planning for activity weekend
4. Planning for Autumn
   Barbeque
5. Any other business
6. Date of next meeting

*Figure 2.1 Typical agenda*

## Question 2.1

*Should an agenda be distributed a few weeks before the meeting takes place or at the meeting, in case people forget to bring their copy with them?*

### Business letter

The layout of business letters has to follow standards that are commonly used. The position of basic information is normally set up as a blank form or template, allowing the typist to quickly fill in the areas created. This ensures a standard layout and speeds up the preparation time. The following example shows the areas or zones we need to create.

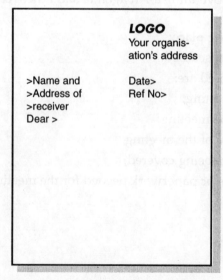

**LOGO**
Your organis-
ation's address

>Name and          Date>
>Address of        Ref No>
>receiver
Dear >

*Figure 2.2 Business letter layout*

The position of any logo used and the sender's address will depend on the house-style created. The pointer '>' shows the typist the position to move to and begin entering the appropriate data. In designing the position of the receiving address, we must remember that its position is important if we are using envelopes with view windows, i.e. the letter must fold to display the address in the correct position of a window envelope. The key zones we have created are:

- name of receiver;
- receiving address;
- date;
- reference.

In many systems it is possible to automatically generate the date field with today's date.

## Invoice

An **invoice** is the form generated when asking the customer to pay for the goods or services supplied. It is important to provide reference numbers that uniquely identify each individual invoice. These invoice numbers enable a finance department to keep track of the invoice system, e.g. when a customer pays by quoting the invoice number, the payment can be credited to the correct account. A list of outstanding or unpaid invoices can be then kept, so that reminders can be sent (have you ever received a 'red' telephone bill in your house because you have forgotten to pay?). The form must include the following information:

- both the supplier's and customer's addresses;
- relevant dates;
- reference numbers, e.g. customer's order number, invoice number;
- description of goods or services;
- VAT as appropriate;
- total payment required and date due.

An example of an invoice is shown in figure 2.3.

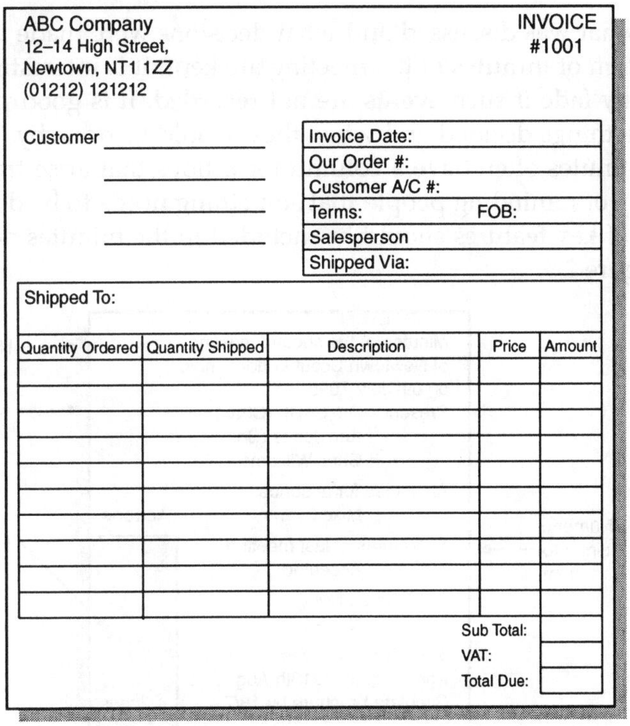

ABC Company
12–14 High Street,
Newtown, NT1 1ZZ
(01212) 121212

INVOICE
#1001

Customer

Invoice Date:
Our Order #:
Customer A/C #:
Terms: FOB:
Salesperson
Shipped Via:

Shipped To:

| Quantity Ordered | Quantity Shipped | Description | Price | Amount |
|---|---|---|---|---|

Sub Total:
VAT:
Total Due:

*Figure 2.3 Example invoice*

### Memoranda

A **memorandum** is used for communication inside an organisation. Hence the need for addressing is reduced because each of the organisation's locations will be well known internally. If multiple locations exist, they may well be given abbreviations, such as MAN1 for a central Manchester office and MAN2 for the manufacturing location. The structure doesn't have to be quite so formal because the external image isn't now critical. It is more important that concise, clear and efficient means of internal communication are created. The following example shows the typical structure.

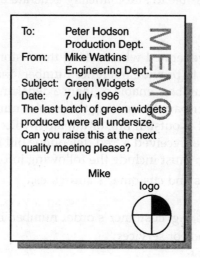

To:     Peter Hodson
        Production Dept.
From:   Mike Watkins
        Engineering Dept.
Subject: Green Widgets
Date:    7 July 1996
The last batch of green widgets produced were all undersize. Can you raise this at the next quality meeting please?

Mike

logo

*Figure 2.4 Example memo*

### Minutes

To remember what was discussed and what decisions were made at meetings, a record of the events in the form of **minutes** of the meeting are kept. It is interesting how people's memories can conveniently fade if such events are not recorded. It is good practice to record who was going to do the things decided and when they should be done by. These are frequently called the 'actions'. Minutes often have a column for actions that arise from the meeting and give a convenient way of reminding people that something needs to be done.

A number of key features should be included in the minutes document. These are clearly indicated in figure 2.5.

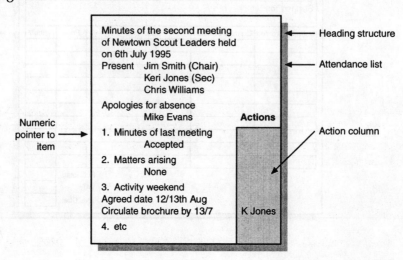

Minutes of the second meeting of Newtown Scout Leaders held on 6th July 1995 ← Heading structure
Present   Jim Smith (Chair) ← Attendance list
          Keri Jones (Sec)
          Chris Williams

Apologies for absence
          Mike Evans                **Actions**

Numeric pointer to item → 1. Minutes of last meeting
          Accepted                      ╱ Action column

2. Matters arising
          None

3. Activity weekend
Agreed date 12/13th Aug
Circulate brochure by 13/7      K Jones

4. etc

*Figure 2.5 Typical minutes layout*

The numeric pointer usually identifies the topic using the same number as the agenda associated with the meeting. The format or contents of each of the topics raised is frequently recorded in brief statements rather than an essay style.

## Question 2.2

*Why do you think an action column is a convenient way of reminding someone that they need to do something?*

## Question 2.3

*How wide should we make the action column?*

## Newsletter

A newsletter is normally produced to keep the intended reader informed about the activities of a group or organisation. It is one of the most important formats to get right in a commercial organisation because the image of the organisation can be so widely seen. The introduction of Desk Top Publishing packages for microcomputers has meant that many features of full publishing can be easily achieved by everyone. The simple construction of columns of print, just like a newspaper, and the use of graphics and tables can create quite a professional appearance.

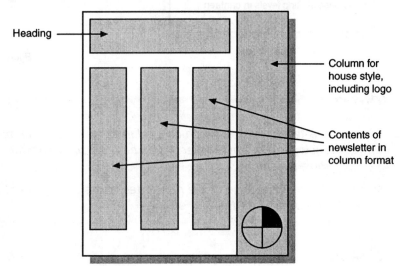

*Figure 2.6 Possible newsletter layout*

The layout in figure 2.6 is just an example of how you can use columns and headings to create a housestyle. There are many good alternative approaches that you could use, e.g. some columns can be combined to create short, fat areas rather than all long thin areas. This will be covered in Element 2.1.2.

## Question 2.4

*Is it essential to have a column for house style as shown in figure 2.6?*

### Report

A report provides an opportunity to record a little more detail on a particular topic or issue. There are many thousands of reports written each day. They range from small investigations on sales performance, productivity or technical reports through to major national surveys, such as a report on the national curriculum.

Normally the report is requested by somebody or a group of people. In the same way it might be one or more people who construct the report. Both of these are identified in the header. The format of any report may vary quite a lot, but will generally contain the key points indicated in figure 2.7. It is helpful to have an introductory paragraph to inform the reader what the purpose of this report is.

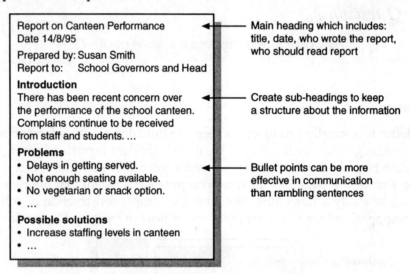

Figure 2.7 Typical report layout

### Task 2.1    PC 1, PC 6                                    C2.2

Create a newsletter which uses columns for a club or organisation which you know well. This newsletter should be A5 in size (see figure 2.10) and at least three pages long.

For the front page of the newsletter, create a template of the header which may be used for the next edition.

### Task 2.2    PC 1, PC 6                              C2.1, C2.2

Create an agenda and a set of minutes for a discussion group between a small team of you and a few colleagues. The group may take the topic of this task as its theme.

## 2.1.2 Page attributes and layouts

### Orientation

The orientation of the page may be in either:

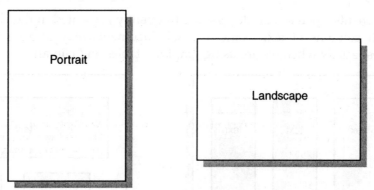

*Figure 2.8 Page orientation*

The particular orientation used will be influenced by the type of document and the page contents and its layout. For example, if you were constructing a table of information with a number of columns, the presentation would be better in landscape format.

| Item | Number sold | Value per item | Total | VAT rate | Gross total |
|------|-------------|----------------|-------|----------|-------------|
| Chair | 2 | £ 69.99 | £ 139.98 | 17.5% | £ 164.48 |
| Table | 1 | £ 160.00 | £ 160.00 | 17.5% | £ 188.00 |

*Figure 2.9 Landscape format for sales description table*

## Question 2.5

*Can you identify another situation which would be better in landscape than portrait orientation?*

### Paper size

There are standard sizes of paper available in what is known as the 'A' series. Each change in number means the page size is twice as big (or half the size) of the next in the range. Approximate sizes within the range are shown in figure 2.10.

| A3 | 420 * 292 mm |
|----|--------------|
| A4 | 210 * 296 mm |
| A5 | 105 * 148 mm |

*Figure 2.10 Size of paper*

In choosing the size of paper for any document we should remember:
- will it need to be filed in a normal size filing cabinet?
- will it need to be read at a distance, e.g. on noticeboards?

- will it need to be put in a notebook folder or personal organiser?
- what is the purpose of the document?

## Column layout

Some documents (such as newsletters) are frequently presented in the classic style of a newspaper with columns of text. Some internal documents may also be enhanced by having columns, especially when we are using graphics, tables and clip art.

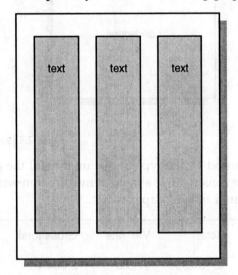 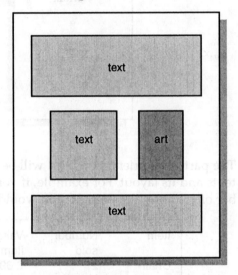

*Figure 2.11 Examples of different column layouts*

## Fonts

Different styles of **font** can be used to suit the particular purpose of the document. In a formal business document a traditional font (such as Times, New York or Palatino) would be selected. For a club newsletter, a less formal font can be selected. Element 2.2.2 looks at this issue again when we consider graphical design.

*Figure 2.12 Examples of fonts*

Once the font style has been selected, the size of the font has to be chosen. For standard documents, this is normally 10 or 12 point. Large sizes are selected for particular features, such as headings, front pages, display posters or a presentation document (which will be projected on an overhead slide).

Times 10 point
Times 12 point
Times 14 point
Times 18 point

*Figure 2.13 Typeface size*

## Question 2.6

*Should we change fonts within a single document to emphasise particular words or sections?*

### Headers and footers

Many wordprocessing packages provide the facilities to put a **header** or **footer** on every page. The information can be either **fixed** or **variable**. Fixed information could be the title of the document or chapter in a book. Variable information could be the date and time. For example, if the date footer was implemented, then today's date would be printed in any listing taken today. If it was printed tomorrow, then tomorrow's date would be printed. The position and layout of any selected element can be set up as you wish. Figure 2.14 shows a footer window in WORD, with the range of tools available for use in setting your footer. WORD is the Microsoft wordprocessing package that I used to prepare this text. Other good examples also exist such as WordPerfect. In particular, the icons for page numbering, date and time are shown in the menu bar and have been selected in this example.

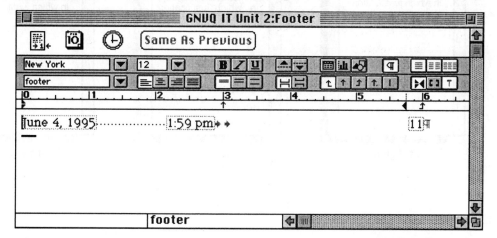

*Figure 2.14 Example footer window*

## Question 2.7

*What is the header on this page of the book?*

### Indents and tabulations

It is common practice to show the relationship of paragraphs in a text by **indenting** the whole paragraph. The result is often known as a **sub-paragraph**. If we only wish to move a single piece of data to the next pre-set position, then we use a **tab (tabulation)** function. Columns of data are usually set up by using a tab feature to get each entry aligned, rather than trying to use the space bar to get alignment. Both features çan be set up on a ruler using the tools shown in figure 2.15. In this figure, the tabulations have been automatically set up at each ½ inch mark (sorry it's an American package working in inches and not a metric system! Still, here in the UK we are not completely metric because we still use miles).

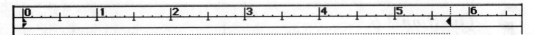

*Figure 2.15 Example of a ruler*

### Justification and alignment

The layout of the page can be selected to have the contents aligned in one of **several ways**:

- left alignment;
- right alignment;
- justified alignment.

The appearance of the document using the **justified** alignment approach is better when the typeface is small. If it is much bigger than 10 point, then the appearance is often one of distorted spacing between words.

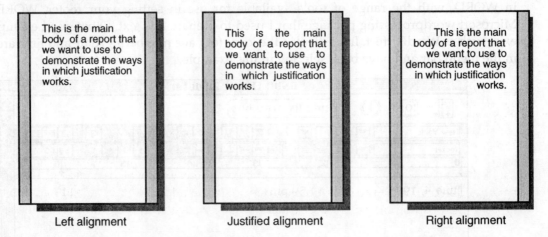

*Figure 2.16 Alignment*

### Line spacing

The space between lines of text can be changed by the wordprocessing (or DTP) package. In a normal presentation, you would set one line space between each row. If you know that the document is a draft and needs the reader to proof read the copy, you could double space (two line spaces) the text. This would give room for the reader to write down any comments or changes needed.

It may be that one and a half line spacing is appropriate, especially if the reader is known to have a sight impairment, or if rows of data are presented. In this case, keeping a clear gap between the data across the page helps.

| Lines of text with one line spacing | Lines of text with one and a half line spacing | Lines of text with two line spacing |

*Figure 2.17 Line spacing*

## Margins

The page layout needs to know how much space you want to leave around the edges of the paper to present the information effectively. These spaces or **margins** will reflect a few basic issues. If the document is going to be filed in a folder or bound in some way, the left hand side of the page needs to be wide enough to do this without loosing the ability to still see the left hand edge of the page. A report may well be produced and have multiple copies made with the pages backed up by printing on both sides of the page. In this case the right hand margin needs to be as wide as the left hand side.

All of the document should have the same basic margins. If we reviewed our business letter layout in figure 2.2, the name and address area would be included in the margin setting as well as the contents of the letter. All wordprocessing packages have a facility for setting the left and right hand margins. Most also allow you to set the format of how big the space at the top and the bottom of the page should be. This can either be achieved using the ruler provided on the package or the margins routine as shown in figure 2.18.

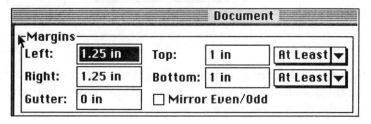

*Figure 2.18 Setting margins*

## Page numbering

In any document of more than one or two pages it is normal to give each page a number. This helps a reader to locate or identify the information quickly. A book index wouldn't be much use if the pages weren't numbered. Several conventions exist which include putting the number either on one of the top or bottom corners, or in the middle of the page. If material has been typeset, the position may alternate corners on either page as in the example of this book.

### Task 2.3     PC 2, PC 3                                                    C 2.2

*Now that you recognise the need for page attributes, such as margins, page numbering, columns and document notes, look at your work from task 2.1. Edit the layout to include the page attributes covered above. Not all the attributes need to be used in each of the four documents. However all the above page attributes must be used at least once.*

### 2.1.3 Enter data and edit document

The data in a document may exist in a number of different formats including:

- graphics;
- tables;
- text.

Each of these data types need their own set of editing tools to manipulate or modify the format. The editing range is discussed within each of the data types.

#### Graphics

This could take various formats (as seen in the next element). The basic format could be a graphical representation of tabular information. The data in figure 2.19 could be represented as:

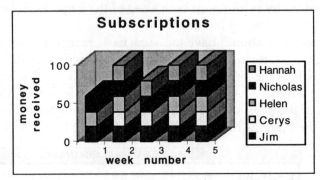

*Figure 2.19 Graphical representation*

Alternatively, artwork known as **clip art** or diagrams constructed in a drawing package can be imported into the document. Of course the size and position within the document is important in trying to get the right appearance.

Here is a example of clip art which can be used whenever we are showing something relating to detection or investigation. Perhaps this is someone trying to find the last bug in their program!

*Figure 2.20 Clip art*

There are many graphics and presentation software packages which allow us to create such documents, including Claris Impact, CorelDRAW and Microsoft PowerPoint. Many of the packages provide a file containing prepared clip art which may be used. To get the material into the right position and of the right size needs some manipulation within the package. Basic edit tools for graphics include:

- copy;
- move;
- rotate;
- size.

For example a box with a line can demonstrate some of the characteristics.

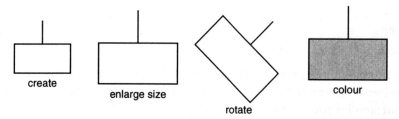

create     enlarge size     rotate     colour

*Figure 2.21 Graphics manipulation*

Copying and moving graphics usually occurs when you are creating a document. The graphic is often copied from the package in which is was created and pasted into the new document. Once it has been sized it may be appropriate to move its position within the document to achieve a more pleasing overall effect. In figure 2.20 the clip art has been made smaller than the original on the clip art file and positioned on the right hand side of the page.

## Tables

Some wordprocessing packages allow you to create tables of data directly. If your package doesn't give you these features, if you want tables of information, numerical data or formula created data, then it needs to be created in another package (such as a spreadsheet) and copied into the wordprocessed document. Copying like this is known as **importing** material.

| Subscriptions in pence | | | | | | |
|---|---|---|---|---|---|---|
| | | | | | | |
| **name** | **Week1** | **Week 2** | **Week 3** | **Week 4** | **Week 5** | **Total** |
| Jim | 20 | 20 | 20 | 20 | 20 | 100 |
| Cerys | | 20 | 20 | 20 | 20 | 80 |
| Helen | 20 | 20 | | 20 | 20 | 80 |
| Nicholas | 20 | 20 | 20 | 20 | 20 | 100 |
| Hannah | | 20 | 20 | 20 | 20 | 80 |

*Figure 2.22 Imported table from a spreadsheet*

Tables have the basic structure of rows and columns to create a grid or matrix effect. Each grid point contains an item. An item is simply a piece of data which has a particular format. The range of formats is considered in Element 2.3.4.

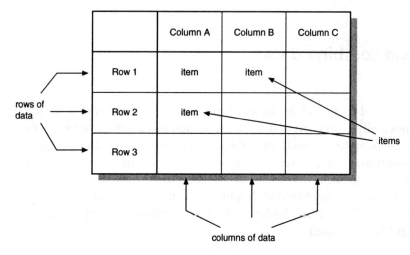

*Figure 2.23 Table structure*

Once a table has been established, the edit tools allow us to insert or delete another:

- row;
- column;
- data item.

Additionally, the size of the row or column can be changed to make the space available for the data item smaller or larger. In figure 2.22 it would be possible to have smaller columns, but it is unlikely that smaller rows could be achieved.

### Text

The bulk of data held on many computer systems is in text format. Data entry is normally via the keyboard and the text is stored in one of the standard formats (such as ASCII or EBCDIC), the format details of which are covered in Unit 4.

The preparation of a text-based document using a wordprocessor is rarely completed without some change being required to it. This may be a small adjustment to the layout. Most word-processors provide a good range of edit facilities for text including:

- copy;
- delete;
- enhance;
- insert;
- move.

Each edit facility usually requires you to select the appropriate text and then begin the action. Some of these edit functions, such as a move, are a combination of basic edit functions like cut and paste (i.e. cut out from one area and paste into another). An enhancement to text may be a simple change (e.g. to a word to put the text in bold, underlined or in italics) to highlight its position or importance. Frequently text that has been prepared elsewhere can be re-used by copying it from the original document and inserting the text into the new document.

## *Question 2.8*

*Are there any enhancements in the format of text on this page of the book?*

## 2.1.4 Find and combine data

### Find

Files are retrieved from disk by locating the file by its name and reading it into main memory. They are normally stored on disk in some structured manner, which group files together that belong to the same topic. Such groupings of files are known as directories or folders. A directory (or folder) may contain within it more directories (or folders), so that a hierarchical structure may be established.

As an example, on my Macintosh which uses folders, I have a folder for the application programme WORD. Within this folder is the file containing the application itself and a series of folders that I have created.

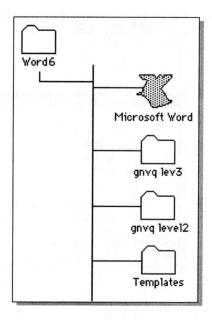

*Figure 2.24 Hierarchy of file structures*

Although the hierarchy of folders is not normally seen like this figure on my window, that is how it is represented in the same style as the directory structure of DOS systems. The folders on my Macintosh are normally seen as:

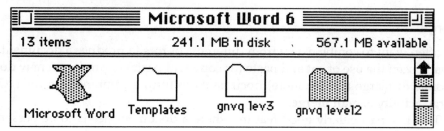

*Figure 2.25 Macintosh folder representation*

When you are trying to locate a file, you would normally search through the hierarchical system, i.e. a directory search (or folder search) until you reach the file you wanted. Of course, in a multi-user system, the file may have been created by others and be in their directory structure. You may or may not have access privileges to search in such areas.

It is entirely possible (in my case quite likely!) that you could forget or may not know where the file is located. In such cases it is normal to use the system to search for the file. This search may only have partial information, because you may not be absolutely sure of the filename. Every time a possible ID is made during the search, then it is displayed. Also displayed is an outline of where it is located to help you determine which of the occurrences (if any) is the file you are seeking.

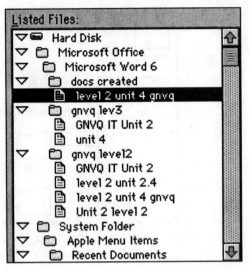

*Figure 2.26 Search for a file containing filename 'unit'*

## *Question 2.9*

*From the information provided in figure 2.26, can you name the files that exist in*

### Merge

We often want to combine data from different sources to produce a document. Indeed we have already seen the use of cut and paste (or copy and paste) to produce a new document. It is also possible to merge two (or more) documents to form a combined product. One example of a merge activity is **mail merge**.

This is a particularly good feature where a document needs to be personalised but many such personalised copies are generated. A standard letter that is sent to a number of people is a typical application. We would create a list of information which will be used for every distribution. This list may be created by direct data entry into the list or generated from a database.

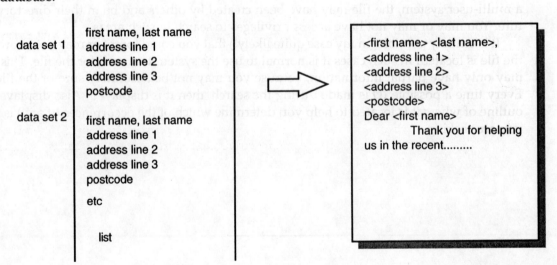

*Figure 2.27 Mail merge*

Each letter produced will take one set of the data from the list and substitute this into the letter. As many personalised letters would then be produced, as there were sets of data on the list. If another letter were produced tomorrow, then only the single master letter needs creating and multiple individual copies can be generated again, each with their individual or personalised information.

## 2.1.5 Saving using filenames plus accuracy and security checks

### Filenames

It is good practice to use a convention for naming files so that they meaningfully represent their content and show any sequence relative to other documents. Hence it might read club_minutes1.doc or club_minutes2.doc, etc. Note that many systems do not like spaces in the filenames, so we use an underscore character instead. Also, many systems like a filename extension (such as .doc or .xls) to indicate the application area that has created the data structure.

### Question 2.10

*Does a DOS based system like to use filename extensions?*

## Accuracy

Any document with an error in it detracts from the communication that is being attempted. The larger the document, the more difficult it is to remove all the little glitches. Wordprocessors can help us remove some spelling errors but will not detect misused words or words used in the wrong context. Grammar checkers are beginning to emerge which help in this area. Basically, the main approach to accuracy checks are:

- proof reading;
- spell checking.

### Proof read

This provides a check that will hopefully spot all the errors. It is a visual check on the document. Unfortunately there is a tendency to read what you expect to see and not what is actually there.

### Question 2.11

*When proof reading a document prepared with two line spacing, can you think of a potential problem that could occur when the final copy is made with one line spacing?*

## Question 2.12

*Identify in the following text what would be noted by spell-checker and what could be subsequently spotted by proof reading.*

*"It was good to sea you again at the recent meeting. Thr venew is two close to the rail station and the noice level is high".*

## Question 2.13

*Proof read the following text to determine if an error exists.*

*It is difficult to proof read a document that you have created because the the text is so familiar, you read what you expect to see.*

### Spell-checker

A complete check on a document or part of a document against the dictionary database can be undertaken. There may be new words that are correctly spelt but were not known to the supplied dictionary. Facilities to add your personal dictionary which will be part of a spell-check are available in many packages. For example Microsoft Word doesn't have my town name included, but I use it regularly in correspondence. Hence I have included it in my user dictionary and it no longer flags a possible error.

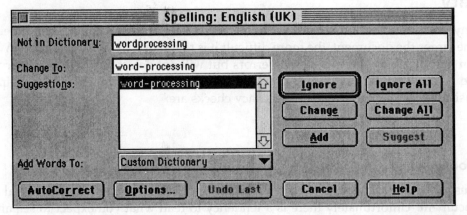

*Figure 2.28 Spell-checker*

### Security checks

Security checks help us keep all the documents safe and secure, reducing the risk of any data loss at any stage where the document is being updated or altered. The broad issues that should be considered include:

- backup;
- confidentiality;
- copyright;
- theft;
- source documents.

### File saving and back-ups

A version of Murphy's Law says "What can go wrong, will go wrong". Computer systems and in particular new releases of software, are prone to containing errors. Have you ever entered data, not saved the file and 'lost' it trying to do something to it? Although this rarely happens, it is new environments, such as implementing new versions of software, that often create such situations. The lesson is save your file regularly, probably every 30 minutes or less. This can be set to happen automatically in many wordprocessing packages. Of course the disk copy which contains this saved file could get damaged or corrupted. Hence back-up copies should be taken at regular intervals. This may be at the end of a session in a computer laboratory or at times of the day when you take a break. It is advisable to use two back-up disks and alternate the one onto which you take the copy. Certainly, daily back-ups of important files must occur. Network systems probably do this for you automatically.

Data held on computer systems is a valuable asset to any business and should be carefully protected. Some data may be confidential or personal information or covered by the Data Protection Act. It is good practice to keep to regular security routines to protect information.

### Confidentiality

It should be recognised that access to some data must be restricted and the originator may be required by their organisation to take precautions to protect it. It may be that the file can be secured either by networked security software or on a local disk with special security software. To access protected data requires the use of a password which was set up when the document was first protected.

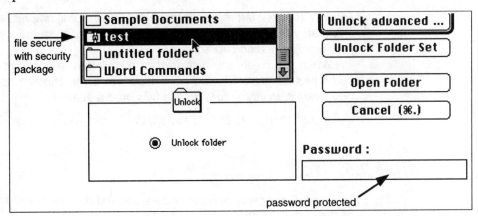

*Figure 2.29 Folder protected by security software*

Some organisations require their employees to sign an agreement of non-disclosure because the data is so sensitive. This means the employee must not release any data or information about the company to anyone else and the non-disclosure agreement can become part of the job contract. To disclose the data and let outside organisations or people see it would break the agreement and could result in dismissal.

### Copyright

To write a book, a piece of software, or to create a database, requires a considerable effort. To protect that work and stop others from copying it needs a conscious effort. Copyright protection is available and makes any infringement illegal. Hence copying a piece of software or data in breach of its copyright is an illegal activity. So is copying a music cassette onto a blank tape!

### Theft

Unfortunately theft of computer systems, both hardware and software is all too common. Indeed sometimes you may not even be aware that someone has stolen a copy of your software or data. To protect systems we could:

- physically secure the hardware;
- introduce protection of the software or data to prevent unauthorised use;
- use procedures to control unauthorised copying or removal of software or data;
- prevent illegal software being imported into your system.

### Source documents

Data is often generated initially in a different format than a computer's digital representation. It is then keyed in to create the computer's digital representation. Until the data has been successfully entered and back-up copies have been taken, the original source of the information (e.g. paper based forms) should be kept just in case we need to recreate from that source in the event of a major error or accident.

## 2.1.6 Produce documents and suggest improvements

### *Task 2.4*   PC 4, PC 5                                        *C 2.3*

*Enhance the newsletter from task 2.1 to contain some graphics and a table of information, which may be created in another package and imported into your wordprocessing package.*

*When you create the first draft of text, before you import any graphics and tables, save the file and back it up. Once the imported data has been positioned correctly, secure the file by saving it again.*

*Use a spell-checker to correct any spelling errors and proof read the layout.*

### *Task 2.5*   PC 3                                              *C 2.4*

*The publishers of your newsletter have decided that they would like the name of the current contributors in a footer at the bottom of the page. Edit your newsletter to include that information.*

### *Task 2.6*   PC 4, PC 6

*The publisher has now recognised that distribution of your newsletter needs to be managed. They have asked if a mail-merge facility could be used. Set up a mail list of at least four people to be recipients of the newsletter. Position on your newsletter an area to indicate the name of the recipient... that could be the top corner of the page! Print the newsletter using the mail-merge facility.*

Having produced your own newsletter and made several modifications, it is worth reviewing the style and layout. Getting feedback from independent people, especially the people for whom the newsletter was originally intended, is a possible step forward. It is also worth reviewing what was produced against the original specification. Does it conform exactly? Have you deviated from the specification? Have you had to make assumptions because the specification in the task wasn't detailed enough?

## *Task 2.7*   PC 6                                        *C2.1*

*Review your document from task 2.6 and note any improvements that could be made. If possible review a similar production from another group of students to see if their work could be improved. Offer them constructive feedback.*

# *Process graphic designs*

## Introduction

This element builds on the work achieved in Element 2.1. It is largely a practical element based on drawing or presentational packages. Here's your opportunity to become a computer artist! Most organisations understand that effective communication, especially in presentations at seminars or training sessions, are a key issue. The presentation software packages available (such as Microsoft's PowerPoint, Claris' Impact and CorelDRAW) all allow the creation of good quality graphics. They may be sequenced to automatically or manually present a slide show. Alternatively, they can be copied onto acetates for overhead projection.

## 2.2.1 Graphic design software

### Bit map and vector graphics

A graphic file can be represented in two basic ways. The whole drawing could be seen as a file containing a series of dots. Each minute item (or dot) in the graphic is held as a single **bit** of information in the file. In fact several bits of information will be held for each dot, if it is a colour picture. We can change any bit in the graphic as an individual piece of information, but we can't edit complete features that are made up of dots. So we couldn't say that an individual line (or any other feature) within a big image could separately be made shorter, leaving the rest of the image the same.

In a vector graphic, each element is defined in vector format which means we know a start point, a direction in which the vector is heading and it's length. So we define the graphic by the characteristics of the element. Each characteristic can be edited and manipulated individually within the whole image. So an individual line in a big graphic image could be changed.

Figure 2.33 is an example of a **bit map** image and the straight line in figure 2.35 is a **vector graphic**. Screen dumps, where you take a snap-shot of the screen and save the image, are a good example of bit map creation, as in figure 2.30. Drawing packages offer you tools to create vector graphics.

### *Question 2.14*

*Are the figures in 2.37 bit-maps or vector graphics?*

### *Question 2.15*

*Is the clip art used in figure 2.20 (page 82) based on bit map or vector graphics?*

92

## Chart

Representation of data in chart form is generally recognised as being easier to interpret than wordy statements. Whether the chart is presented as tables or graphic format (such as piecharts and histograms) is influenced by the sophistication of the intended reader. Detail on charts is given in Element 2.2.3. The tables and charts shown are created using software packages that are known as spreadsheets (examples are Excel and Lotus 123). Some packages, such as Works, have a spreadsheet as part of an integrated set of software.

## Slide show presentation

The presentation software packages normally allow you to create a series of graphic pages or slides. In fact it is this presentation software that you would use to create overhead slides. They typically provide a range of templates into which you enter your data – whether it be text or graphic, etc. A series of pages or slides can be grouped together to form a slide show. The order of the pages or slides in the file is called the **slide sequence**. This sequence may of course be re-ordered at any time. Once it is created, the output of the computer system can be projected either onto the monitor or onto a large screen. Large screen presentation can be achieved either by taking the output of the computer to a display panel mounted on top of an overhead projector or directly into a projection system.

In automatic mode, each slide will be projected for a time period which the presenter can specify. Alternatively, a manual operation can be used, with the next slide being displayed on request (e.g. by clicking the mouse).

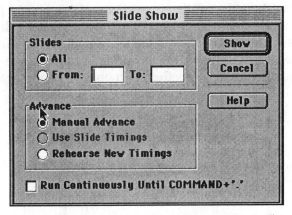

*Figure 2.30 Establishing a slide show*

A typical package which is used to generate presentation slides and which provides a slide show capability is PowerPoint.

## Question 2.16

*Why is a slide show a convenient way to make a presentation?*

**Task 2.8**  PC 1                                                                    *C 2.4*

*Survey the graphic design software packages you have available at your centre. For each package determine which of the following features they support:*

- *bit-map;*
- *vector;*
- *chart;*
- *slide show.*

## 2.2.2 Graphic components to meet design specifications

Most graphical images are made up of a combination of dots, basic lines, shapes and attributes. Once these have been mastered, anything can be constructed, given enough time and patience. The major components will be considered here.

### Attributes

Each diagram drawn can use a range of attributes (such as a style, thickness or fill). Line thickness can be used to show the relative importance of component parts of a diagram. If the diagram represents a manufactured product, then the thickness will represent the physical structure of the product. Thin lines may be fine in printed output, but will not project well if used in presentation software. However the term **line** in presentation software is also used to refer to the border around an object. Together with object fills and shadows, they define the attributes of an object.

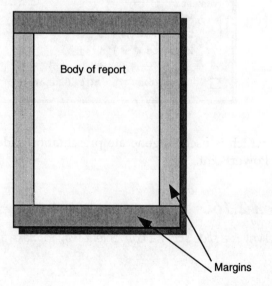

*Figure 2.31 Coloured margins used as border*

94

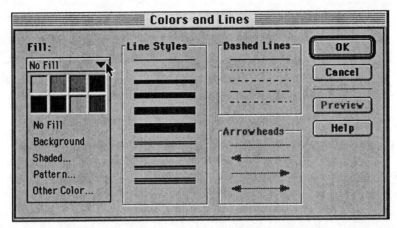

*Figure 2.32 Typical range of fills*

## Brush and spray

A number of presentational packages allow you to create graphics using features that emulate artists 'tools'. Hence you can select a thickness of brush and colour of paint and brush that effect onto the page using the mouse for control. An erase tool to clean up mistakes is usually available. Equally a spray tool with a variety of spray contents is often available to create an aerosol spray effect. You can elect to spray dots, stars, snow, etc. in many packages.

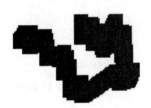

*Figure 2.33 Brush and spray effect*

## Question 2.17

*Is the spray effect shown in figure 2.33 a bit-map image or a vector graphic?*

## Colour

Most computer systems offer colour output. The use of colour on a slide presentation or in a printout can be helpful in making a point more clearly. Colour also adds to the interest level. There are some situations where colour cannot be used cost effectively. For example where pages are printed directly onto acetates to produce overhead slides. The cost of this may be too high for some purposes (e.g. where a large number of slides are used in a college or school). The cost of publishing a book using colour would make its retail price much less attractive to many potential readers.

The option for colouring or shading everything in the range of shapes leaves much to the imagination and creativity of the user of the package.

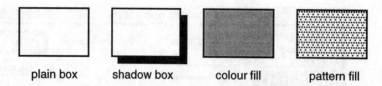

plain box     shadow box     colour fill     pattern fill

*Figure 2.34 Examples of colour and shading*

In selecting the shade or colour, it is worth noting that pale colours do not project well. Bold, strong colours may be needed which may look odd on the monitor, but better on projection.

## Question 2.18

*Do we need to worry about colour combinations?*

## Lines

There are perhaps four basic line formats:

- straight;
- arc;
- curve;
- freehand.

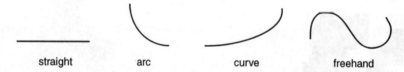

straight     arc     curve     freehand

*Figure 2.35 Basic types of lines*

With these fundamental lines, most other shapes can be constructed. As we saw earlier the width of lines is an attribute which can be helpfully used to represent an object more clearly or accurately.

## Shapes

It would be quite tedious to revert back to building everything from basic lines. The presentation software package is likely to provide a range of shapes to use.

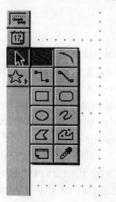

*Figure 2.36 Example of shapes available in Claris Impact*

Typically most packages provide the following shapes:

- rectangles;
- circles;
- polygons.

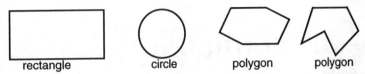

*Figure 2.37 Basic shapes*

### Question 2.19

*Why do we have rectangles rather than a square as a basic shape?*

## Text

The style and size of text in presentations and technical graphic design needs careful consideration. Normal size print at 10 or 12 point is not good when projecting the image for presentation slides. The standard templates supplied with the presentation software have pre-set text size which recognises these display requirements. Using a heading and a series of bullet points is widely recognised as a good style, rather than presenting too much detail on any single slide. Most slide templates have pre-set sizes for bullet points and allow a smaller typeface size to elaborate these main points.

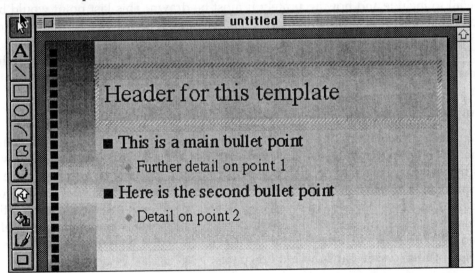

*Figure 2.38 Example template with text features*

### Question 2.20

*What is a **bullet point**?*

If you open a supplied template you will see that the fonts used are the bold, solid and traditional type rather than a fussy style. A font appropriate to the intended audience should be recognised, e.g. a modern style may be more acceptable to a youth club than a business sales presentation!

*Figure 2.39 Presentation font styles*

## Design specifications

In this element we have been looking at the component tools that we use to produce a graphic. Of course we need to have a clear idea of what it is that we are trying to create before we start. This is especially true if the work is being done for someone else. It is important that you understand that we need to specify some design points at an early stage, so that the graphic work produced will meet the needs. We need to know the purpose of the design, how much detail to include and how accurately it must be drawn. This last point would be particularly relevant to manufacturing situations where the graphic shows how a product is to be made and gives the dimensions on the drawing.

We consider the issues behind each of these issues. In Element 2.2.4 we can then proceed to create a graphic.

## Purpose

Preparing presentational and technical graphic design takes a lot longer than one might imagine. The effort put into the preparation should be controlled by the purpose for which the work is being done. For material that will be used many times over, that will have thousands of copies made or that is created for external or commercial work, then there is a good reason for spending time getting the quality right. Smaller, one-off jobs need less consideration, e.g. if you were drawing a map to send to a friend to reach your house, it may not be as carefully prepared and as accurate in scale compared to preparing a map for the location of a business, which was being printed on several thousand brochures.

## Contents and dimensions

The content of the drawing needs to be considered quite carefully. In particular we need to look at who will be using the graphic and how much detail they will need. Hence the purpose is a significant influence. Let us consider a few example situations.

If the document is for a presentation, we should consider that:

- slides with too much information cannot be read easily at a distance;

- slides are usually created to support the presentation and act as a supporting structure, reminding the viewer of the key points;
- too many slides per minute or hour and the viewer will suffer from slide fatigue!

The design needs to consider how best to portray the information without loosing detail. That will influence how much separate documentation will need to be created. For example, if it is a map that is being created, the result may be a series of maps with different levels of information:

- a top level map showing the town in relation to other towns in the region – major roads and motorways will be included;
- a lower level map showing the town only with major features of railway, bus and main roads;
- a detailed map showing the street names and landmarks such as pubs, schools and shops (why is it that people always use pubs as landmarks?).

If the work is a technical drawing, then normally the objects are carefully drawn to scale. The scale should be shown e.g. 1 mm: 100 cm. Normally the units (i.e. mm, cm, miles, etc.) are specified as plus/minus some fixed level or plus/minus a percentage measurement (e.g. ±1 mm or ±1%).

### Question 2.21

*A drawing representing a road map needs an accuracy of ±5%. If a line representing a road is to be 20 cm long, what is the minimum length of the line that we can draw to represent the road?*

Your design or artistic skills can be demonstrated here as you select the width, height, colours and shade. All of these have been previously mentioned. It is only practice and experience that shows you what will work well for a particular situation. We still need to remember that the graphic design needs to fit onto a specified page size which has been selected for the purpose. The way in which output may be presented can then be portrait or landscape and may require margins setting up. All of these issues are a culmination of previous topics and need practice to get perfect.

### Graphic type

We have already seen that bit map and vector graphics exist. Wherever we can work with vector graphics it is more helpful because the size of the file to hold the image is much smaller than a bit map. If we have many bit map images to hold, it is quite common to use a data compression package to reduce the file size.

### Slide show

As we suggested in Element 2.2.1, a series of pages can be placed in a file to form a slide series. These slides can be selected in sequence or have an alternative choice of paths set up (selection) in the more sophisticated versions of software. The display could be simply via the monitor if the group receiving the presentation is small, or projected onto a large screen for bigger groups. Such projection can be through an overhead system or via a panel on top of an OHP.

## Charts and pictures

In any communication it is widely accepted that pictures, diagrams and charts, etc. can more easily convey information to the reader than a text description. Figures 2.19 and 2.22 are examples of the two representations that are both more helpful to the reader than a wordy description of the data. These were generated in a spreadsheet, in this case Excel. The range of charts available include histograms, piecharts, etc. and can be selected within the package to represent the numerical data entered. Figure 2.40 shows a range of charts available.

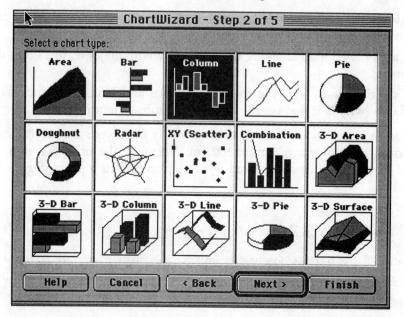

*Figure 2.40 Range of charts*

It is possible that you have an image or picture that you wish to include in a presentation that only exists in paper format. It is relatively easy to scan the picture to create a bit map image of the original. Most pictures exist in bit map format.

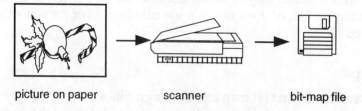

picture on paper            scanner            bit-map file

*Figure 2.41 Scanning process*

To enhance a presentation, it may be helpful to include relevant pictorial information from clip art or diagrams that have been scanned into digital format. A good range of clip art exists and choosing something appropriate is helpful in getting over your message. For example, if you were preparing a document to discuss printers, you could choose an image from one of the following pieces of graphics.

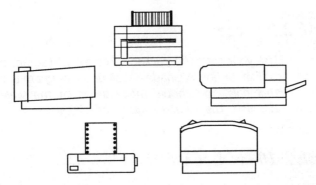

*Figure 2.42 Examples of printer graphics*

## Question 2.22

*Why are there software packages that provide you with clip art rather than let you create your own?*

## 2.2.3 Image and page attributes

The issue of **image attributes** is approached from a number of different directions. These would normally be:

- colours;
- height;
- shade;
- width.

These points have been reviewed earlier in the text. The **page attributes** are:

- margins;
- orientation;
- paper size.

This has also been previously covered, but is presented here as a reminder.

## 2.2.4 Produce and edit graphics

We now have covered all the issues needed to produce a graphic against a specification. The following tasks take us through a series of steps which we need to produce the evidence for this element.

### Task 2.9  PC 2                                                      C 2.3

*Use your software package to draw a diagram of the front of your school, college or house. Shade or colour the diagram to reflect the different building materials. You should make sure that the scale used is displayed on the drawing. The accuracy should be ±20%.*

### Task 2.10  PC 2, PC 4                                               C 2.3

*Use the brush and spray tools to add surrounding detail to the building drawing created in task 2.9 (such as trees, shrubs and paths). You may also import clip art to help.*

### Task 2.11  PC 3, PC 4                                               C2.2

*Take the drawing produced in task 2.10 and reduce its size so that it fits neatly on an A4 page in portrait style. The page should also include a text-based description of how to reach the building by road from some major landmark (e.g. from the railway station, motorway junction or trunk road, etc.). Make sure that there are at least 2 cm or 1 inch margins around the new drawing.*

It is common for 2-D drawings to be plan views (e.g. a road map, a kitchen design, a garden design or an office layout). Care needs to taken over the size of each object to make sure it is scaled to an appropriate size for the drawing. Exaggerating the size of an object by a small amount for clarity is quite acceptable, provided it doesn't create the wrong impression of scale. These drawings are normally vector-based graphics.

## 2.2.5 Graphic images

The manipulation of graphic images is a highly practical issue as far as this unit is concerned. The two activities that need to be demonstrated are:

- save;
- output.

To save a file is straightforward. All the integrated packages support the copying of graphics into a text-based wordprocessed file. Of course the output must be to a printer that supports the formats in which the file is saved. Laser printers supporting postscript standards have become a standard device.

### Task 2.12  PC 5                                                     C2.2

*Print the drawing you have created in task 2.11.*

## 2.2.6 Improvements

It is not unusual for the outcome of any activity to be reviewed or for such a review to think of ways in which improvements can be achieved. It may be that the specification has not been given sufficiently well and the production has not created what was in the originator's mind. It may be that the layout, once produced, gives further ideas on what can be incorporated

*Task 2.13* **PC 6**

*Take the output from task 2.12 and adjust the layout to produce the same information displayed in landscape format.*

# *Process and model numerical data*

## Introduction

Businesses will frequently set up a **model** of their existing or proposed activities. This allows the organisation to see what the likely affect any change would have. If we can model a proposed change rather than do it in real life, then we can avoid doing the things in real life that would have an outcome that we don't want to see happen. At a simple level the model can be based on a spreadsheet. More sophisticated modelling (e.g. based on queuing theory) exists to predict more complex situations. Supermarkets will have modelled what would happen in 30 to 60 minutes time if 100 people arrive at the store over a 10 minute period. Their model will predict the length of the checkout queues depending on how many open checkout positions there are in action. This is a classical problem, but one that is important since you need to know in advance if more checkouts need to be opened if queue lengths mustn't exceed a particular size.

In this element we will concentrate on the use of spreadsheets to provide the level of evidence needed for your portfolio. Other models involve the use of games packages. The modelling approach provides a number of benefits:

- compresses time;
- saves costs;
- safety benefits;
- convenience;
- allows 'what-if' testing.

Most models can easily be set up on personal computers, which are readily available and easy to use. To undertake a modelling test and keep re-running the model with a variety of conditions is normally more convenient than going to the location where an actual test can be carried out, with all the necessary set up procedures involved. Virtual reality brings us closer to providing this as an approach in many situations.

## 2.3.1 Identify computer models

Time invested in setting up the model can be well spent. It can begin as a simple overview, and increasingly become more detailed as we add more information to the system, and as refinements are made to the model. The model could be constructed by setting up a series of related information and combining the various spreadsheets into a single overview. The benefit of this approach is that any small change is seen throughout the whole of the model and its impact recognised. There is no possibility that the computation will miss out one intermediate calculation and do the rest, so the model has greater accuracy than a set of manually-performed calculations. There will be no errors in the mathematical calculations either. Provided we set all formulae up properly and enter the data accurately, the model will be completely accurate throughout.

## Prediction

**Predictive models** are set up to help us work out what will happen in the future, based on a range of issues. Perhaps the most widely-seen predictive model is a weather forecasting system. This takes in a lot of parameters (such as prevailing wind directions, temperatures etc.) and calculates what weather we should expect. Hopefully the calculation is fast enough to give a prediction before the weather happens, otherwise we don't have a very helpful model.

Other examples of predictive models look at the analysis of financial forecasting. Such models are frequently based on spreadsheets, which can provide us with a tool to undertake a range of tests. Such tests can alter one or more of the system variables, so that we can predict what happens if and when the changes are made. These are often referred to as what-if queries on the model.

The example spreadsheet in figure 2.43 is a predictive model. It attempts to show what the profit would be if certain parameters were to change (i.e. it predicts the profit).

For example, consider a possible model of a fictitious hotel spreadsheet. At the moment the hotel charges £50 per night and can sell 50 rooms out of the 75 rooms in the hotel. With current staffing levels there is a fixed cost of £1380 and each occupied room costs £10 per night to service (clean sheets, etc.). We believe the market is price sensitive and a 10% increase in price results in a 10% reduction of guests. The reverse is also believed to be true. A model of this would suggest:

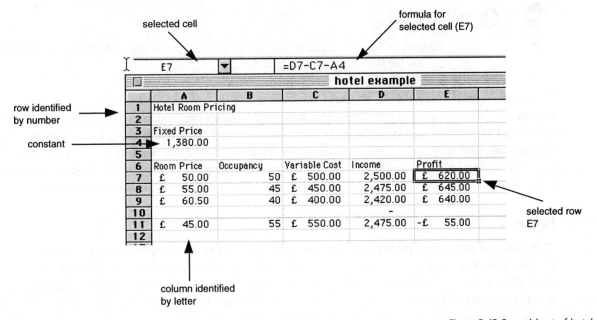

*Figure 2.43 Spreadsheet of hotel*

Further evidence would suggest that if the quality of service were improved by adding more staff (at additional fixed cost of £150 per night), then a further increase of 10% in room bookings can be achieved.

## Gaming

A commonly used game is the business game where teams of players go through a number of knockout rounds. In each round the individual teams will set their marketing and production strategies. The business game models the input from each team and grades which team was the most successful. Successive rounds eliminate the worst performing team(s). Many other games exist involving rules which can be modelled, including many of the new virtual reality games.

Other examples of **gaming models** include the decision making games, where repeated decisions need to be taken, with the opportunity to change the rules (car driving games with increasing levels of difficulty based on driver performance, fit into this category).

## 2.3.2 Data parameters

### Input values

Data input can be from existing information held on database, read directly from sensory devices, or input from the keyboard. The data used in any particular model or processing activity will obviously depend on what it is we are modelling. Typical data elements include:

- numbers;
- date;
- characters;
- formula.

*Question 2.23*

*Given that we are approaching the year 2000, how many digits do we need to set up for the data element of the date?*

The model created in figure 2.43 could have resolved the problem of finding the point where maximum profits occurred without the repeated modelling that we have undertaken. The advanced features of the spreadsheet called **solver** could have been used. Within solver, constraints are allowable, which set the maximum values of variables used in the formula line. For instance, in our hotel example, the maximum occupancy figure is 75 because we don't have any more rooms than this. Hence 75 would be an occupancy constraint in the calculation.

### Formula

The value of some cells in a spreadsheet may be calculated using operators and other variable inputs. The relationship is expressed as a **formula** (e.g. the cell is the sum of all of the cells in the column above). The formula which dictates how the value of such a cell is calculated is not usually displayed in the cell, since this normally displays the result of the calculation. The formula is normally hidden, but if a cell is selected it is displayed elsewhere in the calculation zone. Hence the formula line shows how any cell has been set up or defined.

## 2.3.3 Calculations

Once the variables have been input to the model the relationship between elements can be defined in terms of operators (indeed this could be defined before the data input). The standard operators of arithmetic, relational and logical can be used. An example of a spreadsheet using these operators is shown in figure 2.43. Such operators are often part of a formula which calculate the value of some cells. Constant values as well as variables can be declared to the system and again this can be seen in figure 2.43.

Certainly where repetitive changes are made to the model to undertake what-if queries on the system, it is much more efficient to have established the model than repetitively undertake manual calculations with all the possibilities of an error being introduced. Data integrity checks can also be built into models that will be frequently used to make them more robust and reliable. This helps prevent any inconsistent data being entered.

## 2.3.4 Layout

### Cell formats

Figure 2.23 (page 83) shows the construction of a matrix which is the basic structure of a spreadsheet. A column and a row define any item or **cell**, e.g. column 1, row 2 is a single cell. In a spreadsheet, the columns are usually identified by letters and the rows are identified using numbers. Figure 2.43 shows how a particular cell is identified. Any input cell can have its value changed as part of the modelling. The value held in the cell can have a range of formats which are supported by the spreadsheet. A typical range of formats which can be used are:

- character;
- date;
- number;
- currency;
- scientific.

*Task 2.14*  PC 2                                                                    *N 2.2*

*Use a spreadsheet to set up each of the five data types listed in Element 2.3.4.*

### Entering data

A variety of sources of input which enable data capture by a range of input devices do not restrict us to only using the keyboard for data entry. Equally, the output from our model can be extended beyond the usual numerical display – a typical range of reporting methods were shown in figure 2.40. Data can be exported from the spreadsheet (or other modelling software) and used as input to another system. In Excel (and other packages) you can create and save sets of input values that produce different results as scenarios representing what-if assumptions.

*Task 2.15*  PC 1, PC 3, PC4                                                         *N 2.1*

*Create a spreadsheet as in figure 2.43. Model the impact of the proposed change in service level on the spreadsheet.*

Research has shown that guests are attracted by small additional comforts in the room (e.g. bowls of fruit and sweets, luxury toiletries, etc.). An increase in the variable costs of £5 per night per room would attract another 10% more business.

**Task 2.16** PC 5, PC 6                   *N 2.1, 2.3*

*Model this new set of data on the spreadsheet and produce a report of the output from the original data in figure 2.43, task 2.15 and this task. The report may be in pictorial format to show where maximum profits can be gained.*

It is equally possible to set up a model on a database package such as Access and quiz the model with what-if queries in the form of SQL.

# Use information technology for process control

## Introduction

We can now develop the ideas introduced in Element 1.1 where we examined industrial and commercial information technology systems. The element contains information about sensors and actuators used in control. This knowledge is required to understand what is happening in a control system. Even so, this is only an introduction to the concepts.

One of the advantages of this element is that it integrates with material elsewhere in the Intermediate level GNVQ. Hence in doing some of the tasks in this element, the evidence gained will be of use to you elsewhere within the qualification.

## 2.4.1 Uses of process control systems

### Environmental control

Control is a very important part of our everyday lives. If there were no control we would have chaos. A naturally occurring example is the weather which is a form of environmental control managing the water cycle. Also, we often want to control the environment in our homes or place of work, etc. The most common form of environmental control found in the home is a central heating system. The central heating system is used to control the temperature at a comfortable level in a range of about 18°C to 24°C.

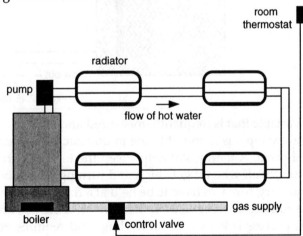

*Figure 2.44 The central heating control system*

In the control system shown in figure 2.44, the gas supply provides the boiler with fuel which is burnt to heat up the water. A pump is then used to circulate this hot water around the central heating system. As the hot water circulates, the radiators heat up and consequently warm the rooms. To stop the room from becoming too hot, a thermostat is used. When the temperature of the room reaches a pre-set value, determined by the thermostat, the gas supply is shut off from the boiler. The boiler and the circulating hot water cool down, resulting in the radiators giving off less heat to their surroundings and eventually causing the room temperature to fall. When it falls below the pre-set value, the thermostat switches on the gas supply to the boiler. This heats up the water and the radiators and the process repeats itself.

### Question 2.24

*How do we monitor the temperature in figure 2.44?*

### Process production control

Let us consider an example of a simple **process production control** system. In an industrial system, the level of liquids in tanks can be achieved in a number of ways. Figure 2.45 shows a probe being used to measure the level of liquid in the tank. The output from the probe uses some electronic or mechanical type circuit which opens and closes an inlet valve to stop or allow the flow of water into the tank. The probe can use a number of different techniques to give its output, such as capacitance and resistance. Whatever the nature of the output from the probe, it is proportional to the level of liquid in the tank. Hence it can be used as an indicator or used for a control device to open and shut an inlet valve.

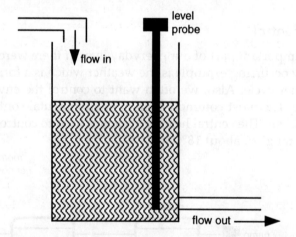

*Figure 2.45 The industrial level controller for liquids*

Temperature is a variable that is frequently measured and used to control the heat of ovens and furnaces. A typical example is found at home in our kitchens where we set the oven temperature to the desired point. A thermostat helps keep the temperature up to the set level, by cutting the heating supply off when it gets high and turning it back on when it drops below.

Similarly in industry, furnaces have to be held at a fixed temperature. In the example shown in figure 2.46, the furnace is being used to heat up steel blocks, known as ingots, to a certain temperature. This process is known as 'annealing' and requires good temperature control. If the temperature falls below that required, the process of annealing does not work. Should the temperature get too high, energy is wasted in heating the furnace more than necessary which is expensive.

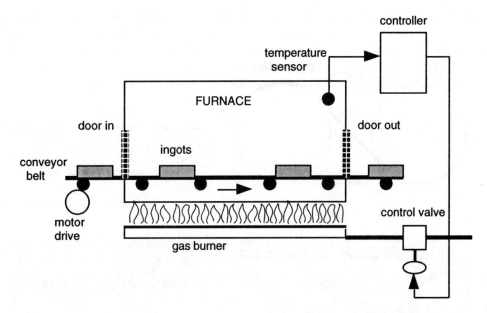

*Figure 2.46 The temperature control of a furnace*

Keeping the temperature of the furnace at a constant temperature is quite complicated and requires sophisticated control. A computer is able to provide this control. Pre-set values of temperature would be stored in its memory and the computer would monitor the temperature of the furnace using a suitably connected sensor. The measured temperature would then be compared to that stored in the memory, and the difference would be used to open or shut the control valve, feeding gas to the furnace gas burners.

### Question 2.25

*Can you think of another domestic appliance where we need to control the temperature?*

Other examples of process production control systems occur in the oil refining industry with petrochemical plant control. Quite sophisticated systems exist in this industry.

### Task 2.17  PC 1

*Investigate and describe how a control system in the petrochemical plant industry works.*

### Quality control

An example of **quality control** can be seen in the manufacture of paper. The thickness of paper during its manufacture is very important. If it is too thin, there is the danger that it will break or tear.

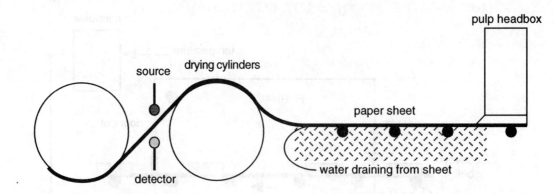

*Figure 2.47 Controlling the thickness of paper*

### *Task 2.18* PC 1, PC 2, PC3                                    *C 2.4*

*Describe how the temperature control works in the oven of your kitchen at home.*

*SAFETY NOTE : DO NOT TAMPER WITH THE COOKER AT HOME.*

Figure 2.47 shows the manufacturing process of paper. The pulp is mainly in the form of water. It comes from the headbox and is drained on a wire mesh. The very delicate, wet sheet of paper is then dried on heated cylinders to form the sheet of paper. The thickness of the paper is determined by means of measuring the amount of radiation that passes through the paper from a radioactive source. The more radiation that the detector measures, the thinner the paper. The quality control is provided by ensuring the correct thickness is maintained throughout a production run.

## Security

A typical example of a control system used for security would be an anti-theft device, similar to the type used in museums and art galleries. The sensor used for this system consists of a transmitter producing a beam of light (a laser beam) or sound, and a receiver which detects the presence of the beam. If the beam is broken by someone passing through it, an alarm is sounded, doors are shut or the police are called automatically. Other examples of **security control** systems are:

- automated video camera;
- timer locks within large bank and vault security systems;
- car security ignition disabling systems.

### *Task 2.19* PC 1, PC 3                                    *C 2.4*

*Describe how we could prevent clothes being stolen from a shop using anti-theft devices.*

## 2.4.2 Stages in a given process control system

In the systems that we are considering, there is always an input and an output. If we change the input to the system then the output changes. For example, if we turn the gas setting higher on a cooker hob, then the heat generated by the burning gas is greater. In this example, any control over the system was by manual intervention and any monitoring of the impact of the output was human (based on visual and audible monitoring, such as a saucepan boiling over!). Figure 2.48 represents a simplistic model of this.

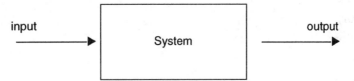

*Figure 2.48 System inputs and outputs*

This figure hasn't shown the stage in which we monitored the output and manually turned the gas level up or down. If we were to consider the actions in this example we can identify three stages, which apply to most other systems:

- sense condition;
- compare existing condition with desired condition;
- adjust system to achieve output desired.

### Question 2.26

*In the example of a saucepan on a hob, how would we sense the output condition we are seeking to achieve?*

### Question 2.27

*In question 2.26, how did we compare the existing conditions with the desired condition?*

### Question 2.28

*In question 2.26, how would we adjust the system and is the response immediate?*

### Sense conditions

To know what the current output level is, we monitor what is happening to the system. Monitoring is normally done with a sensor which provides us with an automatic system, rather than relying on a human (have you ever let the saucepan boil over because you weren't monitoring?). Examples of sensors will be covered in Element 2.4.3.

### Compare conditions

Of course the assumption we have made so far is that we know what we want to achieve as the system output. In our previous example should the saucepan be simmering or boiling vigorously? In any system we are trying to control, we must identify what it is that we are trying to achieve. Typically we may be trying to control properties, such as:

- temperature;
- length;
- weight;
- colour;
- position;
- time.

For example, in a washing machine there are a number of control values that we would want to set by selecting the wash programme. In a simplistic view they might be seen as:

- fill the machine with water … measured by the height of water;
- measure the water temperature … raise the temperature if necessary;
- rotate drums in both directions … a fixed number, pre-programmed;
- drain water … water still leaving?
- spin drum … timer?

Each of the wash cycle stages is assumed to have a desired level which is pre-established. This is true for most systems.

## Question 2.29

*How is the pre-established value of a kitchen oven and a central heating system known?*

How accurately we maintain this value is an important issue. For example, in a central heating system, are we happy for the room temperature to go a few degrees over the set value before switching off? Equally, can the temperature fall a few degrees below the value before switching back on? Depending on our view of control, we could be making frequent adjustments to the system or less frequent, coarser adjustments. The measure of how close we need to keep the output to the preferred value is known as **tolerance**.

### Tolerances

To have perfect control would be very expensive and in the vast majority of applications this is not required anyway. Hence, we say that adequate control has been achieved if the actual value is within a percentage of the desired value. In the case of the furnace the desired temperature may be 500°C with a tolerance of ± 5°C. This would mean that the maximum temperature could vary in the range of 495°C to 505°C and would be satisfactorily within tolerance.

## Question 2.30

*What would be the operating temperature range of a domestic oven which is set to 180°C if the tolerance is (i) ± 5°C; (ii) ± 2%?*

### Adjust system to achieve output

Once we have compared the existing output against the pre-set value, we know whether it matches the desired level, within the tolerance range set up, or whether it falls outside those limits. If it is outside, then we need to signal back to the input stage that action (or continued action) is required.

**Feedback** is the term used in a process control system where part (or all) of the output signal is fed back into the input of the system to achieve the comparisons we have noted. Such a system is generally known as a **closed-loop** system, as shown in the next figure.

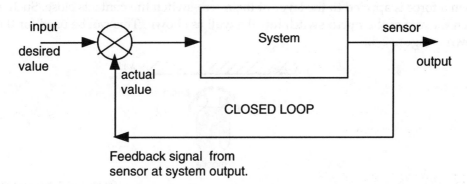

*Figure 2.49 A simple closed-loop feedback control system*

However, not all systems require feedback, for example, where the output always responds in the way it is intended (i.e. the actual value accurately follows the desired value so there is no error and as such there is no need for feedback). Such a system is known as an **open-loop** control system. Figure 2.48 is an open-loop system.

## 2.4.3 Components of process control systems

### Sensors

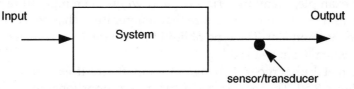

*Figure 2.50 A block diagram of a simple control system*

A **sensor** (or **transducer** as it is sometimes called) is an essential part of a control system because it gives information about what is actually happening in the system. For example, in some of the control systems quoted previously, the thermostat would be sensing the actual temperature of the room or boiler. A range of sensors are available and can be selected for particular applications. A range of key sensors are discussed here.

### Contact sensor

A **contact sensor** has to make physical contact with an object. The cheapest and simplest form of contact sensor would be a micro-switch.

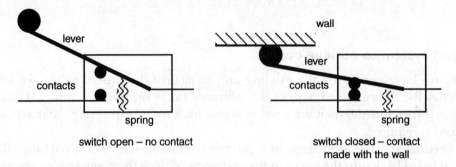

*Figure 2.51 A micro-switch*

When a force is applied to the lever of the micro-switch the contacts close. Such a force occurs when the end of the micro-switch hits the wall as shown. This can be used for the mobile unit shown in figure 2.52.

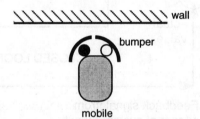

*Figure 2.52 A micro-switch contact detector*

The bumper is connected to the micro-switches, one for each half. If both switches are closed a signal will control the mobile so as to move back away from the wall. If the left-hand bumper hits an object its micro-switch will close, causing a control signal to move the mobile towards the right, away from the object. On the other hand if the right-hand bumper hits an object, the resulting control will cause the mobile to move towards the left.

### Heat sensors

The effect of temperature on substances or materials is used because the effect is a feature that can be measured. Such features that change in this way are called **parameters** of the substance. Indeed, anything that in some way changes with temperature variation can be used as a **heat sensor**. For example, many materials expand when the temperature increases and this effect can be used as an indicator to measure that temperature change. A very well known example of this is the thermometer. The type of liquid inside the thermometer dictates the temperature range over which it can be used.

When a metal undergoes a change in temperature it expands and increases in length as shown in figure 2.53. The increase in length $x$, is proportional to the temperature change and the original length $l$. This is given by :

$$x = l\,a\,D_t \text{ metres}$$

where $l$ is the original length in metres, $a$ is the coefficient of linear expansion in m per m °C, and $D_t$ is the change in temperature in degrees Celsius, °C.

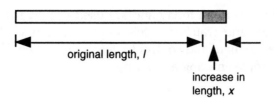

*Figure 2.53 A metal bar which has increased in length due to temperature*

Two different metals can be joined together to form a bi-metallic strip. When the temperature changes the two materials expand at a different rate causing the strip to bend. The rate at which it bends is proportional to the temperature increase and this change can be used to give an indication of the temperature. This is the principle behind the thermostat which we have already used a number of times.

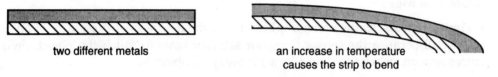

two different metals

an increase in temperature
causes the strip to bend

*Figure 2.54 A bi-metallic strip*

## Task 2.20  PC 4

*Take a glass thermometer and place it into a container of hot water and observe the expansion of the liquid in the column of the thermometer. Record how quickly it responds to the temperature change.*

*What was the temperature range of the thermometer used? How did you select the thermometer for this task?*

## Task 2.21  PC 4

*Heat the end of a bi-metallic strip and observe the expansion of the strip causing it to bend. Describe how it can be used on a thermometer.*

### Light sensors

One example of a **light sensor** is a solar cell. These devices convert light into electrical energy.

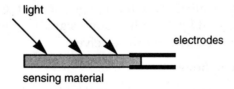

light

electrodes

sensing material

*Figure 2.55 A solar cell*

The sensing material in a solar cell is made from silicon, the same material used for semiconductors. When light shines onto the surface of the sensing device, the photons of light react with the atomic structure of the silicon, converting the light's radiant energy into electrical energy. The electrodes are used to take the electrical energy out from the device to the control system.

Such devices are very common today and are used to power many electronic devices. These range from calculators and watches to telecommunication satellites in outer space. They are usually used in measurement and control to detect the presence or absence of light, e.g. counting the number of people entering a building.

## *Task 2.22*  PC 4, PC 5                                                    *N 2.2*

*Draw a simple diagram to show how a solar cell and a light source can be used to detect and count the number of people entering a building. Are there alternative ways in which this counting may be achieved?*

### Proximity sensor

**Proximity sensors,** as the name implies, detect the nearness or proximity of an object and are very useful because the sensor does not actually have to touch the object. Frequently these devices rely on an echo to detect how far away an object is.

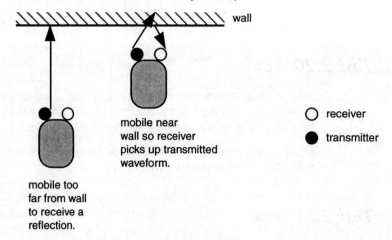

*Figure 2.56 Mobiles using proximity detectors*

The transmitter sends out a burst of signals which hit a surface and are reflected back to the mobile. The reflected signal is picked up by the receiver. The time it takes for the signal to travel to and from the wall is proportional to the distance the object is away from the wall. Hence this distance can be easily calculated. The type of signal transmitted depends upon the type of transmitter used and the types of surface used for the wall. If the wall is a smooth surface and white, or even better has a mirror type finish, light can be the transmitted signal and the detector a photodetector. Infrared light or ultrasound signals could also be used. Naturally a different sensor would have to be used for the receiver.

### Sound sensor and microphones

The most common form of **sound sensor** is the microphone. A microphone is found in the mouth-piece of a telephone, used in cassette tape recorders, etc. The microphone converts sound waves into electrical signals, which in the case of a telephone is ideal for transmitting through telephone wires. There are a number of ways in which sound waves can be converted into an electrical signal, but the majority of the devices include a diaphragm. The diaphragm is used to convert the sound waves into a movement and then this movement is detected and converted into an electrical signal.

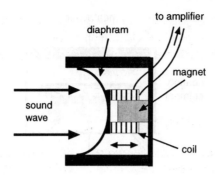

*Figure 2.57 A microphone*

In figure 2.57 the movement of the diaphragm is detected by a coil moving up and down a magnet. As this happens the coil 'cuts' the lines of magnetic field causing a voltage to be generated. This voltage is then an electrical replica of the sound wave.

## Processors

A **processor** is a device which can perform logical and arithmetical operations.

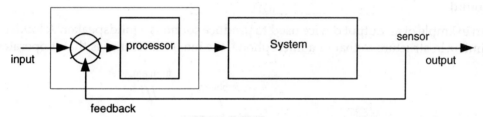

*Figure 2.58 The processor as the brain of the system*

The processor is an integral part of the control system. It is the unit that has input ports to read signals. It has the capability of performing arithmetic calculations (such as comparison of output versus required level) and calculating the level of signal that it needs to output to the system. The detail of the routine needed to determine this value is discussed in the next section on control procedures.

## Control procedure

For us to control a system, we must decide how we are going to do it. In particular, what sort of program do I want to write for the processor (i.e. are there any design algorithms?).

An example of a **control** program exists in a washing machine. The program could, say, rotate the drum clockwise for five revolutions, then anti-clockwise for five revolutions. This could be repeated a number of times depending on the wash programme selected. Alternatively, the control could be provided by a timer (e.g. the timer on a microwave oven) or a counter (e.g. select seven balls for the National Lottery).

## Output devices

Examples of **output devices** include heaters to affect temperature, traffic lights, speakers or a motor which is powering some process. In this text we will consider two of these.

### Heaters

A very simple but effective form of control is found in our convection heaters in the home. They are thermostatically controlled so as to control the temperature of the room in which they are placed.

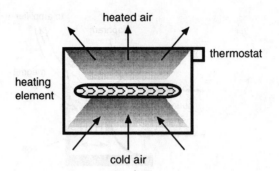

*Figure 2.59 A thermostatically-controlled heater*

The warm air passes out of the top of the heater causing convection currents. These circulating currents heat the room. As the room warms up, the thermostat (which is pre-set to some value) turns off the electric current to the heating element and so the heater cools down. The room temperature falls, the thermostat comes into effect and turns on the current, causing the heating element to heat up, thereby repeating the process.

## Sound

An example of an output device used to produce sound is a loudspeaker. A loudspeaker is very similar in structure to that of a microphone, the major difference is that it operates in reverse.

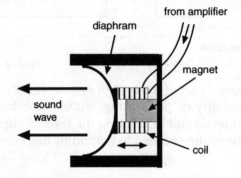

*Figure 2.60 A loudspeaker*

An electrical signal from the amplifier is sent to the coil of the speaker and energises it. The resulting magnetic field from the coil reacts with the magnet's magnetic field causing the coil to move. If the electrical signal from the amplifier represents music the resulting effect is to cause the coils to move back and forth in sympathy with the music. As the diaphragm is connected to the coil it will also move in the same way and pressure waves are set up in the air surrounding the cone. These pressure waves are the sound produced by the speaker.

## Interconnecting devices

In many cases the systems that we have been considering have signals associated with them that are varying or fluctuating with respect to time. Such a signal is called an **analogue signal**. The computer or microprocessor, on the other hand, can only handle digital signals. Therefore a computer has to be connected to a system via a special interface in order to control it. This interconnection is known as the **I/O port** (or **input/output port**).

## 2.4.4 Select and use components to construct a control system for a given specification

To put together a system that is controlled, the appropriate devices have to be chosen and matched. This is done by examining each component by its specification. For a furnace, temperature control components would be used, e.g. thermometers and a temperature controller, which could be a simple thermostat. There are other factors which have to be considered, e.g. the range over which the furnace is to be controlled, how quickly you want the control to occur, the cost of the control system, the type of processor, the type of output device used and the type of control system used. The choice might look easy, but a number of the factors are conflicting. For example, the best control is not necessarily the cheapest to buy.

To build a control system or use a simulation of a control system is probably easier to do if we use a kit or tailor-made package. An example of a control kit is the Feedback's Micamaster MIC957 Traffic Signal Control module.

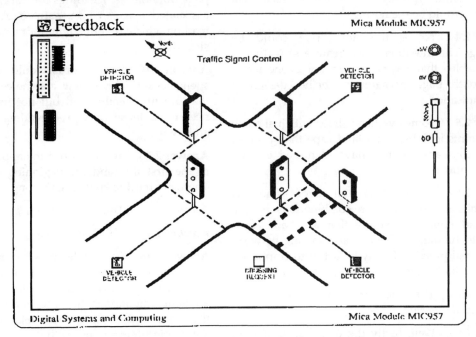

*Figure 2.61 Feedback's Traffic Signal Control Module*

*Task 2.23*  PC 4                                                    *N 2.2*

*Use the Feedback module to set up a test which recognises the vehicle detector sensor used to change a traffic light.*

## 2.4.5 Control system performance and specification improvements

A schematic diagram is used to represent the layout of the process control system to help understand how it works or functions. It is therefore not drawn to scale, nor is it a plan of how the system is actually laid out. There are other more complex diagrams for this purpose. In fact, all the diagrams that make up the figures in this section are in the form of schematic diagrams.

# Answers to questions in Unit 2

**Answer 2.1** If we look at the detail contained in the heading and the body of the agenda, it is all information that is needed before the meeting, especially the time, data and venue.

**Answer 2.2** When the minutes are received, everyone can quickly scan the action column to identify those issues where they need to do something. It is a helpful way of reminding people of the agreed activities.

**Answer 2.3** The width needs to sufficient to contain the names (or at least initials) of the actionees and wide enough to be recognised as the action column. Typically somewhere between 1 cm and 3 cm would be the norm.

**Answer 2.4** No – the housestyle could be anything. The intention is to create a style that is recognisable – that may be a column or a zone across the top of the page or whatever is the best design for the organisation.

**Answer 2.5** Some overhead slides with just a few bullet points look better on landscape than portrait layout. Your answer may have identified equally valid situations.

**Answer 2.6** A limited amount of font change is acceptable, although there are combinations that are good and equally mixtures that are bad. Fonts belong to fundamental types and mixing between types is bad practice. It may be better to emphasise with bold, italics and underlining at the outset.

**Answer 2.7** The header says *2.1 Process commercial documents*.

**Answer 2.8** Well, firstly the question itself is in italics and boxed in. There are some capital letters used to indicate product names. Major features are introduced using a bullet point •, which assists the reader and enhances the text format.

**Answer 2.9** The folder named gnvq level2 (which has an icon that looks like a folder) has beneath it four icons of documents that are contained within it. The indentation of the icon means that the documents are part of the folder directly above the indent. Hence the files in the folder are:

- GNVQ IT Unit 2
- level 2 unit 2.4
- level 2 unit 4 gnvq
- unit 2 level 2

It looks to me like I haven't been using a very strict file naming convention. That's because the developments of this text have taken place over many months and when I create files, I have simply used a name that indicates the contents. When this work is complete, I will go through all the files and tidy them up, renaming all files to follow the same naming convention. At the moment, it looks a little untidy, but at least the contents are recognisable.

**Answer 2.10** Yes, the range of extensions includes .doc (for document) and .xls (for an Excel spreadsheet).

**Answer 2.11** The layout of the document changes quite a lot. Diagrams and text can get separated by page boundaries. Headings for paragraphs and the associated text can be separated. A further proof reading will be required after the change to check for such detail.

**Answer 2.12** Some words would be detected by spell-checker: Thr, venew and noice. Other words that are incorrectly used but not incorrectly spelt need to be detected by proof reading. They are 'sea' and 'two'.

**Answer 2.13** Yes, the word the appears at the end of the first line and the beginning of the second. These are hard to spot when wrong.

**Answer 2.14** These are a vector graphics.

**Answer 2.15** This is a bit map.

**Answer 2.16** Each slide show can have the slides set up in the sequence required, i.e. they can be re-sequenced from an earlier presentation. Once set, no accidents can happen, like a set of acetates falling on the floor and loosing their relative position. If automatic timing is used, the presenter would not have to worry about changing the slides, they can concentrate on the speech.

Small changes to the content of an individual slide can be made without having to reprint an overhead. This is a helpful tool to businesses who make a lot of use of slide presentations.

**Answer 2.17** Again, this is a bit map.

**Answer 2.18** It is as important as the combination of clothes that you wear. The contrast between background and any detail needs to be sharp, e.g. orange on red would not show very clearly.

**Answer 2.19** A square is only a special case of a rectangle. Hence, if we have a facility to draw a rectangle then we can always construct a square.

**Answer 2.20**   It is a few words that state the main point or heading of a section of the presentation. There is little or no detail provided but they provide a framework to the reader of how the topic is being introduced and the sequence in which points are being raised.

**Answer 2.21**   Since 5% of 20 is 1, then a line drawn to the stated accuracy must be no shorter than (20 − 1), i.e. 19 cm. It must be no longer than 21 cm.

**Answer 2.22**   Drawing clip art can be quite slow. If a good range can be supplied as part of the package, then these can be used in combinations to provide the impact you are seeking. Figure 2.41 was constructed from clip art provided within a package.

**Answer 2.23**   It has been common for the year to be represented by two digits, e.g. 96 is the year in which I first wrote this. Of course when we go into the new millennium we should use four digits for the year otherwise we will end up with 00. If we only had 00, then it would be quite difficult to calculate how many years there are between two dates using subtraction, i.e. between 96 and 01.

**Answer 2.24**   The thermostat is the monitoring device that is used to see if the room temperature has reached the desired level.

**Answer 2.25**   Your answer could be better than mine here, but examples are the washing machine, an immersion heater or an electric iron.

**Answer 2.26**   The output condition we are seeking could be to boil the contents or just to let it simmer. How we monitor this could vary slightly but is likely to be a visual check. The alternative is to listen until we hear it boiling, but that often results in a spillage!

**Answer 2.27**   Once we know what we want, our visual inspection will check whether that condition has been reached yet, or whether it is being approached, since we get an early sign that the contents are beginning to boil.

**Answer 2.28**   As the condition is reached (or being reached) then we adjust the heat level. The ability to begin turning down the heat before it boils is an example of good process control. The response to the heat adjustment is quicker in the case of gas, whereas an electric ring has to cool down and takes longer to respond to change.

**Answer 2.29**   Whatever the user selects on the thermostat dial is accepted by the system as the value to achieve. Presumably the fact that it was within a value that could be set, then it is a temperature that can be reached.

**Answer 2.30**   In the first case the range is 175 to 185 degrees. In the second case the range is 176.4 to 183.6 degrees.

# Unit 2 Sample Test Paper

1  Which of the following documents tells you where a meeting is being held and what will be discussed?

   A  business letter
   B  memorandum
   C  agenda
   D  newsletter

2  After a meeting the secretary of the meeting writes a short set of notes, with the key points of discussion and actions. What is this document called?

   A  action list
   B  memorandum
   C  agenda
   D  minutes

3  A document is prepared to inform a customer of how much money they are now required to pay following the supply of goods or services. What is this document called?

   A  memorandum
   B  delivery note
   C  invoice
   D  report

4  A document is prepared to let your employees know what is happening on a range of interesting company topics. What is this document called?

   A  report
   B  newsletter
   C  business letter
   D  paper

5  A document is needed which requires a lot of columns of information. What is likely to be the presentation style?

   A  landscape
   B  portrait
   C  orientation
   D  justified

6  The line that appears on the top of each page of this book has used which layout feature?

   A  footer
   B  header
   C  title
   D  orientation

7  A mistake has been made in preparing a report and a paragraph of text needs to be moved to another page. Which edit feature is used?

   A  delete
   B  insert
   C  move
   D  copy

Questions 8 to 10 share the following answer options.

The tax man has details of each tax payer on a computer system. The following answers represent data accuracy and security.

   A  Data Protection Act
   B  spell checker
   C  copyright
   D  backup

8  How would you locate words that had been keyed in incorrectly?

9  How would you make sure that the files are secure?

10  What stops the tax man from illegally using software packages?

11  A diagram of a component part has been drawn for a manufacturing workshop. Which format will be used to occupy the smallest disk space?

   A  bit map
   B  vector
   C  chart
   D  slideshow

12  Which graphic format is not a general purpose shape?

   A  square
   B  rectangle
   C  line
   D  polygon

13  What text enhancements are used on page headers in this book?

   A  bold
   B  underline
   C  colour
   D  italics

14  Which is the most common size of paper used to write business letters?

A  M4
B  A4
C  A3
D  foolscap

15  Which page attribute ensures you can file a document and still read the contents?

A  orientation
B  paper size
C  margins
D  graphic type

16  Which feature of a spreadsheet represents elements of vertical data?

A  cells
B  columns
C  rows
D  titles

17  What type of numerical model examines the pattern of winning the National Lottery numbers and offers you a selection of numbers for next week?

A  relational
B  chance
C  gaming
D  prediction

18  Which of the following is not a valid spreadsheet data type?

A  character
B  number
C  formula
D  arithmetic

19  What does cell F9 on a spreadsheet represent?

A  row F, column 9
B  column F, row 9
C  row cell, column F9
D  column cell, row F9

20  The data in a cell containing the arithmetic total of a column of numbers is required as a rounded figure. Which feature allows you to round up a figure?

A  total
B  column width
C  comparison
D  function

21  What type of sensor is used on a washing machine to indicate the water intake is now sufficient and the wash programme can continue?

A  heat
B  proximity
C  sound
D  contact

22  What type of sensor is used in a washing machine to control the water temperature?

A  heat
B  light
C  proximity
D  contact

23  In sensing the water in question 21, which of the following actions would not be part of the control process?

A  sense existing temperature
B  compute the temperature needed
C  compare temperature with that required by the wash programme
D  turn on the water heater if necessary

24  Which is a process control output device

A  retina scanner
B  security sensor
C  water sprinkler
D  response time

25  What type of sensor is used in a traffic light control system?

A  proximity
B  sound
C  contact
D  light

by **Mike Watkins**

# *Organisations and information technology*

Organisations are everywhere, throughout our lives we will be part of many organisations, we may form new organisations and we will interact with numerous organisations. In this unit the terms 'organisation', 'business' and 'business organisation' will be used interchangeably.

Each day our lives will have been affected by many different organisations. If you awake to a radio alarm the first thing you hear will be the output from a local radio station, breakfast may involve milk from the local milkman, cereals from a multinational company and newspaper from a national news organisation. You may travel to school or college using a local bus company. Your school or college is an organisation; course fees may be paid by local government, a GNVQ course from a national educational organisation, the computer systems from multinational companies, books from international publishers and so on.

The organisations that we mentioned above are very different from one another. The breakfast milk is delivered by a small private local firm, employing less than ten people, and selling a small range of products. The private bus company may employ up to twenty people to provide a local bus and taxi service. The local radio station may be part of a larger public broadcasting corporation that employs hundreds of people to provide a radio and television service and financed by national government. The school or college is a public organisation financed by local and national government to provide an education service. The computer system hardware may be supplied from a private national electronics company employing thousands of people in production, sales and distribution of its extensive product range. The cereal company may be part of a huge multinational conglomerate which employs tens of thousands of people worldwide in the production of its vast range of products. However they all exist to provide a service or a product to their customers or clients and most of them will face competition from other organisations offering similar services or products.

All organisations will be handling data and generating or requesting information in carrying out their daily activities. Data and information will flow internally within organisations from one part to another and externally between organisations. Information technology has an important role in most organisations today in support of their activities, and many rely on it for their survival.

In this unit you will learn how information technology is used within organisations. We examine the different types of organisations, how they are structured and how they operate. We investigate the flow of information in organisations: how data is handled within an the organisation and the security and safety issues that arise.

# Examine the flow of information in organisations

To function competently as an information technology (IT) professional, a certain amount of knowledge and understanding of organisations and their environment is required. It is not possible to design and develop IT systems for use within organisations, unless there is some familiarity with the workings of an organisation. This element will review organisations: the various types of organisation, their structure and operation, the type and flow of information that is encountered in organisations.

Organisations may be different from one another, but they will all possess the following features in a variety of forms.

*Figure 3.1 The organisation components and its environment*

- Organisations are formed or exist in order to achieve some recognised pre-determined **purpose**: its **goal** or **mission**. An organisation will usually have a primary goal: for a business enterprise it is usually to be profitable for its owner(s), and for a government organisation it might be to provide a (quality) service and value for taxpayers' money. In achieving the primary goal, a number of sub-goals are usually realised, e.g. for a breakfast cereal business to be profitable it might have the sub-goals of providing a quality product, increasing its market share and the efficient utilisation of resources.

- Organisations have an **internal structure** – they are organised. How a particular organisation is structured will depend on its type, purpose, size, history and so on. Structure is influenced by how the organisation operates. Structure can also influence the organisation – many go through re-structuring in order to improve their operation. The local newsagent will have a different structure from that of a national electronics company.

- An organisation interacts with an **external environment** that can affect or influence how it operates. It has customers for its services or products and competitors that provide similar products or services. It interacts with local and national government departments; it may have suppliers and may interact with financial institutions. For example,

127

the restaurant business is very competitive and this affects the prices charged and wages paid, it also has to meet hygiene, building and safety regulations.

- Organisations require **resources** to set up in the first place and to operate subsequently. There are three types: **people, money** and **physical resources** (equipment, buildings and materials); how these are mixed depends on the nature of the organisation and how it operates. The resources may change during the lifetime of an organisation. One organisation such as jewellery manufacturer may be described as labour intensive because it employs many people to assemble costume jewellery, whereas another such as a electricity generator may employ few people but have a costly investment in technological equipment.

- **Systems** are manual or computerised working methods that help an organisation to run smoothly. Systems are closely linked to the structure and operation of the organisation. As an organisation grows it will need to develop structure and the associated administrative systems, in order for it to function effectively. Systems are concerned with receiving, processing and storing data and information which is needed in order for the organisation to communicate effectively within itself, and with the outside world. A local plumber will have a single system that embraces a number of business activities that involve little internal communication: he/she may do the actual plumbing in the day and the administrative paperwork in the evening – dealing with payments to suppliers and invoices to and payments from customers. A large national company will have separated systems, each employing many administrative personnel and requiring a great deal of internal communication.

- **Culture** sets the image or style of the organisation. It is concerned with how the organisation behaves, its tradition and how people act and react, their attitudes, beliefs and expectations. Culture is coupled to the organisation's goals and mission, and affects employee welfare, working conditions, job satisfaction, motivation and participation. The culture of the organisation affects its social responsibility, to the environment and to its local community as an employer.

## *Task 3.1*  PC 1

*This is a class or group task. Obtain the mission statement for your school or college. Discuss it by referring to the features of an organisation listed above. If there is no mission statement, then have a discussion about your school or college using the six features listed above as a guide, and aim to produce as an outcome a list of goals for drawing up such a mission statement.*

## 3.1.1 **Types of organisation**

An **organisation** is a group of people who work together to achieve some common purpose. Organisations exist in all shapes and sizes, a business organisation may be a single person or a huge multinational owned by thousands of shareholders.

# Organisation categories

Organisations can be classified in many ways. Initially there are three broad categories:

- **industrial and agricultural** organisations are involved in the processing of raw materials or the manufacture of products or construction, e.g. ICI, Rover cars, Wimpey Construction, Farming of all types;
- **commercial** organisations supply and sell goods or services to their customers, e.g. Virgin Records, Marks and Spencer, Abbey National Bank, Prudential Insurance;
- **public service** organisations are local or national government funded to provide services for public and business via a civil service, e.g. Local Education Authority, National Health Service, Glamorgan University, Government Statistics Office.

Organisations can also be categorised as belonging to a particular sector of industry. There are three sectors as follows.

- **Primary** sector includes agriculture, fishing and the extraction industries such as oil, forestry, coal mining and quarrying. These organisations supply the raw materials for the next sector.
- **Secondary** sector includes the manufacturing and construction industry. These organisations turn raw materials into semi-finished components, such as chemicals, textiles, steel and bricks; and products such as electrical white goods, cars, furniture clothes, food, tools, roads, bridges and buildings.
- **Tertiary** sector includes the service industries of distribution of freight, raw materials and finished goods, wholesale and retailing of products, travel, tourism and leisure, finance, health and education.

An organisation can be categorised by their size of area of operation as follows.

- **Local** organisations are known only within a small geographical area, a town or region and meet the needs of individuals or other organisations within their immediate area.
- **National** organisations offer their services throughout a country, meeting the needs of individuals or other organisations all over the country. They may operate from regional offices, one of which will be head office.
- **Multinational** organisations cross national borders and operate in many different countries. They see a world marketplace and aim to meet the needs of individuals or other organisations worldwide. The parent company will usually be based in the country of origin. They have diverse business interests, are very powerful organisations, and can influence governments.

An organisation can be categorised by ownership as follows.

- **Public** organisations are owned by the state and are run from government finance for the benefit of the community. These consist of national government departments, local government, government agencies, trusts and public or nationalised companies.
- **Private** organisations are owned by one or a group of private individuals. They are run essentially from profit, to make more profits. There are a number of different legal forms of organisation as follows (related to the size and complexity of operation), this affects their structure, how they operate and their liability.

Size,
Complexity,
Number of
Locations

- **Sole trader**: where there is just one owner who put up capital for the business. The owner benefits from any profits made and is totally liable for any debts incurred. Sole traders tend to be local, e.g. plumber, hairdresser, corner shop.

- **Partnership**: where a group of no more than twenty individuals put up capital and own the organisation. The details of the partnership are set out in a legal document called the Deed of Partnership and includes rules, voting rights and how profits and losses are to be shared. Each partner is liable for all the businesses debts. They may initially be local but may operate nationally, e.g. a popular form for GP practices, architects and accountants.

- **Private and public limited company (plc)**: this is a common form of business organisation, having two or more shareholders. Public limited companies have their shares traded on the Stock Exchange. The law requires that articles and memoranda of association (that includes the nature of the business and names and addresses of directors) are presented to the Registrar of Companies to receive a Certificate of Incorporation to start trading. The plc has unlimited liability, whereas the directors and shareholders have limited liability. They may operate locally, nationally or be multinational.

Other types of organisation ownership includes trusts, charities, co-operatives and members clubs.

## Question 3.1

*Which of these is a public service organisation?*

A   *a water company*

B   *an education authority*

C   *a corner shop*

D   *a health farm*

## Question 3.2

*Which of these is a commercial organisation?*

A   *a health authority*

B   *a coal mine*

C   *a retail clothes chain*

D   *a building company*

## Question 3.3

*Which of these is an industrial organisation?*

A   a car engine plant

B   a health farm

C   a retail clothes chain

D   a university

## Question 3.4

*In which sector does British Telecom operate?*

A   manufacturing

B   secondary

C   tertiary

D   telecommunication

## Question 3.5

*In which sector does National Power operate?*

A   supply

B   secondary

C   primary

D   energy

## Question 3.6

*In which sector does a fruit farmer operate?*

A   primary

B   secondary

C   agriculture

D   food

## Question 3.7

*Which of these organisations is in the public sector?*

A   British Gas

B   British Airways

C   British Telecom

D   British Council

### Task 3.2    PC 1

*Prepare a one page report identifying two organisations from each of the commercial, industrial and public services. For each one, briefly describe its purpose and classify it according to the other categories given previously in this unit.*

## Organisation structure

Small organisations of just a few employees can operate quite effectively with little or no formal structure, just knowing 'who is the boss'. As an organisation goes through the stages of growth and employs more people and expands its operations, it will need to develop a formal structure to maintain control, to be effective and efficient. The structure of an organisation can be represented by an organisation chart. The chart shows, specialist positions of responsibility and authority, associations between positions, functional division and formal lines of authority and communication. Such a chart should give an indication of the size of the organisation and how it organises itself.

Most organisation charts are hierarchical and triangular, narrow at the top, wider at the base and divided horizontally into a number of management levels. Figure 3.2 shows such a structure for a small software house CBS Ltd. It shows lines of reporting and areas of responsibility, and gives an indication of the functional division of the company.

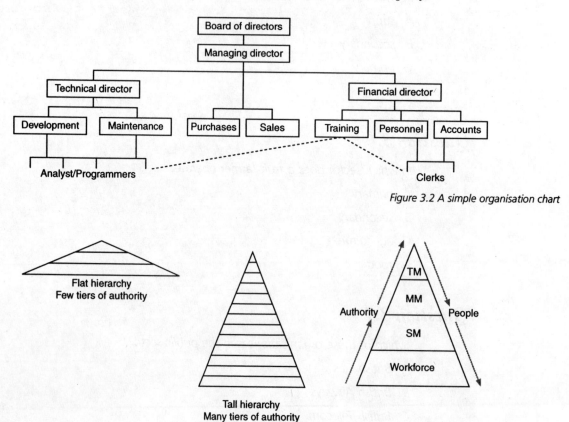

Figure 3.2 A simple organisation chart

Figure 3.3 Hierarchical structures and levels of management

Figure 3.3 shows the hierarchical structures and levels of management. These are as follows.

- **TM** is **top management**, the chief executive or managing director plus other directors. The managing director (MD) has authority over all the staff and is responsible to the board of directors and ultimately the shareholders; the other directors have functional responsibility, for example, marketing director.
- **MM** is **middle management**, for example, the head of a department. The head of department (HOD) has authority over members of a department, is responsible for their work and reports to the MD or a director.
- **SM** is **supervisory management**, for example, the section supervisor, chargehand or shift leader. Supervisory management has authority over a section or team within a department, is responsible for their work and reports to the HOD.
- **Workforce** consists of office, shop and factory workers who carry out the organisations operations (its day-to-day repetitive tasks).

**Flat hierarchies** have many people on the same level and a small number of management levels. Small manufacturing companies may have this structure where there are working directors who actively supervise the workforce they are responsible for. There is no middle management and some supervisory management. Small software houses may also have this sort of structure.

**Tall hierarchies** have a definite chain of command and formal status is important, for example, in the armed forces. As organisations grow and become national or multinational so the number of tiers will grow, for example, store manager, regional manager, national manager, European manager.

The majority of organisations have a four tier structure of top, middle and supervisory management overseeing a workforce. For many business organisations a flat three- or four-tiered structure will normally be more effective than one having many tiers, as this is too bureaucratic. However, for some organisations like those in the retail trade or banking, there is no alternative to a multi-layered structure.

The vertical division of the CBS Ltd structure chart in figure 3.2 shows the functional structure of the organisation, how it splits itself operationally and who is responsible for each activity. The lines from one level to the next indicate formal reporting structures or line management.

### Task 3.3   PC 1, PC 2

*Prepare an organisational chart for your school or college or any organisation you have access to or have read about. Put titles to the positions of responsibility.*

### Question 3.8

*Which of these organisation tiers has the most authority?*

*A  workforce*

*B  supervisory*

*C  middle*

## Question 3.9

*Which of these organisation levels has the most people?*

*A   workforce*

*B   supervisory*

*C   middle*

*D   top*

## 3.1.2   Functions of an organisation

**Internally,** a business organisation will normally be divided vertically into a number of functional units each serving a particular need of the organisation (as shown in figure 3.4). Most organisations will have functional areas, such as sales and marketing, finance and accounts, purchasing and operations. However, not all organisation will have the bottom row of functional areas in figure 3.4, such as production or research and development, and some functions may be combined.

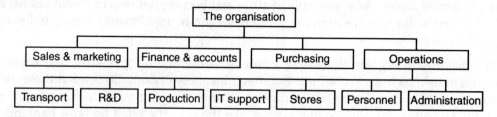

*Figure 3.4 Internal functions of an organisation*

In carrying out normal business, most organisations will interact **externally** with customers that purchase products or services, suppliers from whom raw materials and other supplies are purchased, and government departments or agencies.

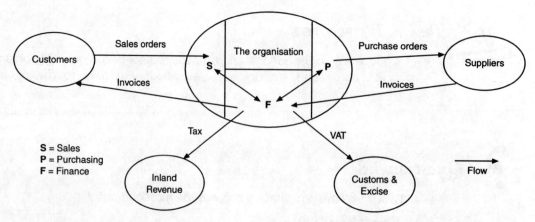

*Figure 3.5 Internal and external functions of an organisation*

## Internal functions

Dividing an organisation into internal functional units has the following benefits:

- divides up a complex structure into more manageable parts;
- reduces the scope of the work done within a functional unit, allowing it to concentrate on and specialise in its own activities within a defined boundary.

However, there now exists a need for communication between the functional areas – an information flow.

The major functional units of a business organisation are **finance, sales, purchasing** and **operations**. Operations can be further divided as follows (but this will depend on the nature of the organisation).

- **Sales and marketing** deals externally with customers or clients that wish to buy products or services from the organisation.
  1. External information flow:
     (a) receipt of sales enquiries from customer;
     (b) quotation responses to customer;
     (c) taking sales orders from customer;
     (d) acknowledgement of order to customer;
     (e) customer after sales liaison;
     (f) promoting products, advertising campaigns;
     (g) finding new customers and securing of new business;
     (h) awareness of competitors.
  2. Internal information flow:
     (a) check availability of stock products to/from stores;
     (b) allocate stock to order, to stores;
     (c) customer and sales order details to accounts;
     (d) made to order sales to production;
     (e) new customer details to accounts;
     (f) customer credit status from accounts;
     (g) provide sales reports;
     (h) salesperson sales and expense details to personnel.
- **Finance** or **accounts** maintains the organisations accounts. It deals with the flow of money within the organisation and all its financial aspects. It is responsible for keeping books or ledgers that record all financial transactions. Accounts will have some communication with all other internal functions and have many dealings externally.
  1. External information flow:
     (a) invoices or bills to customers for sales orders;
     (b) monthly statements to customers;
     (c) chasing of debts;
     (d) collecting customer payments;
     (e) invoices from suppliers;
     (f) paying of suppliers;
     (g) paying and providing financial information to government, income tax and VAT returns;

    (h) liaison with organisation's auditors;

    (i) handle customer or supplier account enquiries;

    (j) liaison with organisation's financiers.

  2. Internal information flows:

    (a) receipt of sales order details;

    (b) receipt of purchase order details;

    (c) monitoring of actual costs against budgets;

    (d) manage and maintain accounts ledgers;

    (e) produce periodic financial reports;

    (f) monitor stores' stock costs and undertake regular stock taking;

    (g) make up of employee wages;

    (h) liaison with production regarding work in progress and costs.

- **Purchasing** is the buying function that deals with suppliers of products and services to the organisation – it is the supplier's customer. It must order and buy in materials as cost effectively as possible (e.g. direct materials, raw materials, components needed for production of products; consumable materials to supply support activities; energy and any other service or expertise required).

  1. External information flows:

    (a) request quotations from suppliers for materials or services;

    (b) receipt of estimates from suppliers;

    (c) issue purchase orders to suppliers;

  2. Internal information flows:

    (a) new supplier details to accounts;

    (b) supplier and purchase order details to accounts;

    (c) receipt of goods received note;

    (d) purchase requirements from stores, production and other function units;

    (e) provide purchasing reports.

- **Stores** manages and controls the stock of parts and raw materials issued to production and received from suppliers via purchasing. It also manages the stock of finished goods received by being bought in or manufactured and issued to customers to meet their orders placed with sales. Stores interacts with both sales and purchasing.

  1. External information flows:

    (a) receipt of goods received note from supplier;

    (b) issue of despatch note to customer;

    (c) customer returns;

  2. Internal information flows:

    (a) material issue notes from production;

    (b) stock availability enquiry from sales;

    (c) finished goods stock availability to sales;

    (d) purchase requisitions to purchasing;

    (e) goods received note to purchasing.

- **Production** manufactures the organisation's product range. It involves planning, scheduling of the production operations to meet deadlines, maintenance of machinery and monitoring for quality and wastage; it may also include research and development of new production techniques.

  1. External information flows:

     (a) liaison with suppliers of bought in materials and services;

     (b) liaison with customers regarding product progress;

  2. Internal information flows:

     (a) materials issue notes to stores;

     (b) employee job time cards to accounts and personnel;

     (c) work in progress to accounts;

     (d) purchase requisitions to purchasing;

     (e) production schedules and reports;

     (f) design and production drawings to and from research and development (R&D).

- **Personnel** ensures that all areas are provided with the employees and skills required. This includes: employee selection, training and development, welfare, pay and conditions and industrial relations. Personnel also maintains employee personal and pay records.

- **Administration** provides a centralised service to other areas, such as reprographics, mail room, leasing, insurance and legal services, word processing, DTP and graphic design, office supplies, and health and safety legislation.

- **Research and development (R&D)** seeks to keep the organisation ahead of its competitors and works closely with production. This includes: design drawings, the development and testing of new prototype products and materials, and the improvement and update of existing items.

- **Transport** manages and co-ordinates the organisation's vehicle fleet, personnel cars, buses, delivery vans, tankers and trucks. It also negotiates, purchases or leases the organisation's vehicle requirements with dealers. The maintenance of vehicles may be done internally or externally, but the service, insurance and registration records are kept up-to-date by the transport unit.

- **IT support** manages and maintains the organisation's IT systems. It aquires computer hardware and software to meet users' requirements and provides facilities for their maintenance. It also manages and supports the organisation's IT information systems on a day-to-day basis, including security and backup, and training. IT support also has an awareness of developments in the IT field and seeks to use and develop IT to maintain the competitiveness and effectiveness of the organisation.

## Question 3.10

*Which of these functions keeps company accounts?*

*A  Sales and marketing*

*B  Finance*

*C  Purchasing*

*D  Production*

### Question 3.11

Which of these functions is responsible for finding alternative suppliers?

A   Sales and marketing

B   Finance

C   Purchasing

D   Production

### Question 3.12

Which of these functions do new customers contact who wish to purchase a product?

A   Sales and marketing

B   Finance

C   Purchasing

D   Production

### Task 3.4    PC 2

Choose one of the organisations you identified in Task 3.2 (or another you have studied or read about). List and then briefly describe its internal and external functions.

## 3.1.3   Types of information

**Data** is raw facts and figures that are generated during the day to day activities of an organisation; they are found on documents, on forms and in IT systems.

**Information** is data that has been filtered and organised in some way to be more meaningful to people who use it.

The four levels of the internal organisation structure (top, middle and supervisory management, and the workforce), perform different tasks and so they need different types of information and data to carry out these tasks effectively.

**Internal and external information**

Information is received from both external and internal sources and is then combined to operate the organisation as effectively as possible. This helps the decision making about the future of the organisation.

- **External information** includes opportunities and constraints revealed by such things as government policies, financial trends, customer needs and preferences, technology and manpower developments, supplier resource availability and cost trends, news, events and public opinion (in addition to the operations information described previously);

- **Internal information** is generated from the organisation going about its daily business. The workforce handles operational data by processing transactions and this generates operations information. This operational transaction data from the lowest level is processed to provide information for the supervisory level. At the supervisory level the information received from below is processed to provide information for the middle level and so on, this process is known as **information filtering**.

# Growth in data and information requirements

The growth in data/information requirements is the result of trends in today's society to increase the size of organisations, whatever their activity – be it commercial, industrial or public service. Information technology may have stimulated this growth, in that good IT facilities can aid the effectiveness of an organisation and hence its growth. The agricultural society of the past was replaced by the manufacturing society, and the manufacturing society is now being replaced by the information society (based on the percentages employed in these general activities).

# Stages of growth

**Small organisations** are characterised by having only a few employees (often just one or two) concerned with the data/information processing activity, who may also carry out other duties concerned with the principle business activity. For example, a plumber may take orders, schedule work, order materials and actually carry out the plumbing activity and another member of the family may 'do the books'.

Information is held on paper and in people's heads. Each person has easy access to most of the information and the same piece of paper can be viewed by all people it affects. Business discussion will involve the recall of information from people's heads, with immediate cross-checking and validation. The data/information is characterised by:

- easy access to relevant data;
- most data need be recorded once only;
- data is reliable because it is heavily cross-checked;
- data is up-to-date because it is in small manageable quantities;
- the data/information processing is efficient and does not inhibit the implementation of management policies, and so the organisation grows.

As the organisation grows it becomes more difficult to manage and the **first stage of growth** occurs. For example, the plumber may see business expanding and employ another plumber, and then take on an apprentice. The work scheduling operation becomes more involved, as does the payroll, and in general more management of the business is required. New business opportunities may also present themselves, such as carrying out boiler maintenance. This growth will often result in the organisation being split into smaller management departments, each having its own clerical systems for data/information processing and its own paper files. This will often involve a degree of data duplication that is necessary to allow each department to function in a self-contained way – the growth continues. For example, our plumber/business owner begins to see a conflict between management and being 'on the tools'.

The manual clerical systems begin to be overloaded, IT is introduced and the **second stage of growth** occurs. The IT solution will have a number of sub-systems that essentially automates the clerical functions within the boundaries of the departments. Each sub-system will have its own data files as before and the data duplication persists. The IT solution may temporally improve the situation but as growth continues the old problems begin to reoccur and the systems begin to creak at the seams. The IT system may require multiple updates of duplicated data; this may not be done simultaneously thus causing inconsistencies and the need for a great deal of reconciliation and further updating. Management have difficulty extracting reliable and relevant information at a time when it would be most useful. It becomes very difficult to co-ordinate different departments and systems integration becomes an IT aim.

The **third stage of growth** will involve the integration of systems across the different departments. The aims for instigating systems integration are:

- to provide easy and rapid access to relevant data;
- to record data only once to achieve data consistency and improve data reliability;
- to keep data up to date and provide up to date information.

Small organisations carried out these goals easily, but growth results in the need to restructure the organisation – and as growth continues this becomes more of a problem. The size and complexity of the data/information requirements of a large organisation need to be sorted out using IT.

## Management decision making

The effect of information should be to reduce uncertainty, increase predictability and provide effective monitoring and control. The different levels of management within an organisation will be required to make the following decisions which will affect the organisation in different ways.

- **Strategic decisions** are long term, have a time span of years, and are made by top management. They are based on mainly external information and personal judgement, and produce planning policies concerned with the organisation's mission and objectives. Internal information supplied by middle management will be in the form of 'one off' reports, 'what if' reports and long-term 'trend analysis'. Within a business organisation, strategic decisions will be concerned with which markets to move into, whether to diversify production, their capital investments, and the allocation of resources to major functions. At a university, a strategic decision might be concerned with whether a capital investment should be made by building new student residences on campus to ensure that all new first year students can be offered a room on campus.

- **Tactical decisions** are medium term, have a time span of months, and are made by middle management. They are based on a mix of internal and external information, with less personal judgement, and produce policies to help the organisation meet its strategic aims and objectives. Internal information supplied by supervisory management includes periodic reports, actual information summarised by period or region, 'what if' reports, and short-term trend analysis. Within a business organisation, tactical decisions will be concerned with planning cash flows, work scheduling, and marketing initiatives. A university tactical decision would be whether to set up a new course in Multimedia to attract additional students.

- **Operational decisions** are short term, have an immediate time span, are made by supervisory management and control the organisation's activities which are linked to the organisation's tactical plan. Internal information will be obtained from monitoring the operations of the workforce (for a short period, a day or a week). Within a business organisation, operational decisions will be concerned with control of stock levels and credit control. A university operational decision will be concerned with whether staff should write the syllabus in the modules of the new course.

Managers at all levels often request **exception reports** which provide information on anything that has occurred that is not according to plan or not normal. These will normally require some corrective action which should be taken as quickly as possible. Non-exceptions means that things are operating according to plan and no or little corrective action is necessary.

| Planning level | Time span | Detail level | Sources | Personal judgement | Frequency |
|---|---|---|---|---|---|
| *Strategic* | Long term | Summarised | Mainly external | High and uncertain | Infrequent |
| *Tactical* | | | | | |
| *Operational* | Immediate | Very details | Internal | Low and certain | Frequent |

*Figure 3.6 Decision making summary table*

## Question 3.13

A decision to build a new car engine factory is taken by which organisation level?

A  workforce

B  supervisory

C  middle

D  top

## Question 3.14

A decision to increase production of a particular product to meet increased demand is taken by which organisation level?

A  workforce

B  supervisory

C  middle

D  top

## Question 3.15

A decision to not set up a customer account is taken by which organisation level?

A  workforce

B  supervisory

C  middle

D  top

## Question 3.16

*A decision to offer an alternative product to a customer is taken by which organisation level?*

*A workforce*

*B supervisory*

*C middle*

*D top*

## Quality of information

The aim of processing data to provide information, is to increase understanding and assist the organisation in making informed decisions. The value of information depends on when and how it was obtained. Its quality depends on the following characteristics.

- **Clarity and brevity** – it should not be too detailed, be specific, not ambiguous, and meet the needs of the recipient of the information.
- **Timely** – it should be as timely and up-to-date as possibe (information tends to lose its value as it ages).
- **Accurate** – it should be without errors and relate to its usage (again meet the needs of its recipient).
- **Verifiable** – it should be possible to check the information, with identifiable sources and an audit trail for summaries.
- **Relevant** – its content should aid decision making (unnecessary information will complicate matters).
- **Complete** – all important details should be present (incomplete information is often worthless).

## Operations information

Operations information flows at the workforce level: internally within and between the functions of an organisation, or externally between the organisation function and an external entity. Each functional unit in the organisation will use and generate information during its daily activities. Data and information will be:

- received into the unit;
- processed, recorded and stored;
- passed out of the unit as responses.

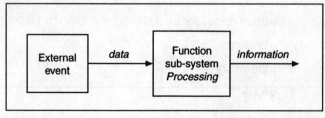

*Figure 3.7 Function produces information from data*

## Sales and marketing

Sales and marketing deals with the organisation's customers, its market place and its competitors. Its primary function is sales order processing, which basically involves taking an order for products and services from a customer. In commercial organisations the products ordered are supplied from stock, but some items may not be available. In commercial and industrial organisations there may also be a request for a quotation; a need to examine the request, cost and plan it; and a need to provide the customer with a cost and delivery time which, if accepted becomes an order.

| SALES ORDER | | | Order No: 960123 |
|---|---|---|---|

**Mikes Computer Supplies**

| Account no: | B0132 | Order date: | 12/06/1996 |
|---|---|---|---|
| Customer name: | BOATSRUS | Contact: | Mr B Sun |
| Address: | THE WARF | Tel: | 0123 4567890 |
| | NEW BAY | | |
| | NEWPORT | Ref: | BRS06010 |
| | NP1 4ZX | | |

Order details:

| Item code | Item description | Quantity | Unit price |
|---|---|---|---|
| T75/1000 | MW Tower 75 8M, 1 Gbyte | 1 | 750.00 |
| R04M | Additional 4 Mbyte RAM | 2 | 50.00 |
| PIJ720 | Inkjet 720 dot | 1 | 345.00 |
| CD04 | Quad Speed CD ROM | 1 | 60.00 |
| ASB16 | SB16 Sound card | 1 | 85.00 |
| SP003 | Pair qualsound speakers | 1 | 25.00 |

*Additional comments:*

No software to be installed

Configure system with basic DOS

Will collect 24/06/96 am

*Figure 3.8 An example order form*

The order form shown in figure 3.8 is typical of most organisations. Such forms would be completed by sales personnel from a telephone or written order request. The form shows who the customer is, which products are required, the quantity of each one, and when it should be ready. The 'Item code' column ensures the selection of a particular product (this column and the price column may be omitted in some organisations). Some order forms for items like clothes would need to include size and colour columns. There are numerous examples of mail-order forms to be found in product catalogues and magazines.

Sales orders are normally written down onto multi-copy coloured stationery. These sale order forms are then used for local filing and distribution to other departments as information about the sale, for example:

- white and yellow copy to pending order file;
- blue and green copy to stores, green returned to sales;
- yellow copy to accounts.

## Stores

The items described on the order from sales and marketing need to be allocated from stock. Stock records show the current status of a stock item.

| STOCK CARD | | *Mikes Computer Supplies* | | | Use both sides |
|---|---|---|---|---|---|

| *Item code:* | PIJ720 | *Location:* | R03S02 | *Min stock:* | 5 |
|---|---|---|---|---|---|
| *Description:* | Inkjet 720 | *Supplier:* | NorComp | *Re-order qty:* | 10 |
| | | *Tel:* | 01234 543876 | | |

| Date | Receipts | | Issues | | Balance |
|---|---|---|---|---|---|
| | Qty | Supplier | Qty | Customer | 12 |
| 15/05/96 | | | 8 | Glamorgan Uni | 4 |
| 01/06/96 | 10 | NorComp | | | 14 |
| 06/06/96 | | | 2 | New School | 12 |
| 12/06/96 | | | 1 | Boatsrus | 11 |
| | | | | | |

*Figure 3.9 Stock card record showing current balance and stock movements*

For example, in figure 3.9 the sale or issue of eight printers to Glamorgan University caused the stock level to fall to 4; this was below the minimum stock level of 5. Purchasing is requested to place an order with the printer suppliers NorComp for 10 more printers; these are supplied and received into stock raising the balance back to 14.

## Accounts

Once stock has been allocated to fulfil the order, sales and marketing notify accounts personnel of the sales transaction, and then a sales invoice can be prepared for the items supplied. The sales invoice is similar to the order form, except that each detail line is extended with a line total cost, the line costs are totalled to give a total net amount (there will also be any discount due), VAT and carriage charge, and all these are totalled to give an invoiced gross amount due. An example of a sales invoice is shown in figure 3.10.

| INVOICE | | | | Invoice No: 005432 |
|---|---|---|---|---|

*Mikes Computer Supplies*
*Unit 17 IT Park*
*Caerphilly CF12 45XX*

*If we haven't got it, we can get it!*

VAT registration no: 111 4444 55    Invoice date: 20/06/1996
To:   BOATSRUS
      THE WARF               Ref:    BRS06010
      NEW BAY
      NEWPORT
      NP1 4ZX

| Item code | Item description | Quantity | Unit price | Total |
|---|---|---|---|---|
| ASB16 | SB16 Sound card | 1 | 85.00 | 85.00 |
| CD04 | Pana Quad speed CDROM | 1 | 60.00 | 60.00 |
| PIJ720 | Spray Inkjet 720 | 1 | 345.00 | 345.00 |
| | | | | |
| | | | | |
| | | | | |
| | | | Total net | 490.00 |
| | | | VAT @ 17.5% | 85.75 |
| | | | Carriage | 0.00 |
| | | | Total due | 575.75 |

5% discount if settled within 14 days

*Figure 3.10 Example sales invoice*

## Question 3.17

*Which of the following receives a sales invoice?*

A   the sales department

B   the accounts department

C   the stores department

D   the customer

## Purchasing

While sales personnel are receiving sales orders from customers, and accounts personnel are issuing sales invoices, purchasing personnel will be placing purchase orders with suppliers. When items are supplied to the organisation, accounts receive a supplier's sales invoice for the organisation to pay (to accounts this is a **purchase invoice**). Again coloured multi-copy forms are used for filing and distribution.

To summarise

- **sales orders** are triggered externally by customers, **sales invoices** are raised internally to customers;
- **purchase orders** are triggered internally to suppliers, **purchase invoices** are raised externally from suppliers.

Other documents that are raised in the processing and progressing of a sales order include the following (multi-copies are often used to provide an audit trail).

- **Picking list** – issued to stores to enable efficient selection of products from stores and the making up of sales orders.
- **Despatch or packing note** – this accompanies the actual order and has details of all items actually making up the supplied order; it only contains quantities and there is no pricing information.
- **Goods received note** – provides details of goods actually received (similar information to despatch note).
- **Remittance advice** – this is attached to the sales invoice and can be detached and sent with the settlement of the invoice by the customer.
- **Statement of account** – this is a monthly statement sent to customers detailing all financial transactions undertaken between the organisation and customer. It shows the amount owed at the start of the month, each sales invoice amount issued, any payments received during the month, and the account balance outstanding at the end of the month. Regular account customers would tend to settle on statement rather than settle each individual invoice as it is received.

### Industrial information

An organisation in the manufacturing or construction sector will also have information connected with the manufacturing or construction processes. This information includes the design specifications (design drawings, materials specification to be used in manufacture or construction, operations to be used and locations for carrying out any operation). A manufactured product's specification:

- will show its components (or what the product is made of);
- will describe the stages of manufacture, the operations and processes needed to make or assemble the product (or how the product is made);
- may also show where these operations will take place (or where the product is made).

In the motor vehicle industry, assembly line construction of engines, transmission systems and the finished motor vehicle are common place. Such manufacturing methods are also used for electrical goods, like washing machines and televisions. For such systems to operate effectively the production process must be managed, planned, monitored and control. Each sales order that creates a primary demand for, say, 2000 items of a product like a television, will create a secondary demand for the components needed in each television (2000 cases, 2000 screen tubes, 2000 on/off switches, 6000 control dials, 2000 circuit boards and so on). Some items will be common to many products and the secondary demand for them will be even greater. For production to run smoothly there must be no out-of-stock situations. Shortages of items can also cause problems, pushing up prices and reducing production. For example, a shortage of computer RAM chips made them quite expensive, but recent increases in availability has seen prices of RAM fall.

Production control information describes the physical flow of items through the manufacturing process: from receipt of the order, scheduling of production, through production, to final despatch or distribution.

## Question 3.18

*Which of these functions prepares and issues a sales invoice to a customer?*

*A  sales and marketing*

*B  purchasing*

*C  accounts*

*D  stores*

## Question 3.19

*Which of these functions raises a request for more stock of a material?*

*A  sales and marketing .*

*B  purchasing*

*C  accounts*

*D  stores*

**Task 3.5**   **PC 3**

*For the organisation that you chose in Task 3.4, prepare a portfolio of documents that describe the types of information found in that organisation.*

## 3.1.4   Information flow between functions

All the different functions within an organisation communicate with another function and generate an internal flow of information. Some functions also generate external information flows with entities external to the organisation.

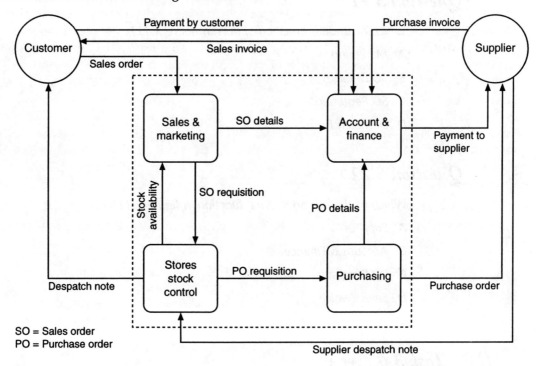

*Figure 3.11 Information flow block diagram*

The diagram in figure 3.11 shows the flow of information (such as paper-based documents) between the different internal and external functions. The dotted line indicates the boundary or scope of the organisation. It does not show the actual flow of goods from the organisation to a customer, or from a supplier to the organisation.

147

# Question 3.20

Which of these is an internal flow in figure 3.11?

A Buying

B SO Details

C Purchase invoice

D Payment by customer

# Question 3.21

Which of these is an external flow in figure 3.11?

A Marketing

B SO Details

C SO Requisition

D Despatch Note

# Question 3.22

Which of these is an internal function in figure 3.11?

A Supplier

B Account & Finance

C PO Details

D Sales Invoice

# Task 3.6   PC 4

For the organisation used in Tasks 3.4 and 3.5, draw a diagram (similar to figure 3.11) that shows the internal and external information flows.

# *Describe data handling systems*

## Data and information resources

Data and information are important and valuable resources of any organisation whether it be private or public, a road haulage company, a building society, a tool hire firm, a school or the Inland Revenue. For an organisation to operate it is essential that its data is as accurate and complete as possible, to provide timely, relevant and clear information to enable effective real-time, short-term and long-term decisions to be made. In the competitive business world, timely and accurate information is a valuable commodity. Creation and maintenance of data, and the provision of information, costs money so it is worthwhile to make the effort to get things right.

The information required by an organisation will change as it responds to its internal operations and external environment. Information is raw data that has been processed (e.g. totalled, averaged, sorted, analysed, evaluated) in such a way that it means something to the organisation. Very often the same raw facts are manipulated in different ways by different information systems of the same organisation. One person's or department's information is another's data.

Data handling systems are concerned with the capture, processing, storage and retrieval of data that underpin the information used by an organisation. Historically this processing of data has been carried out manually by clerks and administrators, but over the years this job has been made easier through use of machines (like the telephone, typewriter, calculator and, in the past fifty years, the computer). Today, most organisations use IT in support of its basic office functions and also to process its data to provide information.

Internally or externally to the organisation, events occur that create data in the form of a transaction that must be processed by the organisation. Some events are time controlled in that they occur on a regular basis and are predictable, for example payroll events occur about the same time each week or month, telephone bills arrive each quarter, and bank statements arrive each month. Other events are random and can occur at any time, for example, the use of a bank's ATM, the purchase of new clothes, and the ordering of a new car – some events occur more frequently than others. Whatever the cause or the frequency, the event will create a transaction that contains **source data** about the event which will need processing.

## Data hierarchy

Within every computerised information processing system there exists a data hierarchy or data organisation pyramid as follows.

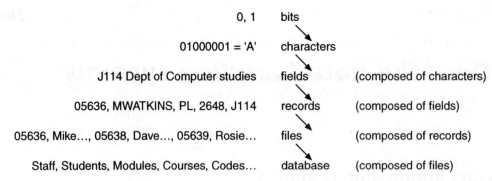

| | | |
|---|---|---|
| 0, 1 | bits | |
| 01000001 = 'A' | characters | |
| J114 Dept of Computer studies | fields | (composed of characters) |
| 05636, MWATKINS, PL, 2648, J114 | records | (composed of fields) |
| 05636, Mike…, 05638, Dave…, 05639, Rosie… | files | (composed of records) |
| Staff, Students, Modules, Courses, Codes… | database | (composed of files) |

*Figure 3.12 The data hierarchy*

## Master and transaction data

**Records** or groups of **fields** are used to record the details of an event. Records of the same type are grouped together in a data **file**. A **database** is a collection of files associated with a particular function of the organisation.

- The sales and marketing function would have a database containing a customer file with a record for each customer; an order file with a record of each order placed; a product file with a record for each product available for sale; and a salesperson file with a record about each salesperson.

- A stores function would have a database containing a stock file with a record for each stock item; an issues file with a record for each issue of items from stores; and a receipts file with a record of each receipt of items into stores.

Some events tend to occur less frequently and may not be a daily occurrence, while others occur very frequently, often hundreds of times a day. For example, a new customer, new employee or new stock item event for an organisation may not occur frequently; whereas many sales orders will be taken each day, many employee pay records will be updated each week, and many issues from stores will occur each day.

These files can be one of two types as follows.

- **Transaction files** – the orders, issues and receipts files are all transaction files. Each record holds the details of the transaction events that have occurred in a working period, day, week or month. Records are added to the transaction files throughout the period. At the end of the period, if batch processing is used, the corresponding master files are updated. The records themselves provide an audit trail and in time they will be archived (printed out and filed) and purged (deleted from the system).

- **Master files** – the customer, product, stock and salesperson files are all permanent master files. They store two types of data about the entity. Relatively static data values (like product name and location), and data that changes when transactions are processed (like stock balance). New records for these files do not occur too often, although their contents get changed when transactions are processed against them. For example, the balance of a stock item is increased with a receipt into stock, and is decreased with an issue from stock. Master files may be updated directly when a transaction occurs, or later on when a batch of transactions is processed. Master files will also need maintenance when other less frequent events occur, for example when there are new customers, or a change in customer address.

## Data take-on

When an IT system is installed to replace a manual system, the first thing that must be done is **data take-on** to build the master files. Only after this has been done and checked out can the system become operational and start processing its transactions. For example, a vehicle leasing company would need initially to take on all its current customer details, all its current contract leases with each customer, all its current vehicles and a summary of their maintenance history to date. After this has been done contract and vehicle transactions can be processed and the files updated, and vehicle maintenance invoices can be processed that will update vehicle mileage and running costs.

### Question 3.23

*Which of these is a transaction record?*

*A   employee person details*

*B   customer details*

*C   employee petrol receipt*

*D   vehicle details*

### Question 3.24

*Which of these is a master record?*

*A   purchase order details*

*B   supplier details*

*C   stock requirement details*

*D   supplier invoice*

## 3.2.1   Methods of processing

For commercial systems, the source data making up a transaction can be processed within an IT system in one of two ways: immediately in **real time**, or later after a number of transactions have been accumulated into a **batch**. How transactions are processed determines how up-to-date the system is. For example, a stock system that processes an item issue immediately will have an up-to-date stock level at all times; whereas a system that accumulates the item issues throughout the day, and processes them all overnight, will only be up-to-date at the start of each day. Generally it is better to keep a system as up-to-date as possible, but it can be an expensive procedure.

## Batch processing

In the past, **batch processing** systems accumulated paper transactions (records) into a suitably sized **batch**, which was then transported to a central computer system and processed as a

**group** by the computer system in one processing run. This was done because the technology of the day could not support any other way of doing things.

Prior to computer processing each batch was given a unique number. This was also attached to each transaction, which was dated. The batch was then subjected to some manual pre-processing (such as totalling the number of transactions in the batch and totalling transaction amount or quantity field to give a batch **hash total**), and then this batch control data was entered onto a batch header record – this enabled the computer system to check that all data in a batch have been entered and reconciled.

Now that technology has advanced, batch processing is still used where there is:

- usually bulk data (hundreds or thousands of transactions to be input and processed);
- **no** requirement for data to be up-to-date immediately;
- where data is processed regularly, e.g. at month end.

Batch processing may involve accumulating the batch directly on-line to a computer file, or off-line to some intermediate portable tape or disk storage (automated data entry using MICR or OMR still batches transactions). Much transaction data occurs naturally in batches (e.g. a day's orders received in the post, the end of month payroll done in department batches, the payroll processing of weekly time cards by the factory), and much bulk volume transaction processing is handled on a batch basis (e.g. the daily update of bank accounts).

Prior to starting a batch processing job on the computer, copies of the files to be updated by the batch are taken – this means the original files can easily be restored if things go wrong. The user has very little interaction with the job, and once started the computer processing of a batch should not be interrupted. During the running of the batch job, the files being updated are not available to any other user or processing job.

Handling data in batches causes delays in processing, from the data originating at its source to seeing the effects in the stored master data. The elapsed delay period must fit in with the system's requirements and be acceptable to the users and anyone or anything affected by the processing. However, using batches improves control over the quality of the input data: lost transactions can be traced to a batch, and some errors in data can also be detected. Batching of data implies a centralisation of the data capture activity or the use of less data capture points. Batch print-outs can highlight any errors detected in the transactions and subsequent corrections can be made. Errors detected in a batch may result in the rejection of the whole batch.

## Transaction processing

**Transaction processing** handles transaction data interactively, on demand and in real-time, processing transactions **one at a time**. Immediately an event occurs the transaction data arising from it is entered into the system, it is captured and processed and the system is updated immediately.

The data entry activity will check that only valid data is entered and show any errors (this is possible for codes but not all data can be validated in this way). The system can also respond with confirmation data (obtained by using the codes to access associated data records in on-line files).

For example, in a purchase ledger accounts application, purchase invoice entry will involve typing at the keyboard a supplier account code; the system will display the code on the VDU screen, use the code to look up the corresponding account record on file and then display the account name, thus giving the operator a check that the name displayed matches that at the head of the invoice.

The processing of the transaction will update related master record data immediately. Locking records accessed by the transaction prevents other users having simultaneous access to them, and this ensures that the update is secure on completion of the transaction. Output from the processing may either be received immediately and fed back to the data source, or at some later time in the form of a period report.

For example, a vehicle tyre depot enters the details of a sale immediately after fitting. This transaction immediately updates the stock file and produces an invoice for the customer.

Transaction processing requires multiple data entry stations or terminals, usually as close to the originating data source as possible. The originating data source may still be paper-based, but many systems today capture data without any transcription to paper. On most general purpose commercial systems, one terminal may handle a variety of transactions, although due to its location one terminal may be dedicated to data entry activities for a particular application. Some systems will have terminals that are highly specialised and may only be used for a particular form of data capture.

Having access to data on-line is the major requirement for transaction processing systems. In addition to the processing of transactions, the system will also be able to provide a quick response to enquiries.

For example, in a tyre depot, a prospective customer telephone enquiry requests the availability of a certain make and size of tyre. The depot employee can use the system to check the stock level, and for out-of-stock items an alternative could be displayed and offered to the caller.

## Question 3.25

Which method processes transaction data one record at a time?

A  batch

B  transmission

C  transaction

D  transcription

## Question 3.26

At which time will a master file be most up-to-date when using batch processing?

A  immediately before the first batch job

B  immediately before the last batch job

C  immediately after the first batch job

D  immediately after the last batch job

## Task 3.7   PC 1

*Using example systems that you have access to (or have read about), describe one batch processing activity and one transaction processing activity. You should include the names of the batch files that are updated, and what their record contents are; and the names of the transaction files, what their record contents are, and what data source generated them. For the batch processing indicate the time allowed to accumulate the batch and describe any pre-processing applied to it.*

## Types of data handling systems

### Bookings

A **bookings** type of reservation system is common in the travel industry and is used by airlines for seat reservations, by hotels for room reservations, by holiday tour operators for holiday reservations and by sea ferry operators for passenger and vehicle reservations. The systems used have the following characteristics:

- the system will be multi-user with access using keyboard, VDU screen and a printer;
- the system will be secure requiring operator identification;
- coding systems will be used to reduce operator dialogue and the amount of transmission;
- all required data files regarding the services provided, and their availability, will be on-line;
- the transaction processing method will be used.

For example, some major holiday tour operators support hundreds of remote terminals, providing access to many different travel agents who make a dial-up remote connection to the system. Other small specialised holiday firms may only support one local head office, with access by their own employees, and the customer communicating with the company directly by telephone.

The agent or operator uses the keyboard and screen to:

- make enquiries about the availability of customers requirements (destination, dates, numbers);
- access travel operators' files on-line and search to retrieve information matching the enquiry;
- make a booking reservation for the customer, the booking is given a unique booking number and is held for a few days;
- confirm the booking and update the booking record – on confirmation of the booking, the customer pays the deposit, and the costed confirmation note is printed.

After this initial interaction, the system will automatically output to the customer via the travel agent:

- within two months of departure a customer computer-printed invoice is sent for payment;

- within two weeks of departure, the computer-printed travel tickets and hotel reservation slip are sent to the customer.

## Payroll

**Payroll processing** is a regular activity carried out every week or every month (some organisations have weekly and monthly payrolls). It may employ batch and transaction processing methods.

- Batch processing will be used to input clock card or time sheet details, batched by department or office. The main payroll run will operate in batch mode by processing all employees.
- Transaction processing will be used to make changes to the individual employee master record details (e.g. changes to the tax code, rate of pay or annual salary).

Input of 'time' data can take several forms and is accumulated on-line in a transaction file:

- paper-based timesheets completed by the employees and signed off by their supervisor are input using a keyboard and screen, with screen forms that match the layout of the timesheet;
- clock cards may be input at end of period using OCR or OMR readers;
- clock in/out times may be collected directly through employee smart cards that are swiped and the transaction time stamped (these devices can also monitor flexitime systems).

Output from the payroll processing system can also take several forms:

- pay slips – impact printed on continuous pre-printed stationery, often in secure envelope form;
- pay cheques – impact printed on continuous pre-printed stationery;
- a record of individual pay details for transmission using BACS system;
- updated payroll master file (new cumulative to date amounts);
- notes and coinage analysis to make up cash wage packets.

These are all regular payroll activities, although there are others that occur lest frequently – like annual printing of P60 tax records. Tax and national insurance figures will also be required periodically.

## Ordering

Sales order processing handles **orders** received from customers. The order may be verbal by telephone, or written by paper (through the post or fax). Mail order companies allow both types of order and provide special purpose order forms – if the order is received verbally it will either be transcribed onto a paper order form or entered directly into the computer system.

Batch or transaction processing methods are used. Verbal orders processed directly will use transaction processing, with several operators accessing the system simultaneously using keyboard and screen-based order forms. Paper-based orders can be entered as a batch and then processed in one batch job run. The order entry system has access to customer and product stock files, which are updated as the order is processed. The system produces printed pick lists and despatch notes for a finished goods warehouse, order details for accounts, and periodic sales reports.

### Invoicing

**Invoicing** is a finance and accounts activity. A sales invoice is produced which is sent to the customer for payment. Invoices are printed on special stationery and batch processing would be used to print a batch of invoices in one print run. The invoice is based on the contents of a processed sales order of actual items supplied – in an integrated system, the processed order details stored in the system are used to generate the associated invoice. Customer details and product details are obtained from the respective files and then the contents are updated. Some systems use transaction mode to produce one-off invoices for despatch with the order.

Some systems require invoices to be printed regularly each month to customers in a monthly batch invoice run. For example, a vehicle leasing system would use the lease contract to generate a monthly invoice automatically to every customer detailing each lease due for payment that month.

### Stock control

**Stock control** is a stores function. The system has a stock master file to keep up-to-date records of each item held. The stock master file holds the stock item records (e.g. item number, description, cost, price, quantity in stock) and this is updated with stock movements as follows:

- issues from stock to sales (despatch notes) or production (requisition note);
- receipts into stock from production or suppliers (goods received notes);
- returns and adjustments.

Stock movements can be:

- recorded using a paper-based system and end-of-period batch processing to update the stock master file;
- entered directly on-line using transaction processing, to update the stock master file immediately;

In manufacturing organisations the majority of data entry may be by keyboard and VDU, but other data capture methods are used in another industry. For example, laser-scanned barcodes for issues used in supermarkets and retail stores provide transaction processing capability, and Kimball tags or punched cards provide a batch processing capability.

### Personal records

**Personal records** embrace many applications and organisations. In addition to payroll and personnel applications, some others are as follows:

- **Medical records** – most GP practices keep computerised records of patients registered with them and most processing is transaction-based. The record holds personal details plus medical history data. It may also operate a computerised appointment system that is updated with patient bookings and produces printed appointments lists for the GPs. In hospitals, patient and bed availability records are kept; on admission a record is created and personal details kept throughout the stay.
- **Student records** – many colleges use a centralised student-administration system to record student details, the course studied, the modules taken and the results obtained. On enrolment at the start of their college studies, the students will complete enrolment forms for entry onto the computer system. During their studies, this record will keep track of their progress by being updated with data from their respective departments. The systems employ a mix of batch and transaction processing.

- **Club membership records** – many sports clubs use membership systems that create member records from forms completed on joining and paying a membership fee. The system can be used to produce mailing lists and annual renewal invoices. Some clubs may have club cards enabling the purchase of services via a smart card – details of cards issued and transactions undertaken are recorded by the system. The system may also be used to record the results of matches and produce regular updated print-outs on performance.

## Question 3.27

Which of these is most likely to be a batch processing job?

A  booking seats at a pop concert

B  producing monthly bank statements

C  editing a spreadsheet

D  handling a customer account enquiry

## Question 3.28

Which of these is most likely to be a transaction processing system?

A  printing electricity bills

B  printing monthly bank statements

C  making an appointment at a GP's surgery

D  printing annual income tax data

## Question 3.29

Why does a factory use a computerised stock system?

A  to buy stock at a lower price

B  to help decide when to re-order materials

C  to improve efficiency of manufacturing

D  to improve accuracy of designs

## Task 3.8    PC 1

*Using example systems you have observed (or have read about) write a short report that describes the two types of data handling system described previously – one should involve the use of predominantly batch processing, the other transaction processing. You should outline the whole system, listing and briefly describing each functional feature. You should describe what you consider to be the key feature in more detail. For example, a library system has the key function of lending books, additional features include book acquisition, book disposal, and user searches.*

## 3.2.2 Objectives of data handling systems

Using IT systems to process data to produce information has several objectives. The speed of operation (particularly where there is bulk data to handle) must meet the requirements of the system. The accuracy or quality of operation is measured by its reliability and the number of errors that occur, if the system is given garbage, it will produce garbage. The IT system must be cost effective, there are initial set up costs and subsequent operational costs. The system should support the decision making process of the organisation.

## Speed

The input, process, output activities have widely different speeds of operation: once in, the computer processing of data is lightening fast; output from the system can be fast but is much slower than processing; input is the slowest activity, as it often has a human element. Capture of data and entry via keyboard and screen is slow and is the bottleneck of many systems. To overcome this, some systems have automated this process to quicken the time taken to enter a transaction. Once in the system, the data can be manipulated at electronic speeds. Bulk printed output from the system can also be time consuming and technology has enabled this process to take less time, but at a cost. Today many organisation systems could not function without an IT system.

## Accuracy

Accuracy is concerned with errors in the data, incorrect data being used in the processing, and the reliability of the system (how often it breaks down). Data entry causes the majority of errors that occur in an IT system; other sources of error include incorrect software, carrying out the wrong processing function and, more rarely, hardware. The IT system processes the data it is given, if garbage is input then the output will also be garbage.

If allowed to go uncorrected, input errors will cost progressively more to correct the longer they remain undetected. In clerical systems, errors are treated on an ad-hoc basis as they are found, but an IT system must plan to detect and correct errors as soon as possible so as to minimise error and future cost.

The keyboard and screen method of data entry is the most error prone as it involves the human operator entering data from a document, a product, or from verbal instructions; automated methods are much less error prone

It is very worthwhile expending considerable effort on the programming of data entry software to validate or check input data for accuracy and allow the human operator to verify their entry.

**Validation** is logical checks made by software on the values of data fields entered into the system. In general, the types of validation check that can be carried out by software on data input are:

- field size or length;
- field type or format, text or numeric or alphanumeric;
- value range and limit checks;
- validity of codes entered (look up codes in a table or file);
- self-checking codes that use check digits;

- presence or absence of field (is it mandatory?);
- further checks include sequence and batch reconciliation.

In transaction entry systems, the errors detected are immediately feedback to the operator, whereas with batch systems an exception report is produced. The system should allow the operator to make a visual verification of data entered, before committing it to be processed.

## Cost

IT systems have a number of cost components:
- the cost of buying and setting up the system initially;
- the cost of maintaining the hardware and software of the IT system;
- the training of personnel to use the system;
- the day-to-day operating costs.

Against these costs must be set the advantages that using the IT system will provide. In many organisations it is the staff costs that are a significant part of the operating costs. By providing an effective IT system staff cost savings may be made, remaining staff can be more effective, the organisation can gain a competitive advantage, operations can be more efficient, and management can have better information that enables more effective decision making.

Advertising of computer products would have businesses believe that the purchase of an IT system hardware and software package will solve all their problems overnight. The truth of the matter is that an IT purchase should be treated like any other capital investment – the implications of installing it should be fully understood as there are many hidden costs.

## Support decision making

Information is organised data, once captured the data can be used to provide management information at all levels. On-line enquiry facilities can aid all levels of the organisation. Exception reporting and warning can aid the supervisory level. Summary or periodic reporting, actuals against budgets or forecast can aid the middle and top levels. Other software tools enable all levels to manipulate the data stored and perform 'what if' processing, carry out trend analysis, and present data in a variety of user-friendly graphical formats.

*Question 3.30*

*Which of these is **not** an objective applied to the use of barcodes?*

*A speed of data entry*

*B accuracy of data entry*

*C improved decision making*

*D cost effective*

**Task 3.9** PC 2

*For the systems described in Task 3.8, describe the objectives of each system using the criteria listed in Section 3.2.2.*

## 3.2.3  Data sources for data handling systems

Historically, data entry has involved transcribing data from one form to another: from its original source to finally being input into the system. This was particularly true of organisations with centralised data-processing departments – they had a multi-user system with enquiry terminals in departments, but data input was a DP department function. The trend in data entry is to move away from centralisation and reduce the number of transcription steps, by capturing data as close to the source as possible. It is also an area where productivity of operators can be increased significantly.

On-line terminals with keyboard and screen data entry facilities, enable transactions to be entered or posted to the system immediately they are received or occur within the source department. This activity is fine for low volume work or where there is a need for a dialogue with the data originator (e.g. a customer), but where there is a need for bulk data input a speedy data input service source-data automation is required.

Automated data-capture methods need to be:

- inexpensive to operate, there may be a more expensive initial set up cost to purchase special equipment;
- reasonably error free and reliable;
- easy to operate and to train staff in its operation;
- fast and able to handle high data volumes.

### Barcodes

Many products sold today have an identifying barcode: a group of lines and spaces printed on their packaging at the time of manufacture or stuck to them later like a label (there is one on the back of this book). The barcode can be optically scanned by a barcode reading device and the numbers printed below the barcode pattern enable us to read the code. The barcode uniquely identifies the product within the organisation – some organisations may use their own system of coding, while others may adhere to an internationally agreed format of 'country of origin code/manufacturer code/product code/check digit'. Barcodes can also be used on membership cards, or on a card next to a terminal to identify a particular type of transaction (such as a library book issue or return).

Barcodes are used in transaction processing systems where their use removes the need for the operator to type in the code; it therefore speeds things up and is less prone to error.

### Document character recognition

There a number of forms of **character recognition** used to capture data, all of which are able to be read or interpreted by us. The data to be read from the document must be placed at set fixed positions on the document, special symbols may be used to indicate the start and end of a field. The main types of character recognition are as follows.

- **Optical character recognition (OCR)** reads printed characters, letters and numbers. Most use a particular stylised print font that can be read optically by the computer input device:
  - OCR-A, 26 capital letters, 10 numeric digits and symbols;
  - OCR-B, capital and lower case letters, numeric digits and more symbols.

  Some may be able to read handwritten printed letters and digits. Not all text on the document is read, only the specific data fields are read from fixed positions.

- **Optical mark recognition (OMR)** reads black marks placed on documents at specified positions. Numbers can be read by marking over digit values in a grid or dial, selections can be read by placing marks in particular boxes.

- **Magnetic ink character recognition (MICR)** reads characters printed using magnetic ink. This is used mainly to input numeric data, a particular stylised print font is used that can read magnetically by the computer input device:
  - E13B, ten numeric digits, 4 symbols;
  - CMC7, ten numeric digits, 26 capital letters, 5 symbols.

- **Turnround documents** are extensive users of character recognition. The document used is either produced by the computer system itself or supplied from a printer, both will have some identifying fields completed, further data is added by the user at specified locations on the document. The document is either captured in that form or will need some minor processing to make the data supplied by the user readable.

Character recognition is used in batch processing systems, particularly where there are high numbers of transactions and where the encoded documents are accumulated over a period and processed at period end. Banking uses MICR for cheque clearance, domestic supply utilities use OCR with OMR for meter reading and billing, education uses OMR for marking of multi-choice examination questions, OCR is used to process payment remittances.

Text, pictures and drawings, can be scanned using document page scanners, however these are not viewed as transactions but their images can be processed and stored in a database for future reference. For example, pieces of text, pictures and drawings would be used in a DTP system; a picture of an employee would be used in a personnel system; a house or building picture in an estate agents; a parts component explosion drawing in a production system. Such systems input one piece at a time and store them on file for subsequent inclusion into the application.

## Electronic files

There are several forms of electronic data sources, from small payment cards to electronic funds transfer as follows.

**Magnetic stripe cards** have been widely used for personal financial transactions. There are several basic forms:

- **credit card** – used to purchase items or services by credit to pay for at some later date, e.g. Access or Visa;
- **cash card** – used in banks and building society automated teller machines (ATM), a secret PIN number is necessary to use the card for cash, e.g. Abbey National cash card;

- **direct debit card** – issued by a bank or building society and used to purchase items or services, the cost is directly debited from the holder's account, e.g. Delta.

Some cards are multi-function providing cash and direct debit facilities and the cards can provide their service in foreign countries worldwide.

This set of cards has been extended by many retail shop organisations issuing their own store card – used to purchase items or services on credit from any shop belonging to that organisation, e.g. Marks and Spencer store card.

The magnetic stripe on the back of the card contains basic details about the account and the card holder and is machine readable. When swiped the data (including this information, the date and where it was used, and details of purchases or service used) is electronically transferred to the appropriate account. For expensive purchases the card can be used to obtain authorisation from the credit card company prior to the transaction going ahead. The card is used in a transaction processing mode, details of each transaction will appear on a monthly statement for the account.

**Smart cards** are similar to magnetic stripe cards, but use a microprocessor chip embedded in the card instead of a magnetic stripe. The chip gives the card greater versatility to support a range of services, can hold far more data and has a processing capability. Their main use to date in the UK is in Satellite TV receivers; the chip holds details of the services the holder has subscribed to and prevents reception of any other service. The chip can be updated with additional services if the holder wishes, the extra data is sent to it via the satellite.

**Electronic point of sale (EPOS)** is used by many shops and stores to capture data at the cash register, that in turn is connected to the store computer system. These systems use transaction processing to input data. The product code of an item sold is entered and used to access its record on the computer file, name and price details are passed back to the terminal for display, and the item's stock balance is updated. Their use enables the retailer to maintain up-to-date information on sales and stock control, and provides useful management information. Keyboard and screen may be used for input, but most systems now use barcodes to input product details. The customer gets a fully itemised printed receipt.

**Electronic funds transfer (EFT)** is used to replace paper financial transactions with an equivalent electronic transaction from one financial institution's account to another. Employees' salaries can be paid directly to their bank account from the employer's bank account using BACSTEL. The direct debit card used to purchase products or services sets up such a transaction from the EPOS terminal, allowing both the customer and retailer accounts to be updated immediately. EFT may use batch processing with BACS details input and transaction processing for EPOS details input.

EFT is now available in homes through use of Viewdata systems like PRESTEL, enabling 'viewers' to check their bank accounts, settle bills and order products or services using their television and telephone lines.

**Electronic mail (E-mail)** allows messages to be transmitted from one subscriber's terminal to another. The mail message is composed and sent by the sender, and on receipt it is held in a 'post office' for viewing when the receiver comes on-line. Each subscriber to the system must have a unique E-mail address code, e.g. MWATKINS@GLAMORGAN.AC.UK. Data files and other attachments can be sent using this and other electronic document transfer facilities. Many UK Universities provide an E-mail template to be completed by prospective students who are then sent course details.

## People

People can be sources of data not available from any other physical source. To obtain data from people a number of methods can be used as follows.

- **Interviews** can be an effective method of obtaining data. An interview will involve at least two people: the interviewer who asks the questions and the interviewee who provides answers to the questions. The answers obtained will need to be transcribed by the interviewer into a form suitable for computer input – this may be done as the interview progresses or afterwards by consulting interview notes made during the interview. A doctor will obtain symptom data from having an interview with patients.

- **Questionnaires** are useful for collecting specific data from a large number of people. Design of a questionnaire is a skill and it should provide data in a form that can easily be processed. Completed questionnaires can be input using OMR or by keyboard and screen (using a screen questionnaire template). Electronic questionnaires are feasible through use of E-mail;

- **Task diaries** are useful for collecting data about the tasks people do in their daily jobs (what they spend their time doing). Like interviews, the data collected will need transcribing for input to the computer.

Input of questionnaire, interview and task diary data would use batch processing, although the input of the interview data can also use transaction processing.

### Question 3.31

How does the EPOS system (used in a CD and video store) identify items sold?

A  from till receipts

B  from customers

C  from barcodes

D  from the manager

### Question 3.32

How does the EPOS system (used in a CD and video store) obtain customer payment?

A  from a payment card

B  from a customer barcode

C  from a membership card

D  from till receipts

### Task 3.10   PC 3

For the systems described in Tasks 3.8 and 3.9, describe the data sources of each system.

## 3.2.4 Methods of data capture

Alternative methods of data capture have been developed in response to the increasing need for information, the need for accurate and fast processing and also the economics of the whole operation. Various technologies have been introduced with the general aim of automating data capture as far as possible, removing or reducing the occurrence of error, and providing the necessary resultant information at a competitive cost. The general trend has been to cut out manual operations wherever possible and replace them with alternative methods which are cheap, error free (or relatively so) and fast. Such systems generally require a high initial investment to set up the information infrastructure which will support the capture system. The general benefits are the reduced reliance on manual input, less errors, faster input and a tendency towards volume independence in the general costing of operations.

This trend may be illustrated with today's adoption of barcodes and laser-reading technology by the retail trade, supermarkets, shops, and DIY stores. In the past a handwritten bill and clerical (machine-assisted) totalling would have been used. From this developed (in chronological order):

- operator entry and non-itemised priced bill;
- operator entry and part-itemised priced bill;
- operator-controlled laser-scanned fully-itemised priced bill;
- user-controlled scanned shopping trolley;
- where next? ('Cable' shopping at home?)

What this shows is an increase in the automated components of the capture and a very much reduced manual contribution. Note that totally automated systems will only gather what they are designed to gather, and for real intelligence, the human factor is of overriding importance.

## Keyboard

Due to the popularity of PCs, keyboards have become increasingly important at the origin (or point of capture) of transaction data. The PCs are not normally in stand-alone mode but connected, via networks, to a centralised or distributed file facility. For low-volume entry, the keyboard skill of the user is relatively unimportant, but as volume of transactions, rise the need for true keyboard skills emerges. Many people spend their working day in front of VDUs and data input via keyboards is now protected by law on various aspects and conditions of the job: **repetitive strain injury (RSI)** and **VDU safety and usability** are just some of the considerations to be borne in mind. The overall observations to be made on keyboard entry of data are that:

- it is the most popular mode of entry;
- many operators are keyboard unskilled;
- manual operations are error prone and costly to detect and correct;
- physical injury can result from lack of or poor training (RSI).

# Mouse

A mouse has limited use in data entry but can be used to control a system. Using the 'point and click' activity, the mouse can replace the requirement to enter commands at the keyboard and provide greater versatility by:

- selecting processing activities (by command buttons and menus);
- selecting options from a set of displayed data values (by radio buttons);
- switching items characteristics on or off.

A mouse is particularly useful for those users who are not regular system users, and find the graphical user interface (GUI) and a mouse more natural than issuing keyboard commands.

The mouse is used in graphics systems to create diagrams and drawings, drawing activities and characteristics are mouse selected from a toolbar.

# Keypad

This is a reduced keyboard in its functionality. Perhaps its most frequent use is to enter limited types of data at the point where the data is created, e.g. data from the factory floor is entered directly on a numerically-controlled machine, or a hand-held electricity meter readers' unit.

# Barcode reader

This device scans barcodes optically using laser technology. The device is either a **static scanner** and the barcode is waved over it, or portable **laser 'wand'** that is waved over the barcode. The barcodes are either printed on packaging or can be produced as labels by bar- code printers when required. The most common occurrence of such codes is on foodstuffs and other goods in the retail market sector. Internationally recognised standard code structures are available but for private internal use in an organisation, code design is at the discretion of the user (though many firms will choose to stay with standard codes where they exist).

Application areas are in, for example, the retail trade, libraries, and shop floor reporting for manufacturing operations. The article can be identified by its barcode and barcodes can also be set up as standard transaction identifiers, e.g. issue of a book, return of a book, transfer of location etc. The read error rate is extremely low and for the right applications, barcodes are an extremely effective means of data capture.

# Optical mark recognition (OMR)

The major use of **optical mark recognition (OMR)** has been in the areas of multiple-choice examination answer scripts and gas or electricity meter reading. However, the National Lottery has made OMR more commonplace and uses a particularly small and simple reading device. The resulting completed document is read by the mark reader which scans the document, and where marks are sensed, they are given the pre-assigned value. The method is limited in its application and can be error prone, requiring human assistance to decipher a choice made.

## Optical character recognition (OCR)

**Optical character recognition (OCR)** is again not a new technology, but with more powerful and cheaper electronics the method has become more widely-used as the price of the system has fallen. The method relies on scanning text presented to the reader in document form. It builds up a pixel image of a character, which is then compared to a stored set (or sets) of characters. In this way, characters can be interpreted and stored internally in the computer. It represents a reasonably cheap and fast way of getting data into computers, but some problems may arise with errors on poor quality input documents. The user needs to be careful in adapting the technology to applications where accuracy needs are high.

Do not confuse this method with the technology of **document image processing (DIP)** which does not interpret documents, but merely stores digitised images available for later recall.

## Magnetic character reader (MICR)

**Magnetic character reader (MICR)** is the earliest attempt at automating data entry. This technology has remained firmly in a single application area, that of banking. We are all familiar with the E13B font of stylised numbers at the bottom of our cheques. These characters are printed in an ink which has ferrous traces in it, capable of being magnetised when put into an **MICR** reader **(magnetic ink character recognition)**. The MICR reader then recognises the magnetic field associated with each character and converts it into the internal character code. The clearing banks may still using this technology for some time to come.

## Sensors

There are many types of sensor that are used in industrial systems as input devices. They can:
- enable the machine to have 'sight', 'hearing', 'touch' and even 'smell' and 'taste';
- detect movement, heat and cold, pressure, flow;
- count and measure length and distance, weight, speed, volume.

Sensors are used to monitor activity or to sense their environment by reacting to their sensed 'image'. The device produces signal data that is passed back to the controlling processor for interpretation. The data received is often time stamped and stored in a data log file that can be inspected as required.

Robots are increasing in numbers in the manufacturing industry and use a variety of sensors. In addition, many devices at home and work employ sensors. For example, a washing machine has a water temperature heat sensor that controls its heater and a water level sensor that controls filling with water, both sensors are connected to an embedded processor. Microphones and speech recognition software enable machines to be trained to react to the spoken command.

## Question 3.33

Which of these is used to select an option from an application menu?

A   a scanner

B   a barcode wand reader

C   a magnetic card reader

D   a mouse

## Question 3.34

Which of these is used in a golf club when a payment card is used to pay for services in an EPOS system?

A   a scanner

B   a barcode reader

C   a magnetic card reader

D   a mouse

## Task 3.11   PC 4

For the systems described in Tasks 3.8 to 3.10, describe the methods of data capture used in each system.

## 3.2.5  Processes of data handling systems

As explained earlier in Unit 1 (1.2.1), data is represented internally in computers by an eight-bit binary code, giving 256 different combinations. These may be ranked in absolute value from 00000000 to 11111111 giving an ordered ranking of code (character) values called the **collating** sequence.

## Question 3.35

Which decimal value is equivalent to binary 11111111?

A   254

B   255

C   256

D   257

This ranking can be applied to any text data field occurring in each record of a file, so that we can sequence records in a file. Records in a file can be sorted or re-arranged into any sequence (ascending or descending) on a number of data fields in every record. The ability of the computer system to manipulate or sort data into different sequences is one of its major benefits for business use.

## Calculating

Business applications will involve the computer processing and manipulating the data. Much of the processing will require **calculations** to be carried out with the various data values.

For example, in a payroll system where employees are hourly paid (as in a shop), an employee's gross pay is calculated by multiplying the hours worked by the rate of pay per hour. Tax is then calculated at 20% of gross pay; take home pay is calculated as gross pay minus tax. This type of calculation would be repeated for every employee, and the tax for each employee can be accumulated into a company total.

Some calculations are performed once at the start of a process, some are repeated many times and others are performed once at the end of a process.

For example, in sales invoice production, the typical calculations carried out are as shown below.

---

***Once** before processing any invoice lines:*
Initialise or set a value:
    Total net amount = 0

***Repeated** for each item line on the invoice:*
Multiplication:
    Total item amount = Quantity × Item price
Tallying or accumulating of lines:
    Total net amount = Total net amount + Total item amount

***Once** after all item lines are processed:*
Multiplication:
    VAT amount = Total net amount × 17.5%
Addition:
    Total invoice amount = Total net amount + VAT amount + Carriage
Subtraction:
    Amount to be paid = Total invoice amount − Discount amount

---

The calculations in most business applications will usually involve repetitive application of simple arithmetic operations (like the ones above). In some applications (such as mortgage calculations) the calculations may be harder, but the computer system handles these just as easily. Industrial applications may require the computer to perform thousands of mathematical, engineering or scientific calculations.

## Sorting

**Sorting** rearranges (or orders) items of data (or records) based on their stored values. For example, a set of examination scripts for a class could be sorted in a number of ways:

- in alphabetic sequence, based on the value of the student's last name (the records are sorted on 'last name');
- in descending numeric sequence based on the value of the percentage mark given (the records are sorted on '%mark').

Figure 3.13 shows the contents of a disk directory sorted into file type, date and size sequence.

| View | Options | Win2 |
|---|---|---|
| √ Tree and Directory | | |
| Tree Only | | |
| Directory Only | | |
| Split | | |
| Name | | |
| √ All File Details | | |
| Partial Details... | | |
| Sort by Name | | |
| √ Sort by Type | | |
| Sort by Size | | |
| Sort by Date | | |
| By File Type... | | |

| File | Size | Date | Time |
|---|---|---|---|
| mcluber.dat | 4096 | 24/12/93 | 15:53:16 |
| select-a.dbf | 4096 | 24/12/93 | 15:33:14 |
| select-d.dbf | 16384 | 24/12/93 | 15:53:18 |
| ashgrove.doc | 12288 | 28/06/95 | 12:56:56 |
| jack2.gif | 21964 | 15/12/95 | 09:48:18 |
| mike2.gif | 90172 | 21/02/96 | 18:41:26 |
| mwatkins.gif | 58004 | 15/12/95 | 09:36:56 |
| useful2.htm | 3337 | 21/02/96 | 18:58:48 |
| cricket.pas | 3372 | 24/12/94 | 12:20:30 |
| landtax.pas | 5819 | 02/11/94 | 11:16:46 |
| mike2.pcx | 130677 | 21/02/96 | 18:38:42 |
| template.txt | 2268 | 19/04/93 | 00:00:00 |
| paint.zip | 1339638 | 15/01/96 | 14:51:58 |
| udrip.zip | 70623 | 01/03/95 | 14:20:26 |

| File | Size | Date | Time |
|---|---|---|---|
| useful2.htm | 3337 | 21/02/96 | 18:58:48 |
| mike2.gif | 90172 | 21/02/96 | 18:41:26 |
| mike2.pcx | 130677 | 21/02/96 | 18:38:42 |
| paint.zip | 1339638 | 15/01/96 | 14:51:58 |
| jack2.gif | 21964 | 15/12/95 | 09:48:18 |
| mwatkins.gif | 58004 | 15/12/95 | 09:36:56 |
| ashgrove.doc | 12288 | 28/06/95 | 12:56:56 |
| udrip.zip | 70623 | 01/03/95 | 14:20:26 |
| cricket.pas | 3372 | 24/12/94 | 12:20:30 |
| landtax.pas | 5819 | 02/11/94 | 11:16:46 |
| select-d.dbf | 16384 | 24/12/93 | 15:53:18 |
| mcluber.dat | 4096 | 24/12/93 | 15:53:16 |
| select-a.dbf | 4096 | 24/12/93 | 15:33:14 |
| template.txt | 2268 | 19/04/93 | 00:00:00 |

| File | Size | Date | Time |
|---|---|---|---|
| paint.zip | 1339638 | 15/01/96 | 14:51:58 |
| mike2.pcx | 130677 | 21/02/96 | 18:38:42 |
| mike2.gif | 90172 | 21/02/96 | 18:41:26 |
| udrip.zip | 70623 | 01/03/95 | 14:20:26 |
| mwatkins.gif | 58004 | 15/12/95 | 09:36:56 |
| jack2.gif | 21964 | 15/12/95 | 09:48:18 |
| select-d.dbf | 16384 | 24/12/93 | 15:53:18 |
| ashgrove.doc | 12288 | 28/06/95 | 12:56:56 |
| landtax.pas | 5819 | 02/11/94 | 11:16:46 |
| mcluber.dat | 4096 | 24/12/93 | 15:53:16 |
| select-a.dbf | 4096 | 24/12/93 | 15:33:14 |
| cricket.pas | 3372 | 24/12/94 | 12:20:30 |
| useful2.htm | 3337 | 21/02/96 | 18:58:48 |
| template.txt | 2268 | 19/04/93 | 00:00:00 |

*Figure 3.13 Disk directory contents arranged by type, date and size*

Sometimes it is necessary to use more than one field, for example:

- two students have the same last name (like 'DAVIES' or 'PATEL'), if this occurs then we will need to look at the first name value (the records are sorted on 'last name/first name');
- two students have the same mark, if this occurs we will look at the last name and then the first name (the records are sorted on '%mark/last name/first name').

Where sorting is based on more than one field, the left to right sequence is important. The left-hand field '%mark' is the **major** sort field and has **most control**, the right-hand field 'first name' is the **minor** sort field and has **least control**.

| Last Name | Initials | Title | Grade | Room | Tel no | E-mail |
|---|---|---|---|---|---|---|
| Hodson | PJ | Mr | 20 | J117 | 2270 | PJHODSON |
| Eyres | DE | Mr | 16 | J113 | 2648 | DEEYRES |
| Jones | CB | Prof | 16 | J211 | 2722 | CBJONES2 |
| Watkins | M | Mr | 16 | J113 | 2648 | MWATKINS |
| Beynon-Davies | P | Dr | 15 | J226 | 2243 | PBEYNOND |
| Jones | BF | Prof | 15 | J210 | 2730 | BFJONES1 |
| Evans | D | Mr | 14 | J130B | 2260 | DEVANS3 |
| Wright | GGL | Mr | 14 | J314 | 2254 | GGLWRIGH |
| Evans | GV | Mr | 12 | J217 | 2247 | GVEVANS |
| Davies | P | Mr | 10 | J217 | 2247 | PDAVIES4 |
| Davies | RA | Dr | 10 | J215 | 2264 | RADAVIES |
| Norris | K | Mr | 10 | J217 | 2247 | KNORRIS |
| Moon | J | Mr | 4 | J225 | 2263 | JMOON |
| Rees | C | Ms | 3 | J130B | 2260 | CREES4 |
| Stubbs | G | Mrs | 2 | J225 | 2263 | GSTUBBS |

*Figure 3.14 Staff records arranged in Grade/Last name order*

| Last Name | Initials | Title | Grade | Room | Tel No | Email |
|---|---|---|---|---|---|---|
| Beynon-Davies | P | Dr | 15 | J226 | 2243 | PBEYNOND |
| Davies | P. | Mr | 10 | J217 | 2247 | PDAVIES4 |
| Davies | RA | Dr | 10 | J215 | 2264 | RADAVIES |
| Evans | D | Mr | 14 | J130B | 2260 | DEVANS3 |
| Evans | GV | Mr | 12 | J217 | 2247 | GVEVANS |
| Eyres | DE | Mr | 16 | J113 | 2648 | DEEYRES |
| Hodson | PJ | Mr | 20 | J117 | 2270 | PJHODSON |
| Jones | BF | Prof | 15 | J210 | 2730 | BFJONES1 |
| Jones | CB | Prof | 16 | J211 | 2722 | CBJONES2 |
| Moon | J | Mr | 4 | J225 | 2263 | JMOON |
| Norris | K | Mr | 10 | J217 | 2247 | KNORRIS |
| Rees | C | Ms | 3 | J130B | 2260 | CREES4 |
| Stubbs | G | Mrs | 2 | J225 | 2263 | GSTUBBS |
| Watkins | M | Mr | 16 | J113 | 2648 | MWATKINS |
| Wright | GGL | Mr | 14 | J314 | 2254 | GGLWRIGH |

*Figure 3.15 Staff records arranged in Last name/Initials order*

| Last Name | Initials | Title | Grade | Room | Tel No | Email |
|---|---|---|---|---|---|---|
| Eyres | DE | Mr | 16 | J113 | 2648 | DEEYRES |
| Watkins | M | Mr | 16 | J113 | 2648 | MWATKINS |
| Hodson | PJ | Mr | 20 | J117 | 2270 | PJHODSON |
| Rees | C | Ms | 3 | J130B | 2260 | CREES4 |
| Evans | D | Mr | 14 | J130B | 2260 | DEVANS3 |
| Jones | BF | Prof | 15 | J210 | 2730 | BFJONES1 |
| Jones | CB | Prof | 16 | J211 | 2722 | CBJONES2 |
| Davies | RA | Dr | 10 | J215 | 2264 | RADAVIES |
| Evans | GV | Mr | 12 | J217 | 2247 | GVEVANS |
| Norris | K | Mr | 10 | J217 | 2247 | KNORRIS |
| Davies | P | Mr | 10 | J217 | 2247 | PDAVIES4 |
| Stubbs | G | Mrs | 2 | J225 | 2263 | GSTUBBS |
| Moon | J | Mr | 4 | J225 | 2263 | JMOON |
| Beynon-Davies | P | Dr | 15 | J226 | 2243 | PBEYNOND |
| Wright | GGL | Mr | 14 | J314 | 2254 | GGLWRIGH |

*Figure 3.16 Staff records arranged in Room No./E-mail name order*

Figures 3.14 to 3.16 show how staff records can be sorted in different ways. Figure 3.17 shows the table sort window for Word 6, that allows up to three sort fields.

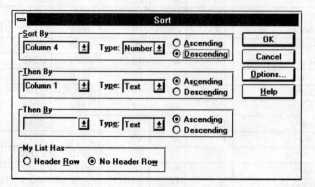

*Figure 3.17 Table sort window from Word 6, allows up to three sort fields*

Records in a data file are usually sequenced by their primary key, but reports can be generated from the file with the data arranged in a different sequence. Prior to printing, the report the file would be sorted (using a sort utility program) into the required sequence.

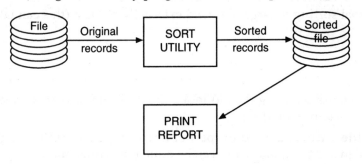

*Figure 3.18 Sort pre-processing for reporting*

A sales invoice file has the fields shown below and is ordered on the unique 'Invoice number' field:

*Invoice number*, Customer number, Agent number, Invoice date, Invoice amount

A report is required that lists the total sales for each agent, where there are sub-totals for each customer the agent deals with. The effect of the sorting groups the data records together (as shown in figure 3.19).

| Agent | Customer | Invoice no | Invoice value | |
|---|---|---|---|---|
| No. 1 | Cust A | 960321 | 123 | |
| | | 960375 | 456 | |
| | | 960433 | <u>789</u> | |
| | | Total | | <u>1368</u> |
| | Cust B | 960325 | 366 | |
| | | 960429 | <u>522</u> | |
| | | Total | | <u>888</u> |
| No. 2 | Cust G | 960322 | 911 | |
| | | 960434 | <u>822</u> | |
| | | Total | | <u>1733</u> |
| No. 3 | Cust B | 960327 | 543 | |
| | | : | | : |

*Figure 3.19 Report structure showing data grouped by sorting*

This file will have been sorted as follows:

| *Major field* | *Intermediate* | *Minor field* |
|---|---|---|
| Agent number/ | Customer id./ | Invoice number |

The major field changes value least frequently and the minor field changes value most frequently in the sorted file.

Sorting is a very time consuming activity, even using a computer system. To sort a few hundred records won't take very long, but to sort tens or hundreds of thousands records will take some time. It is also one of the most valuable of processing activities, as much information is really the same data presented in a different sequence and summarised differently.

The sorting methods fall into two categories:

- **internal sorting** of small quantities of data held totally within the main memory (this will be very fast);
- **external sorting** of large files held externally on disk (this can take some time).

## Searching

Searching involves scanning data to locate the presence or otherwise of an item of data. The data scanned may be stored as:

- **text file** – where a word (or part of a word) is searched for (e.g. locate occurrences of 'own' in a list of names) and can be quite time consuming;
- **tables** – stored totally internally in the main memory, this will be very fast (e.g. search for 'UK' in a table of European Union countries);
- **files of records** – stored externally on disk (or other secondary storage), this can take some time, (e.g. search for a particular student record in a student administration system).

There are two components of a search:

- the search **argument** (the data value to search for), that each piece of data will be compared to for equality;
- the **data** (table, text file, file of records), that contains or might not contain the item required.

Either the search will find occurrence(s) of the argument or it will go through all the data and not find a match. Many searches used in business applications require the one match to single particular piece of data, other searches will provide multiple matches.

For example, you could search the student file for student number '95CS0057', one match only would be possible (or the student is not found). If you searched the student file for a student's last name 'DAVIES', many matches might be possible. A search for a particular book in a library system using its ISBN is another example where one match only is possible (or the ISBN is not found).

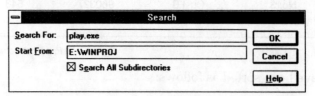

*Figure 3.20 Search window from File manager*

When searching tables (or files of records), how the data records are arranged can help the search process. Suppose we wish to find the telephone number of a member of staff 'Davies M' from the list shown in figures 3.14 to 3.16. Using the table organised as in figure 3.14, we would have to look at every record to find out that the person doesn't exist. Using the table organised as in figure 3.15, we would find out that the person doesn't exist much quicker.

## Question 3.36

How many rows would be scanned in figure 3.16, in order to find out that 'DAVIES M' was not a member of staff?

A  1

B  2

C  8

D  15

By sorting data to facilitate a search, faster searching methods can be used, but remember that sorting takes time and so it may not always be feasible.

## Selecting

**Selecting** is closely associated with searching. It occurs when records or data, which satisfy certain selection criteria, need to be extracted from a set. For example, find all customers who have a credit limit of £500 or more, the customer file needs to be searched record by record, selecting only those with a value in the credit limit field of 500 or more. Selecting could also be used to locate books in a library system that cover a particular topic, such as 'use of IT in libraries'. In selection situations there may be a single record response, or a multiple record response, or none.

## Merging

**Merging** is the process of combining two or more groups of data in the same sequence, to form one group of data in the same sequence. Merging is often used to combine files of records in the same sequence to form one file.

For example, an architect's practice has two offices and the monthly time sheet data for each employee is held in two separate disk files, both in ascending staff number sequence. Prior to processing the time sheet data, the records from the two files are merged to form one file, which will be in ascending staff number sequence.

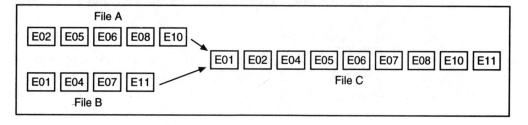

*Figure 3.21 Merging of two files into one, sequenced by Employee no*

173

# Validating

**Validating** is the process of checking the validity of input data. Any incorrect values are trapped before they get processed and will not be used to access records or update files with wrong values.

In batch processing, the batch run (when the transactions are input) is used for validation, with the errors found being highlighted in a printed report. In transaction processing, validation has to be carried out as the transaction data is entered, with error messages displayed on a screen. The checks used may be logical tests applied to the input data values or checking the data against some specific allowable set of values. Validation will not trap all the errors, but will significantly reduce the number getting through.

For example, in a supermarket checkout, application data entry starts with the input of the product code. The product code can be checked by searching the product data file – if a record is found that matches it then it is valid and the name and price of the product can be displayed, if no match is found then the code is rejected and must be re-input.

In a payroll application for part-time sales staff, a data value input will be the hours worked in a week. This value can be checked – for example, that it is at least 1 hour and not more than 20 hours the limits for part-time staff – a value outside these limits is rejected.

In a student application, a data value input would be the sex of the student. This value must be one of the following <'M', 'm', 'F', 'f'>, a value like 'N' would be rejected.

## Question 3.37

Which process would be used to locate a specific property in a computerised estates system?

A  calculating

B  validating

C  searching

D  sorting

## Question 3.38

Which process seeks to ensure that correct data is entered into a system?

A  validating

B  selecting

C  grouping

D  merging

## Question 3.39

Which of the following allows stock records to be listed in store location sequence?

A selecting a location code

B searching for a location code

C calculating a location code

D sorting on location code

## Task 3.12 PC 5

For the systems described in Tasks 3.8 to 3.11, outline the processes used in each system. Try and list a process under each of the headings of Section 3.2.5.

# Use information technology for a data handling activity

## 3.3.1  Database components

A **database** is a collection of data that is organised to provide the user with easy access to information. A database may be paper-based and manual, e.g. a telephone directory is a database of people's telephone numbers, a shopping catalogue is a database of items available for sale.

Computer-based databases are composed of tables or files of related data:

- **table of data** – composed of columns and rows that describe an entity or an object of interest;
- **column** (a single data item or **field**) – identifies and describes a single attribute or property or characteristic of an entity;
- **row** (a set of data values or **record**) – represents a single instance of an entity;
- **relationships** – associations between tables, joined via a column in each table;
- **key indexes** (based on column values) – assist access to table data.

For example, a personal CD collection database would have a CD table, an ARTIST table and a MUSIC TYPE table.

## Fields

**Data fields** are items of data represented by a single column in a table. Each field has:

- a name that is unique in a table, the name identifies the column or field;
- a data value that is stored in it and referred to via the name.

For example, your personal CD table has the following columns or fields:

- **reference number** – given to each CD purchased and is unique, e.g. value 'MW097';
- **title** – the title or name of the CD, e.g. value 'Looking East';
- **artist** – the principal artist or group playing on the CD, e.g. value 'Jackson Brown';
- **year** – the year purchased, e.g. value '1996';
- **type** – a code that represents the type of music, rock, soul, folk etc, e.g. value 'FR';
- **price** – the amount paid, e.g. value '11.99'.

# Data type

The data values that fields have can be classified according to **type**. There are two broad categories:

- **character data** – text alphanumeric or non-numeric data, e.g. artist name or CD title;
- **number data** – an amount or a price.

Number data is usually split into two sub-categories:

- whole numbers or integers (positive or negative numbers that don't have a decimal point or fractional part), e.g. CD year, 1996 or 49, 1024, –273;
- decimal numbers (positive or negative numbers that have a decimal point or fractional part), e.g. CD Price, 11.99 or 17.5, 0.1, 3.142, 1780.75, –8.632543.

There are other more specific data types:

- date – a value arranged in a date format, e.g. 05/06/96 or 05 Jun 1996;
- money – a value arranged in a currency format, usually having two decimal places, e.g. 27.36, 3478.96.

## Question 3.40

*Which of the following has a numeric data type?*

*A   customer discount percentage*

*B   customer postcode*

*C   customer telephone number*

*D   customer address*

# Length

A second characteristic of a field is its maximum size or length, particularly if it is a character field:

- **character field length** – represents the maximum number of characters that can be stored in the field. An artist name field may allow a maximum of 30 characters, an address field is 90 characters (in order to hold the several lines making up an address);
- **number field length** – represents the maximum value, 9s in each digit position that can be stored in the field, e.g. a CD price field might have a maximum size of 99.99, which means no CD could cost more than £99.99;
- **date fields** – have a default length associated with the format chosen to represent the date, e.g. 05/06/96 is 8 characters long.

# Records

The group of data fields referring to a particular entity is a called a **record** or **data group**. A table is a collection of records or rows (a row in the table is a single instance of a table record).

For example, the CD record has the following fields:

Reference number, Title, Artist, Year, Type, Price.

A single instance of a CD record is:

'MW097', 'Looking East', 'Jackson Browne', '1996', 'FR', '11.99'.

## Keys

Each table or record type will consist of a set of columns or fields that characterise it; however, it must also be possible to distinguish one instance of a record or row in a table from another. The **record key** has a unique value for each record instance, this means that the field chosen has a value that is never duplicated or the same as that of another instance of the same record type.

- **Simple or elementary key** – this type of key is made up of a **single** field. For example, in the CD table the field 'Reference number' is used as it is unique to each record instance. There may be several CDs with same values in 'Artist' or 'Year' or 'Type' field, 'Title' may be unique but cannot be guaranteed ('Greatest Hits' is a very popular title). For a student record the field 'Enrolment no.' may be used, as it is unique to each record instance, fields 'Name' or 'Date of Birth' would not be unique. In a product record the field 'Item no.' would be unique. An invoice would have a unique 'Invoice no.' as a field.

- **Compound or composite key** – this type of key is one made up from two or more fields joined together. For example, a cheque record would use 'Bank sort code/Bank account number/Cheque number' to ensure uniqueness, to distinguish one instance of cheque from another. In a golf club competition, a card record would use 'Competition date/Member no.' to distinguish each instance of competition card.

- **Primary key** – is a simple or compound key that makes it possible to distinguish one instance of a record from another instance of the same type. By knowing the primary key value of a record type, a particular instance can be identified and its other field values made known. The primary key:
  - uniquely identifies each instance of a record;
  - must have a value, it can never be null;
  - should not be longer than needed to ensure uniqueness.

  For example, 'CD reference number', 'Student enrolment number', 'Flight number', 'National insurance number', 'Insurance policy number' are all examples of fields that uniquely identify the record type they belong to.

## Question 3.41

*Which of the following would uniquely identify a cheque drawn on an account?*

*A   Bank sort code/Account number/Cheque date*

*B   Account number/Cheque number*

*C   Bank sort code/Account number/Cheque number*

*D   Bank sort code/Account number/Date/Cheque number*

## Question 3.42

*A vehicle record type has the following attributes: Make, Model, Year, Registration Number, Colour, No. of door, Price.*

*Which of the following would be a suitable Primary Key field?*

*A   Make/Model*

*B   Registration Number*

*C   Year/Model/Colour*

*D   Model/Year/Colour*

## Question 3.43

*A patient record type has the following attributes: Patient no., Name, Home address, Ward, Bed no., NI number, Date of birth, Gender, GP name, Admit date.*

*Which of the following would **not** be suitable as a primary key field?*

*A   Patient no.*

*B   Ward/Bed no./Admit date*

*C   Name*

*D   NI number*

## Question 3.44

*How many instances of a record type must a value of a primary key identify?*

*A   Exactly one*

*B   None*

*C   One or more*

*D   Zero or more*

- **Secondary keys** – these are fields other than the primary key that may be used to identify or select records. The data value stored in this type of key does not have to be unique: the secondary key value could identify a group of records that have some common characteristic. Several secondary keys could be defined for one record. For example, in a student record, the primary key would be the 'Enrol no.' field, a secondary key could be a 'grant authority code (GA-code)' field. The 'GA-Code' could be a secondary key allowing access to all student records for an individual authority. In a vehicle record, the 'Year' field would be suitable as a secondary key, it identifies all vehicles made in a particular year.

- **Foreign Key** – this is a field of one record type that has a value that is the primary key value of another record type – it links two record-types together. For example, in a sales order record type, the field customer account number will be a foreign key because it will have a value that uniquely identifies the primary key of the customer record type (see illustration below). Sales orders may be taken from customers who do not have a sales account with the company because they pay by cash, and in this case the field 'Customer account no.' of the record type 'Sales order' has a null value (no value). Should the field 'Customer account no.' of 'Sales order' have a value then it must match one instance of the 'Customer' record type.

**Company sales order application**
Record Types:

| Sales order | Customer |
|---|---|
| **Order number** | **Customer account no.** |
| Order date | Customer name |
| **Customer account no.** | Customer address |
| Order total amount | Balance outstanding |
| | Credit limit |

## Question 3.45

*A hospital system has two record types: 'patient' and 'ward'. A 'patient' record type has the following attributes:*

**Patient no.**, *Name, Home address, Ward id., Bed no., NI number, Date of birth, Gender, GP name, Admit date.*

*Which of the following may be a foreign key?*

*A   Ward id.*

*B   Patient no.*

*C   Bed no.*

*D   Date of birth*

## Task 3.13   PC 1

*For a small database application involving not more than two or three table or record types, identify and define:*

- *each table or record and its purpose;*

- *the name and data type of each field for each table and record;*

- *primary keys, foreign keys to join tables, and any field you believe may be suitable as a secondary key.*

*Draw a diagram to show how the tables or records are related.*

### 3.3.2   Create a database

Microsoft Access is one of several relational-database systems available on microcomputers. The package is part of the Microsoft Office suite and can integrate with other software packages. Access is a desktop relational-database management system, with a built-in applications generator for Windows GUI. It provides extensive facilities for database definition and database application development: using forms, reports and queries. Other desktop products provide similar facilities, such as Paradox, Approach, Dbase for Windows.

Access, like its competitors, provides good support for tables, forms, queries and reports, with easy to use designers (wizards in Access) that provide a step-by-step guide to laying out each item. For example:

- **New**: enters design mode to create new items;

- **Open**: runs an existing item;

- **Design**: modifies an existing item.

The data used by forms and reports can come from single tables, queries or multiple tables. Forms built on one table can have sub-forms based on a second table.

*Figure 3.22 Access Design and Use Window*

## Create/define a table using Access

The design table window is used to name and provide properties of each table column or field (in Access terminology). The field names and their data types are listed in the top pane, and extra properties about a field are shown in the bottom pane (see figure 3.23). Switching between panes is achieved using the mouse or the function key <F6>. Help facilities about data types and other properties are available using the function key <F1>.

The following example demonstrates the facilities of Access, in creating and manipulating two tables: 'Car', that has records about cars for sale; and 'Make', that is a list of car makers and their country of origin. The tables are related: the Car table has a 'make' field that is a foreign key to the matching record in the Make table (the fields of the table are shown clearly in figures 3.26 and 3.27).

A car **must** be made by **one** maker; a maker **may** manufacture **many** cars.

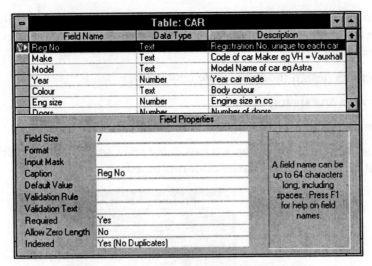

*Figure 3.23 Access table definition window with field property pane*

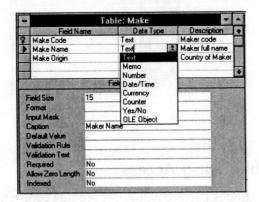

*Figure 3.24 Field data types available in Access*

## Indexes

Each database table should have a primary key that uniquely identifies each row. Specifying a primary key field will create an index for that key field. The index has the format:

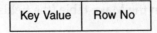

There will be one entry for each key value stored and this entry will be ordered on its key value. Figure 3.25 shows the indexing of the 'Registration number' column. Other table fields may also be indexed. The MOT index would help to locate quickly those vehicles having an MOT due in a particular month. Use of an index will speed up the selection of rows from a table, where a selection is based on an indexed field.

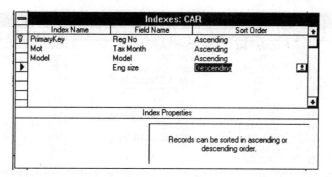

*Figure 3.25 Create and view indexes*

 **Task 3.14** PC 2

*For the database tables defined in Task 3.13, use a desktop relational-database product to create and design the tables.*

### 3.3.3 Edit table data

Once created, a table can be populated (have data entered into it) through using 'Open', which displays a default form. The form design projects the structure of the table onto the screen and provides an easy to use data entry facility. The column headings used in the form are taken from the 'caption' property of each field, if no 'caption' property is specified the table column name is used.

### Append

**Append** adds *new* data records or rows to the table, each new record is appended to the existing data rows, extending the size of the table. A new 'Make' record would be added after the last row.

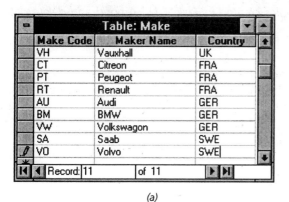

(a)

(b)

*Figure 3.26 The contents of the MAKE table*

Figure 3.26(a) shows the contents of the 'make' table after initial data entry, while 3.26(b) shows how the system has sequenced the data when committing it.

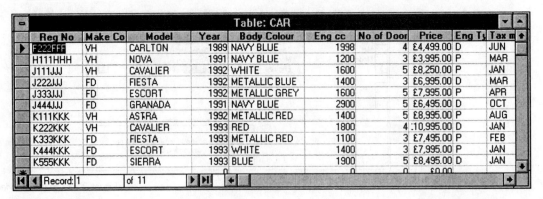

*Figure 3.27 The car table data*

## Amend

**Amend** changes the values of data already stored in the table. The data row and column are selected and that particular field value can then be changed.

For example, in figure 3.27, the price of the Cavalier car, registration K222KKK should be £10,495 not £10,995. The colour of the Granada car, registration J444JJJ, should be metallic blue not navy blue.

## Delete

**Delete** removes existing data records or rows from the table – the row is first selected and the delete operation triggered. Once deleted, the data values held in the row are no longer accessible for processing.

For example, in figure 3.27, the Astra car, registration K111KKK, is sold so its record can be removed.

## *Task 3.15*  PC 3

*Append data to the tables created in Task 3.14. Amend and delete data as appropriate.*

## 3.3.4  Use database facilities

A database package like Access is able to provide facilities for retrieving data from the database in the format of:

- views of complete tables as stored or sorted on a particular data field (examples are shown in figures 3.28 and 3.29);

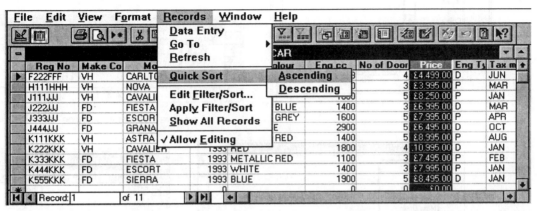

*Figure 3.28 Simple sort selection on displayed table*

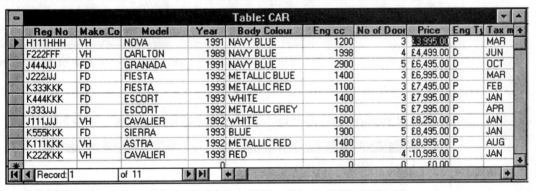

*Figure 3.29 Sorted display*

- querying of the database by table searching and selection of data items from one or more tables (see figures 3.30 to 3.31);

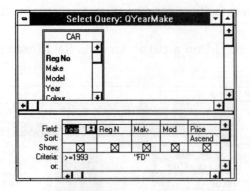

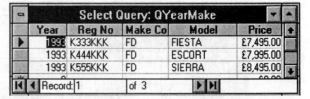

*Figure 3.30 Simple query on 'car' table and its results*

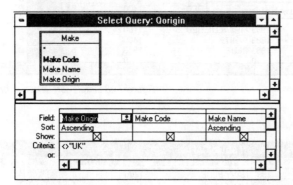

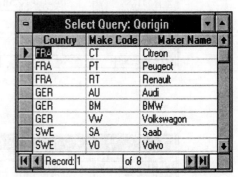

*Figure 3.31 Query on 'make' table of those **not** made in 'UK'*

- generation of reports based on tables or queries (see figures 3.32 to 3.34).

*Figure 3.32 Sales list report of vehicles based on 'car' table*

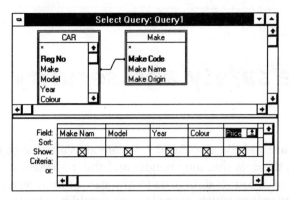

Figure 3.33 A two-table query, based on the join of 'car' to 'make', by 'make' fields

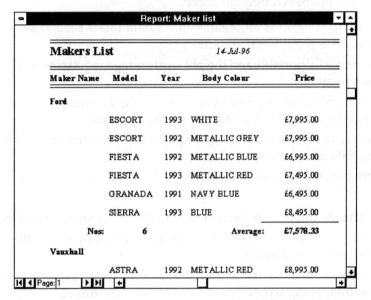

Figure 3.34 Report based on the query of Figure 3.33

## *Task 3.16*  PC 4

*Use the facilities of the database package to produce displays and reports to meet some specified application requirement for the database of Tasks 3.13 to 3.15.*

# *Examine safety and security*

Computer hardware and the associated software are valuable physical resources of any organisation. However, the data that they handle and the information produced are just as valuable, if not more. Loss of accounts data (due to any cause) may result in financial loss, data stored about an organisation's products or customers would be of interest to its competitors, and personal data must not be wrongly disclosed.

Using IT systems to process an organisation's data raises several security issues based on the characteristics of computerised systems:

- data are easily portable and the physical storage requirements to hold megabytes of data are very small;
- application software processing is often highly automated and requires little human intervention; changes to data may not be traceable;
- stored data can be lost through equipment malfunction, natural hazards and human error, data can also be stolen;
- where a system is on-line, unauthorised persons may gain access to data to just read or alter it.

Therefore, data should be kept protected to maintain its security and integrity:

- **security** is protection of data from being accessed by a unauthorised users and keeping it safe from other hazards;
- **integrity** is the correctness or accuracy of data, it is protection of data from authorised users, from being wrongly input, changed or destroyed.

## 3.4.1  Accuracy checks

Accuracy checks are controls that are applied at the data capture and input stage to minimise the chance of incorrect data being entered into a system. There are two general types of check:

- **Validation** – this type of check is applied to the value of a data field, whether it is within an acceptable range, not incomplete and reasonable; it aims to detect illegal or erroneous values;
- **Verification** – this type of check is concerned with the accuracy of data entry (checking what has been entered is the same as that provided for entry), this might involve double entry by re-keying or operator read back.

### Validation checks

As data is entered to a field, the data entry program applies logic checks (associated with that field) to the value entered. If the value is illegal, it is rejected with a meaningful error message displayed and the data value must be re-entered. A particular input field will be subject to at least one of the following standard checks.

- **Range check**: this ensures that the data value lies within some prescribed limits for a field. For example
  - entering a start time of a job in hours and minutes: the hours must range from 0 to 23 and the minutes from 0 to 59;
  - the amount withdrawn from an ATM machine cannot exceed some limit amount fixed for the card, say £50.
- **Consistency or combination check**: this ensures that one data field value is consistent with the value of another data field. For example
  - the due date of a library book to be returned should be a later date than its issue date: the value of a fines field should be greater than zero if the actual return date of a book is later than the due date.
- **Type check**: this ensures that the data value matches a prescribed data type for the field. For example
  - a numeric field should not accept letters or any other non-numeric symbol;
  - a date field should only accept a valid date.
- **Set check**: this ensures that the data value belongs to a prescribed set of discrete values. For example
  - a person's marital status must have a value from the set <'M', 'm', 'S', 's'>;
  - a bank transaction code must have the value from the set <'D', 'W'>.
- **Table look-up check**: this is similar to a set check, but the number of permissible values is much bigger. For example
  - a country code must belong to those of the European Union <'UK', 'GER', 'FRA', 'IRE', etc >.
- **File look-up**: this uses a code to access a record on file directly, the successful retrieval of the record indicating a valid code. Display of the item name that the code identifies would also provide visual validation. For example
  - a product code would be used to access its record in a stock file.
- **Self-checking number or check digit**: this type of check is often used for record identifier codes, such as an account number or product code. One of the characters of the code has an arithmetical relationship with the other characters, should the code be entered incorrectly then it will not check out. Bank account numbers and many bar-code numbers are self-checking.

## Verification

Data can be verified after the data entry process before it is committed. Historically, this meant re-keying, of the data a second time by a different operator. While re-keying, the system would compare the second entry with the value originally entered, and any differences were immediately flagged. With transaction processing, re-keying is no longer feasible, so verification will consist of a visual check of data entered against the source document (or by verbal read back to the data source).

For example, in an on-line sales order system, the data entry operator would enter a product code and read back to the customer the description of the item retrieved from a file and displayed by the system for verification.

Wordprocessing systems have spell checkers and grammar checkers that are used to verify the content of documents.

**Correctness**

**Correctness** is checking of data and the information it produces to ensure that it is meaningful – fully-validated and verified data can still produce meaningless information. For application data, this is often associated with reasonableness and rules or guidelines that specify how to ensure the integrity of data.

For example, a report may not contain any spelling mistakes, but may still contain misuse of words such as 'stationery' instead of 'stationary', or 'uses' instead of 'user'. Wages of £800 per week to a data entry operator seems unreasonable, if normally they are paid at £5 per hour. An electricity bill of £1000 for a quarter to an old age pensioner may have been calculated from validated meter readings but may also seem to be unreasonable.

The system should flag results that seem out of the ordinary, these are then subject to further investigation by clerical staff.

## Question 3.46

How does a data entry clerk check that they have entered the correct staff number from a timesheet?

A  by entering the staff number twice

B  by validating the staff number

C  by comparing the name displayed on a VDU to the name on the time sheet

D  by looking up a list of valid staff numbers

## Question 3.47

New supplier data (such as account number, name and address, telephone number) are prepared using data entry forms. Which is a verification check of the entered supplier data?

A  comparing the screen data with that on the application form

B  making sure that the postcode contains letters and numbers

C  counting the number of letters in the name

D  checking that the supplier is based in the UK

## Question 3.48

Which is used to validate the data entry of a library book ISBN number?

A  a range check

B  a type check

C  a check digit

D  a set check

*Task 3.17* PC 1

*For the database application developed in Tasks 3.13 to 3.16, specify validation checks for some of the input data fields. Using the validation feature of the field properties, apply the checks to the fields of the application. Test the validation features by entering invalid data values.*

## 3.4.2 Security checks

There are a number of security controls that can be used to ensure the safety of system data from destruction (natural or otherwise), and illegal access. The system and its data are at risk in a number of ways as follows.

- **Physically** – tapes or disks can be damaged or destroyed by fire, flood or vandalism, mislaid or stolen, and can be copied. They may also be susceptible to environmental aspects of temperature, humidity, dust and magnetic fields.

- **Corruption** – the data contents of files may be damaged or destroyed due to a hardware or software faults or through processing the wrong files.

- **Hacking** – loss of data confidentiality through access by unauthorised users.

Controls must be implemented that minimise the chances of these risks occurring, or minimise the effects of such risks on the operation of the system.

### Backup

'Backup' and 'restore' is a procedure that is used to take regular copies ('dumps') of application data files.

- The **backup** involves copying application files or databases from the permanent hard disk to some permanent exchangeable media like a floppy or tape. Backup of large files or databases to tape can take a long time.

- Should the hard disk files get corrupted, they can be **restored** from the backup media – any updates to the file since the backup was taken would need to be re-processed, either by re-keying, or from a transaction log file.

Currently floppies are only feasible for quite small files of less than 5 mbytes, however the increasing availability of portable zip disks will increase this to 100 mbytes. Backups should be taken regularly as part of the daily processing routine (say last thing in the afternoon). Temporary copies of files can also be taken onto another hard disk directory prior to carrying out some major processing run, this will be faster than taking a normal backup.

For some applications, three generations of master and associated transaction files are kept. The most recent and up-to-date file is called the **son,** a previous generation is the **father,** and an earlier third generation is the **grandfather.** The earlier generations can be used to recreate the next generation, the 'father' files can recreate a new 'son' file, 'grandfather' files can recreate new 'fathers'.

File backups, copies and earlier generations should be stored safely, using fireproof safes, away from the processing work station. It is customary to store the oldest generations in a different building. Failure to backup data files will normally lead to disaster.

## Confidentiality

Within an organisation the data it stores with its IT system has a value not only to it, but to other organisations. It would be improper to share (or 'disclose') data or information available on the system to any third party outside the organisation. For instance, if an organisation has collected data about a customer it should not disclose that information to a second customer, who may be a competitor of the first. Also, within the organisation, access to data and information should be restricted to those who have authority to access and use it.

Access controls prevent unauthorised access to the system as a whole, or to a particular application, or to segments of an application. In addition to preventing access, the type of access allowed can be controlled, for example, read only, read and write, read and copy.

User identification and passwords are commonly used to grant access and type of access.

- **User identification** – each authorised user of a system is allocated a unique user name which must be used to gain access. This name can be used at different levels within an application and can be logged to provide an access audit trail. Personal details like an identification card, a voice print and a fingerprint are also possibilities.
- **Passwords** – these are associated with users, or pieces of software, or data files, and should be private or restricted. Passwords are the most common form of user authentication. They should never be permanent and should be changed on a regular basis to help prevent unauthorised use.

Whatever controls are used, no system is totally secure from unauthorised access – not all incidents of 'hacking in' are reported due to organisations not wanting their systems to be thought of as insecure, but enough reach the press each year.

## Copyright

Any software purchased is usually subject to a licence agreement with the manufacturer or supplier. This means that the software cannot be copied for use on another machine or by another individual, although security backup is allowed. Organisations wishing to use multiple copies of a piece of software will buy the number of required licences, or negotiate a site or organisation licence that allows copying of the software for use within the organisation. In general, each copy of a piece of software must be authorised – the exception being freeware.

Software is classed as a literary work and as such is subject to the Copyright, Designs and Patents Act 1988. The Act gives protection to software writers and makes it illegal to copy or adapt the software without the agreement of the copyright owner.

Copyright also applies to data, particularly data used in multimedia applications that use video film clips, photographs, drawings and quotes from literary texts. Use of such source data can be barred under copyright or may require payment for use. The availability of access to the World Wide Web on the Internet has raised many copyright issues.

## Regular saving

When working with general office products (such as wordprocessors, spreadsheets, presentation and database software), it is good practice to regularly save work in the event of hardware failure. If current work is lost, the saved copy can be loaded and a small amount of work redone.

## Question 3.49

What stops an unauthorised user gaining access to stored data?

A  copywriting the access software

B  allocating access passwords

C  validating data

D  taking regular backups

## Question 3.50

Which is the process that recovers data following a system failure?

A  backup

B  restore

C  saving

D  undeleting

## 3.4.3  Health and safety

On the face of it, computer systems don't appear to be particularly dangerous or life threatening, but there are aspects of their use that can have an impact on users' health and safety. Dangers that arise from repeated use of a keyboard and VDU include the following.

- **Stress** – use of a computer workstation can cause stress in a number of ways. **Repetitive strain injury (RSI)** can cause serious and lasting aches and pains to the arms, wrists and fingers caused by using a keyboard for too long a time without a break. **Eyestrain** can be produced by the glare and flickering of the screen, poor screen design, poor use of colour, and location of the screen relative to the user. Eyestrain is often associated with migraines and headaches. **Backache** can be produced through use of unsuitable seating, the positioning of equipment, and the lifting of equipment.

- **Radiation** – this is given off by the VDU screen. Some studies claim that this can cause illness or health defects.

- **Hazards** – the computer is an electrical piece of equipment and as such will be subject to normal electrical faults and fire risk. The health and safety measures associated with any electrical item used in an office environment should be applied to computer systems. Computer systems also require extensive use of external cabling between components, these must not be hazardous or form an obstruction.

- **Working practices** – employees have a responsibility to partake in safe working practices by not lifting heavy equipment, by dealing with any hazards, by being aware of the fire drill, by using equipment correctly and taking regular breaks.

- **Legislation** – the Health and Safety at Work Act 1974 applies to the use of computers, and employees who suffer illness or injury from the use of computer terminals may be able to sue their employers for negligence. There are several pieces of European legislation that has clauses covering periods of work, analysis and assessment of usability and fit for purpose of IT systems, and technical requirements.

## Question 3.51

*What can be caused by using a keyboard for a long period of time?*

A   electric shocks

B   repetitive strain injury

C   respiratory problems

D   injury by fire

## Question 3.52

*Which hazard is present when a VDU is switched on?*

A   radiation

B   fire

C   repetitive strain injury

D   obstruction

## Task 3.18   PC 4

*This is a task for groups of two or three students. Prepare a presentation that highlights the health and safety issues concerned with the use of IT systems. The presentation should apply to an IT user department and could be in the form of:*

- *some warning notices, each dealing with a particular health or safety aspect;*
- *a warning poster presentation that covers a number of health and/or safety issues;*
- *a health and safety manual.*

## 3.4.4   Obligations of users

The biggest threat to the security of an organisation's IT system is often the untrustworthiness and incompetence of its own employees. Someone who is very incompetent can cause as much harm as someone who is dishonest. These characteristics of staff are not new, but they have a greater significance when staff have access to IT systems and the data stored within. The organisation should take steps to uphold the security and integrity of its IT systems, but their users have responsibilities too.

### Confidentiality of data

It is important to recognise that an IT user has access to private information that arises from business relationships. It would be improper if information gathered from one client was passed on to another (possibly a competitor of the first). Personal data stored on an IT system is subject to the Data Protection Act, that in addition to giving individuals rights of access to data held, has rules about disclosure.

## Copyright

As stated earlier, software and data are classed as a literary work and as such are subject to the same copyright laws. An IT user should only use software that is legally licensed to them or their employer – copying of software for personal use is illegal. A user purchasing a software product will be given a unique software licence for that product. This usually allows them to:

- install the software on the hard disk of a single computer only;
- if supplied on disk, to copy the original disks for back-up purposes only.

Where networks are used, installed software will have a network licence that defines the number of simultaneous users the product is licensed for.

Copyright also applies to new software developed on a computer system and involves two concepts concerned with authorship and ownership. Normally, an employee writing a computer program will be the author of that program, but the employer will own the copyright. Employer and employees may agree to any other arrangement, as may be the case with universities and student projects.

Data classified as computer-generated works is covered under copyright law and includes:

- works created using a computer, such as files, wordprocessed documents, CAD drawings and a spreadsheet report;
- works created by a computer, such as automatic generation of weather forecasts, simulations;
- intermediate works, that lie between computer-created works and works created using a computer; it includes bespoke software products developed for a specific application (such as a vehicle leasing system).

## Responsible attitude to uncensored or private materials

Users of IT systems must have a responsible attitude with regard to their ability to access the data and information stored on their own, and other, systems. A user should ensure that someone else does not use the user's facilities to breach system security, and gain access to private materials that they are not entitled to see. A user who accidentally breaches the security of a system and gains access to materials they are not entitled to see, should not take advantage of that opportunity and should report the incident.

For many years, pornographic and other sexual material have been available to computer users mainly through supply on disks and CD-ROM (the media replacing glossy magazines and video tape). Today, the Internet poses particular problems with the facilities it provides for users to 'surf' the World Wide Web and the non-regulation of material that is stored on it. While the web can provide extensive access to very useful and valuable information, this will include pornographic and sexual material. Users of all types and ages can have access to and be contacted via the World Wide Web.

Many parents are concerned regarding their children accessing this unsuitable material, or being contacted by paedophiles. Several Internet-access-service providers are taking steps to monitor and censor material stored on the World Wide Web to prevent its misuse. Software is also becoming available that has knowledge of 'dangerous' sites and will not allow access to them.

However, many World Wide Web users view it as the ultimate uncensored medium, that is independent of any political or financial control and censorship, and is administered by its users. The computer system is a multi-media facility allowing the display of text, graphics, pictures and video together with sound. How it is used is the responsibility of the individual.

## Theft

Theft of computer **hardware** became one of the major crimes of 1995/1996, with organisations loosing millions of pounds worth of equipment. The most valuable components are the memory chips (these are small, easily removed and installed, highly portable and virtually untraceable). There are many cases where not all of the memory has been removed, the system remains operational, and the theft is not detected for some time.

Theft of **software** is largely concerned with breach of copyright and the use of unlicensed software products. This is often viewed as less of a crime by users, but is major cause of loss of revenue to software suppliers. This can be achieved by copying (backing up) installed software off hard disks or by 'borrowing' the original disks or CD-ROM. It is possible to obtain 'pirated' copies of many of the most popular software products complete with documentation. However, don't leave source disks or CD-ROMs lying around as they are likely to get 'lost'.

Theft of **data** from a computer system is also a rising crime. **Hacking** into on-line systems to gain access to confidential files has been frequently reported. However, many incidents go unreported because the organisation does not wish to make public the knowledge that its system's security has been breached. Most hacking is concerned with gaining access, viewing or copying data and leaving undetected, however, some incidents have corrupted data. However, the greatest threat to data security is from within, through unauthorised copying of data onto floppy disks, or theft of data disks left lying around by the organisation's own employees.

The Computer Misuse Act 1990 is the legal response to the threat of hacking and viruses, it covers the offences of unauthorised access to, and unauthorised modification of data or programs.

## Virus checking

A computer virus is a particularly nasty piece of software designed to affect the health of a computer system and pose a major threat to the security of the system. Viruses have been deliberately developed to infect every type of program and data, and to replicate themselves without the user being aware of their existence, until disaster strikes. Viruses move from one computer system to another over networks or via floppy disk files – the Internet provides a worldwide virus transportation medium. To minimise the threat of viruses, the following steps will help protect the system.

- Use vaccine or anti-virus software, that detect and remove known viruses – they disinfect the infected system. Such software is constantly being updated as new virus strains are detected. Most systems run virus-checking software when starting up the computer system each day.

- Do not use or load unauthorised software obtained from an unknown source.

- Limit the use of floppy disks across different computers, don't allow users to insert disks or load software that they have brought into work.

- Make sure that users are aware of the dangers of viruses and where they might originate from.

## Question 3.53

What do you infringe, by copying for personal use some application software from your school or college system?

A   copyright

B   security

C   confidentiality

## Task 3.19   PC 2, PC 4

This is a task for groups of two or three students. Prepare a presentation that highlights the security and obligations of the user aspects of IT systems. The presentation should apply to a IT department (or IT application user group) and could be in the form of:

- some reminder notices, each dealing with a particular security and/or obligation issue;
- a reminder poster presentation that covers a number of security and/or obligation issues;
- a security and obligations guide.

### EU and UK copyright and data protection legislation

**Copyright** is part of the branch of the law that deals with **intellectual property rights**, this also includes patent law, trade marks, designs and related areas. They apply to the development, exploitation and use of computer hardware, software and data, and cover both the product and the people involved. The rights are designed to provide remedies against those who steal the fruits of another person's ideas and includes the following.

- **Copyright law** – that protects works from being copied or used without permission.
- **Patent law** – that is concerned with inventions such as a new printer design.
- **Law of confidence** – that protects information such as trade secrets, business know-how, lists of clients and contacts, personal information and even ideas for a new computer program.
- **Law of designs** – that covers registration of designs like computer furniture and is closely associated with copyright law. It includes **semiconductor regulations,** that protect integrated circuits designs.
- **Trade marks and passing-off** – that covers registration of a distinctive trademark, like the Apple logo. 'Passing-off' covers action against anyone who 'passes off' their goods or services as being those of someone else having a 'good' reputation.

There are many horror stories about people who have had data wrongly attributed to them, or who have received unsolicited (junk) mail from organisations they have had no previous dealings with. Data protection legislation seeks to provide a system of checks and balances to prevent the abuse of computer power.

The **Data Protection Act 1984** relates to data concerning individual persons that is stored and processed by computer. It aims to control the storage and use of **personal data** by **data users.** It provides a system of data registration, monitoring and control under the direction of a **Registrar** who has powers of enforcement and prosecution. The Act is based on the Council for Europe Convention on Data Protection and the main features of the UK act are:

- unless exempt, all data users who hold or provide services in respect of computerised personal data, must register with the Data Protection Registrar;
- the registrar maintains a register of data users that includes details of their name and address, the description of personal data held, a description of data sources, a description of receivers that the data may be disclosed to, identities of data subjects requesting access to the data;
- exceptions to registration include employee data used solely for processing of wages and pensions, accounting data used solely for accounting purposes, medical records;
- the data user must comply with the principles of the Act and any requirements placed on them by the registrar.

The Act establishes rights in law for the data subjects and allows them to:

- obtain access to personal data of which they are the subject;
- seek compensation for damages caused by loss of, or inaccurate, or misleading data about themselves;
- apply to have inaccurate data to be put right or removed.

The data protection principles of the Act are that:

- personal data shall be obtained and processed fairly and lawfully;
- personal data shall be held only for one or more specified and lawful purposes;
- personal data shall not be used or disclosed in any manner incompatible with its specified purpose;
- personal data held shall be relevant and adequate for its purpose and not be excessive;
- personal data shall be accurate and kept up-to-date;
- personal data shall not be kept for longer than is necessary;
- an individual is entitled to access any data held and have such data corrected or erased;
- appropriate security measures shall be taken against unauthorised access and against accidental loss or destruction.

These reasonable principles must be applied by the data users and such organisations should develop a data protection policy to enable them to comply with the Act. The Act is an attempt to protect individuals' interests within the information age with its great dependence on IT to hold and process records.

The Act has not provided total freedom of information, and there are exemptions or partial exemptions. Exemptions from the whole of the Act include national security, payroll and accounts, and domestic records (your personal diary on computer), information required by law to be made available to the public (registers of electors, births, marriages and deaths). In some circumstances, data users may be exempted from allowing the data subject access to their data, these include crime and taxation, health and social work data.

## Question 3.54

Which is covered by the Data Protection Act?

A  software packages

B  sales figures

C  personal data

D  product details

## Question 3.55

What must a building society do that keeps data about clients?

A  keep client data secure

B  store the client data for at least two years

C  allow anyone access to the client data

D  send counter clerks on IT courses

## Task 3.20  PC 4

*This is a task for groups of two or three students. Prepare a presentation that highlights the principle features of The Data Protection Act. The presentation should describe the role of the registrar, the obligations of the data user, and the rights of the data subject, with respect to an application that uses an IT system to hold and process personal data. The application can be one you have investigated, read about in the library or discussed as a case study.*

# Answers to questions in Unit 3

| | | | | |
|---|---|---|---|---|
| Answer 3.1 | B | | Answer 3.29 | B |
| Answer 3.2 | C | | Answer 3.30 | C |
| Answer 3.3 | A | | Answer 3.31 | C |
| Answer 3.4 | C | | Answer 3.32 | A |
| Answer 3.5 | B | | Answer 3.33 | D |
| Answer 3.6 | A | | Answer 3.34 | C |
| Answer 3.7 | D | | Answer 3.35 | B |
| Answer 3.8 | D | | Answer 3.36 | D |
| Answer 3.9 | A | | Answer 3.37 | C |
| Answer 3.10 | B | | Answer 3.38 | A |
| Answer 3.11 | C | | Answer 3.39 | D |
| Answer 3.12 | A | | Answer 3.40 | A |
| Answer 3.13 | D | | Answer 3.41 | C |
| Answer 3.14 | C | | Answer 3.42 | B |
| Answer 3.15 | B | | Answer 3.43 | C |
| Answer 3.16 | A | | Answer 3.44 | A |
| Answer 3.17 | D | | Answer 3.45 | A |
| Answer 3.18 | C | | Answer 3.46 | C |
| Answer 3.19 | D | | Answer 3.47 | A |
| Answer 3.20 | B | | Answer 3.48 | C |
| Answer 3.21 | D | | Answer 3.49 | B |
| Answer 3.22 | B | | Answer 3.50 | B |
| Answer 3.23 | C | | Answer 3.51 | B |
| Answer 3.24 | B | | Answer 3.52 | A |
| Answer 3.25 | C | | Answer 3.53 | A |
| Answer 3.26 | D | | Answer 3.54 | C |
| Answer 3.27 | B | | Answer 3.55 | A |
| Answer 3.28 | C | | | |

# Unit 3 Sample Test Paper

Questions 1 to 3 refer to the following.

Newsagents sell magazines, delivered to them through the mail. The magazines are printed by a publishing organisation using paper supplied by a paper manufacturer who uses timber supplied by a forestry company.

1  Which organisation is in the primary sector?

    A   the newsagent
    B   the publishing organisation
    C   the paper manufacturer
    D   the forestry company

2  Which sector does the paper manufacturer work in?

    A   the tertiary sector
    B   the secondary sector
    C   the primary sector
    D   the public sector

3  Which is a public organisation?

    A   the magazine
    B   the newsagent
    C   the mail service
    D   the forestry company

Questions 4 to 14 relate to the following.

A T-shirt and sweatshirt manufacturer has a factory to make its products that it sells to shops. It buys its fabric and other raw materials from suppliers. It advertises its products in sports and leisure magazines.

4  Which department is reponsible for advertising an organisation's products?

    A   personnel
    B   production
    C   purchasing
    D   sales and marketing

5  Which department would advise on staff recruitment?

    A   personnel
    B   production
    C   purchasing
    D   sales and marketing

6  Which department obtains the best prices for the supply of an organisation's fabrics?

    A   personnel
    B   production
    C   purchasing
    D   sales and marketing

7  Which type of information tells factory supervisors when machines need routine maintenance?

    A   marketing information
    B   operational information
    C   sales information
    D   supplier information

8  Which information flows from the accounts department to shops?

    A   supplier invoice
    B   purchase order
    C   sales invoices
    D   sales orders

9  Which information flows from purchasing department to fabric suppliers?

    A   supplier invoice
    B   purchase order
    C   sales invoices
    D   sales orders

10  Which performs an external function?

    A   purchasing
    B   production
    C   accounts
    D   shops

## Data handling

11  Which is most likely to be a batch processing activity?

    A   taking a sales order from a shop
    B   handling a shop account enquiry
    C   producing employee weekly payslips
    D   editing a product advertisement

12  Which is most lilely to be a transaction processing system?

    A   printing weekly sales reports
    B   printing shop sales invoices
    C   printing quarterly VAT returns
    D   taking a shop sales order

13 Why does the factory use a computerised stock control system?

    A  to buy fabric at the lowest price
    B  to help decide when to order new fabric
    C  to increase factory throughput
    D  to improve the quality of production

14 Why does the company store its personnel records on its computer system?

    A  more records can be kept
    B  records are more accurate
    C  personnel enquiries are more quickly handled
    D  no manual records are needed

15 A university's student services department stores information about some students' special needs. How is the special needs data obtained?

    A  from a questionnaire
    B  from an interview
    C  from a GP prescription
    D  from a magnetic tape

16 A CD and video store uses an electronic point of sale (EPOS) system to update stock levels. How does the system identify the items that have been sold?

    A  from till receipts
    B  from customer questionnaires
    C  from customer interviews
    D  from a barcode

17 A restaurant system displays a menu to the waiter. Which of the following is used to select an option from the menu screen?

    A  a customer
    B  a barcode reader
    C  a mouse
    D  a magnetic stripe card reader

18 A customer pays for a meal using a magnetic stripe payment card. Which is used to update the customer account?

    A  a magnetic stripe card reader
    B  electronic funds transfer (EFT)
    C  electronic point of sale (EPOS)
    D  bankers automated clearing systems (BACS)

Questions 19 to 26 relate to the following.

A video rental organisation uses a computer system to store data about videos it has for hire and its members who are borrowers of videos.

19 Which process locates a specific video in the system?

    A  calculating
    B  sorting
    C  verifying
    D  searching

20 Which process ensures that correct borrower information has been entered?

    A  validating
    B  selecting
    C  grouping
    D  merging

21 Which will be used to store the value of a video's rental rate?

    A  a character
    B  a field
    C  a record
    D  a file

22 Which has a numeric data type?

    A  video play time
    B  borrower postcode
    C  borrower telephone number
    D  video title

23 Which is a primary key for the borrower file?

    A  postcode
    B  telephone number
    C  borrower initials
    D  borrower identification number

24 Which will allow a print out of borrowers in postcode sequence?

    A  selection of a postcode
    B  searching for a postcode
    C  sorting on postcode
    D  merging on postcode

25 Which is used to list videos on loan that are overdue for return?

    A  sorting on return date
    B  searching by comparing dates
    C  selection using on an index
    D  merging on return date

**Safety and Security**

26 There are no videos with a play time that exceeds 240 minutes. Which accuracy check is used to ensure this when creating a video record?

A verification
B field length
C invalid character
D within range

Questions 27 to 35 relate to the following.

A software mail order company uses a computerised sales order processing system. New customers fill out data entry forms. Existing customers can place orders by telephone by telling data entry clerks the product codes they want. On entry of a product code the system displays the matching product description and other related data.

27 How do clerks check that customers have provided the correct product codes?

A by entering the product code twice
B by checking the product stock level
C by validating the product code
D by reading the product description to customers

28 Which of the following is a verification check of new customer data?

A comparing screen data with that on the data entry form
B making sure the postcode has letters and numbers
C counting the letters in the name
D checking that the address is in the UK

29 Which of the following stops unauthorised people looking at the customer data?

A copyrighting the software
B allocating user system passwords
C validation of data entry
D regularly backing up the data

30 Which of the following allows data to be recovered if the computer system is stolen?

A copyrighting the software
B allocating user system passwords
C validation of data entry
D regularly backing up the data

31 A data entry clerk is off sick with repetitive strain injury (RSI). What is the most likely cause of RSI?

A poor quality VDU
B poor office lighting
C using the wrong type of chair
D keying in for long periods

32 What should data entry clerks do to reduce the risk of eye strain?

A adjust their chairs properly
B take regular breaks away from the VDU
C reduce their working day
D use the latest software

33 A software package user guide is difficult to understand. What does this cause?

A backache
B eye strain
C operator stress
D repetitive strain injury

34 An accountant has bought a single user licence for an accounting suite of software. Where can the software be installed?

A on a network fileserver
B on one computer only
C on all computers in one office
D on one computer in the office and on a second computer at home

35 Wrongful access to personal data has been detected. What should the IT manager do?

A dismiss all IT operations staff
B reload the system software and restore all data files
C review data and system security procedures
D revise data record formats

by **Peter Hodson**

# *Communications and Information Technology*

## Introduction

Most students find this a challenging but interesting unit. Although the unit starts with the descriptive part, it changes into being a unit which needs to have practical experience of using a network and transferring electronic files. For any of you who are already surfing the Internet, this will be an easy practical session. For those of you who are new to this area and have wondered what networks were all about, then this is another chance to get involved.

The extent to which your practical sessions will take you will depend on the equipment to which you have access. Maybe you have an Internet account at home, so some of the work can be done there. Best of luck on your network voyage.

# *Describe electronic communication systems*

## Introduction

The first part of this element describes a range of electronic communication systems, in particular:

- broadcast systems;
- networks;
- telephones;
- facsimile.

To underpin the remaining elements in this unit, the ideas involved in protocols are covered. This is followed by a description of the various modes of communication. This element also provides the knowledge base to support the practical emphasis of Element 4.2.

## 4.1.1 Electronic communication systems

This is an important aspect of Information Technology. Without **electronic communications systems** we would not have seen such widespread use of general electronic equipment or the development of fax machines, automatic telling machines, travel booking systems, etc. The ability to send and receive information over any distance is a significant contribution to the technological developments that have occurred. The transfer speed of this information has radically changed the ways in which people expect communication systems to work. For example, I have just watched Hong Kong celebrating their New Year on the television whilst in the UK it was still several hours before midnight and New Year's Day. Pictures and sound are transmitted around the world in seconds.

Companies and organisations expect to send data around the world quickly to ensure information or company instructions are delivered and acted upon without delay. There have been projects where the design has been undertaken by joint teams in the UK and USA. Work undertaken by the UK team during the day was picked up at the end of the day by the USA (the start of their day shift, working seven hours behind the UK), who then continued the development. The following morning (UK time) the UK team resumed the work and so the cycle of development continued. This is just an example of the impact that communication systems can have on an organisation.

In this opening element we will cover a range of electronic communication systems. Although this is not a complete list, it is sufficient to cover the range of systems required by the unit.

### Broadcast systems

**Broadcast systems** have been around for a very long time. Indeed you may consider speech as being a broadcast system which uses the airwaves as a transmission medium. There is, of course, a limitation on how far such a broadcast can travel.

 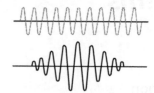

*Figure 4.1 Speech waves and analogue signals*

Electronic broadcast systems can exist in both audio and video forms and have been evolving with the advances made in technology. Radio broadcasting is typical of the early broadcast systems, with transmitting stations sending signals over the airwaves on an allocated frequency and receiving stations tuned into the frequency of the station. A number of radio stations, each using their allocated frequencies could share the transmission media (the airwaves). A radio could receive any of the frequencies, but the end-users tune their radios into the station or frequency required.

*Figure 4.2 Radio transmission*

One of the big developments of the century was the introduction of television transmissions. To be able to send pictures as well as sound needed a larger frequency block for each channel than had been necessary for radio. A viewer selects the channel they wish to view by selecting one of a number of frequency bands that the television set has been tuned into. The broadcasting authority allocates frequencies in the UK and Europe to give adequate separation between these allocated frequencies and to ensure that there is no interference between the transmissions. Hence BBC1, BBC2, ITV and Channel 4/S4C will each broadcast in a separate frequency channel.

### Question 4.1

*Can you think of another example of a broadcast system that has been in place for a long time and another one that is relatively new?*

Innovation continues to bring new systems into existence. As an example, mobile phones are a new development that is based on cell broadcasting. The technology has divided the country into areas known as cells and each mobile phone transmits and receives within the cell in which it is currently located. As the phone moves to an adjacent area, then the new cell takes over the role of transmitting and receiving for that individual handset.

*Figure 4.3 Mobile phone*

### Task 4.1    PC 1                                                      *C2.4*

*Investigate and report on how either the mobile telephone or satellite television broadcasts operate.*

Other examples of the broadcast systems being used include the use of ship and aircraft transmissions to their appropriate control centres, e.g. their navigation systems receive navigation signals from beacons. Emergency services have their own broadcast systems for communicating messages.

## Wide area networks (WANs)

We noted earlier that organisations or businesses had benefited from the ability to send data over long distances through **wide area networks (WANs)**, hopefully with no more direct involvement by the end-user than if the communication was over very short distances. In an ideal situation the communication systems are transparent to the user (i.e. the user doesn't realise that communications are actually happening). For example, you can get money from an automatic telling machine anywhere in the world ... provided you have some money in your account! Whether the machine is inside your bank's local branch office or in Hong Kong or New Zealand makes no difference to the way in which you use the system. We often diagrammatically represent the connection between any two or more points by a 'cloud'. This can represent a simple connection or a very large series of interconnected networks.

*Figure 4.4 Network concept*

Services which involve distances further than the boundary points of your office block or factory area must use communication systems that are provided by the **public telephone companies** (or PTTs as they are internationally known). In the UK, British Telecom and Mercury are examples of PTTs. There are a range of network services available from these organisations such as:

- dial-up lines;
- leased lines;
- ISDN (Integrated Services Data Network);
- telex.

## Question 4.2

*Can you think of another network service that is available from a PTT?*

Historically, we had a telephone network which carried voice traffic using **analogue signalling**. This was a public switched telephone network. The word **switched** is used to indicate that once a subscriber had dialled the number, exchange relays were switched to form a connection between both ends. A connection between two points might well consist of a whole series of lines between various exchanges, whose relays have made the line connections. When the need to carry digital signals over these existing networks was identified, a new device called a **modem** was introduced. This device allowed an analogue signal (known as a **carrier**) to be modified to represent the digital data that was to be transmitted. At the other end of the line, a second modem converted the transmission back into the digital format that was needed by the electronic devices attached.

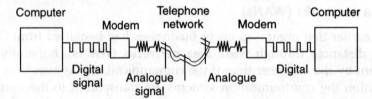

*Figure 4.5 Analogue network carrying digital data*

Hence it was just as common to see a modem device as it was to see a telephone handset wherever there was a need to send digital information.

*Figure 4.6 Modem and telephone*

Changes to the telephone networks over the last decade have seen a rapid replacement of the analogue signalling equipment, with a network that carries signals between distant locations in **digital** format. All the old relay telephone exchanges have been replaced with electronic equipment. Hence the attachment of electronic communication equipment is enhanced. Of course, we now have to convert all the voice traffic (which is analogue) into a digital format to transmit across the network and then convert it back to analogue signalling at the destination end so the original speech input can be recognised … the human ear isn't adept to receive '0's and '1's.

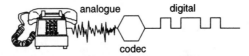

*Figure 4.7 Digital network carrying analogue information*

Wide area networks can be run as either private or public networks. A **private** wide area network is set up by an organisation by leasing lines between locations from a PTT for exclusive use of that organisation. For example, a company with three offices in London, Cardiff and Newcastle may lease a line between each of these locations. All communications between the offices can then be channelled by the company through these facilities. No other organisation or member of the public will be transmitting on these dedicated wide area network facilities. **Public** networks are those set up for general use (such as X.25). Many networks will have added value services to which the public may wish to subscribe and connect, e.g. CompuServe or BTNet.

### Local area networks (LANs)

A common arrangement within an organisation is to connect a number of local devices together on a local network which is restricted in the distances over which it operates. It is normal to see a **LAN (local area network)** restricted to a building, office or campus, i.e. within the boundary points of an organisation's site. These limits are based on the practical issues of where an organisation is able to install the cabling needed to connect the devices. They can only install cable in areas which they own and control. A LAN is also restricted by how far a signal can travel down a cable without significant distortion. We can make a connection to a wide area network from the local area network to talk to distant locations outside the area of the organisation's site. In most cases the local area network is a locally operated and owned network. Typical examples of LANs are Ethernet and Token Rings. In other cases it may be that the local cluster is based on a concentrator of some sort that belongs to the wide area network suppliers and does not have to be managed and operated by the local organisation. In either approach, the intention is to set up a local environment in which devices can communicate quickly and efficiently with a mechanism to 'talk' to more distant devices whenever there is a need. An example could be a LAN with several PCs and a laser printer.

### Telephone

As we have already seen, the telephone network has been modernised and is essentially a digital network which carries both voice and data. The normal household telephone point expects an analogue input but digital connection points can be provided by the PTTs. Hence, a wide range of services can be supported by the telephone network. Developments are in hand to provide entertainment channels on the digital links. Already millions of people connect to the Internet and exchange information with the other Internet users and services around the world.

### Task 4.2   PC 1

What range of services are available from a PTT for the home subscriber to purchase?

### Task 4.3   PC 1

What additional facilities may be offered to a large maintenance organisation?

## Facsimile

A communication system that has survived the introduction of high tech products is a **facsimile**, or **fax machine** as they are more commonly known.

*Figure 4.8 Facsimile machine*

The device scans the paper copy that is input and represents the image on the paper in a digital format of '0's and '1's. What the fax system is primarily doing is representing the white and grey areas on the paper by a '1' or a '0'. By scanning across the paper an image of the content can be constructed. The more scans across the paper needed to make up a page, the better the quality of the image captured. Of course in this scanning technique a lot of long strings of '0's or '1's can be generated. To make the data transmission more efficient, it is common to compress the data before transmission. For example, if we were sending a string of one hundred zeroes as (100 * 0) rather than 000000 … 0000. The data is transmitted over a network and the receiving fax recreates the paper-based copy of the source input.

### Task 4.4   PC 1                                                                C2.4

Investigate the standard method used by a fax machine to represent a scanned document.

Various events have occurred which have strengthened the role of the fax. Postal strikes at various times have left organisations with fax machines as the simplest way of getting paper-based material to distant locations. Having used this method, there is a growing recognition that the benefits gained by such speed of transmission give a commercial advantage. Because people still like to see written communication, it is helpful to send information so it can arrive in printed format at the destination. A more recent development has been the introduction of fax transmission capability on a card slotted directly into computer systems. This allows computer generated material to exist as an electronic document and to be sent directly from the computer to the remotely located fax, without having to print at the sending end. It creates a big advantage, since paper copy at the sending end isn't really needed and the original copy can be electronically filed. Indeed in a local area network, one fax system on the network could take the transmissions from all the other connected devices and be a central despatch point.

Each fax station is uniquely identified using the same numbering system as the telephone network. Indeed a telephone number could be either a voice line or a fax line or be a joint number between both.

## 4.1.2 Protocols

To send data between two or more points, each end must agree on the approach to be taken or the convention to be used. Different arrangements have existed for a long time. For example, scouts have used semaphore flags, Red Indians have used smoke signals, etc. It would be no use using semaphore flags at one end and smoke signals at the other, hence we need to agree the convention for signalling. In establishing the **protocols** for electronic communication there needs to be agreement on the settings to a range of parameters. These parameters are established to make sure both ends will follow the same rules and will be able to understand what the other end is saying. An analogy is seen in common speech. If someone comes up to you and says 'Good Morning' you expect the rest of the speech to be spoken in English. However if the opening greeting is 'Hola', you may expect the rest to be in Spanish!

The impact of each of the settings has a significance which is beyond the scope of this text, but the individual topics needed for this element are introduced here.

### Baud rate

To transfer data between two devices there are a few basic points to be examined. Let us consider the simplest of physical connections shown below.

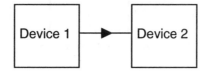

*Figure 4.9 Simple serial connection*

If this connection is a single strand of copper wire then exchange of data can only be by a serial sequence of bits flowing along the transmission media. Electrically this won't be exactly true because a return circuit is needed (i.e. two wires), but for the purpose of understanding principles we can consider this as a single connection. Data can only flow in one direction at any instant in time along this single connection. For convenience, the bits are frequently grouped together to represent a character, typically eight bits at a time (i.e. a letter of the alphabet, a number or a symbol such as an '!'). Each bit is usually represented on the copper wire as a voltage level. The normal arrangement is for a 'zero' to be represented by a positive voltage and a 'one' to be represented by a negative voltage. To ensure that each device is capable of sending to or receiving from other devices, international standards have been established.

The speed at which we can send data, or bits, along a connection is obviously important. Every good data communications designer will try to get as fast a connection as possible. The number of bits that can be sent in a second is called the data transmission rate, often quoted as bits per second (bps or bits/s). The signal on the connection, which represents this data, is the activity that, strictly speaking, controls the speed. The faster the signal changes, the more bits per second can be sent. In engineering terms the rate at which the signal changes is called the band rate. Of course, when a signal level sends one bit at a time, then the band rate and the bit per second have the same value.

The makers of various equipment (i.e. the vendors) have chosen RSR23C or V24 interfaces on their devices. These international standards include the signalling conventions. The more recent **X.21** standard has been in place for quite a while, but migration to this has been slow. Fortunately, special arrangements to link this new standard of X.21 and RS232C have been introduced to accommodate this slow acceptance, so bits can be transferred between X.21 and RS232C. These standards show how bits may be serially transmitted.

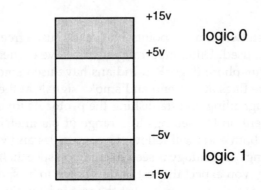

*Figure 4.10 RS232C Voltage levels*

Normally the voltage levels used in RS232C signalling are +12v or -12v, although a voltage level between +5v and +15v will be interpreted as a 'zero' and equally a 'one' will be interpreted by a signal in the -5v to -15v range. A voltage level in the shaded areas of figure 4.10 should be recognised as a signal representing a bit. Using this standard the bit stream 01010 may be represented by the signal levels in figure 4.11.

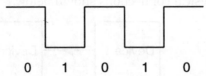

*Figure 4.11 Typical bit stream*

## Question 4.3

*Draw the signal levels that would represent 10101, using the standard in figure 4.11.*

## Question 4.4

*Draw the signal levels that would represent the bit stream 10100 using the same standard.*

## Question 4.5

*In answering question 4.4, were there any particular difficulties in representing the last two bits?*

Each bit needs to be represented for a given length of time at the required voltage level on the copper wire. The length or duration of the signal has to be sufficiently long for the receiving end to recognise the incoming signal and record it accurately. Hence, if the duration of a signal was 1 second, then the receiving end has a full second to identify the voltage level and the transmission rate would be 1 bit per second. If each change of signal occurred after 10 ms, such that each bit was sent in this length of time, then in a 1 second period we could send 100 of these signals, i.e. we could send 100 bits in 1 second. This is usually stated as 100 bps or 100 bit/s (i.e. bits per second).

## Question 4.6

*What is the time length of each bit's signal when the transmission speed is 300 bps?*

## Question 4.7

*If the data rate were 1600 bps, what would be the duration of each signal level?*

### Data bit representation and parity checks

As noted earlier, bits are often grouped into eight bits to represent a character. There are several different bit representations of a character, two of which are **ASCII** and **EBCDIC**. Table 4.1 is the ASCII representation which is the most widely used, especially outside the IBM user base. It should be noted from this table that we use only seven bits to uniquely represent the range of characters. Hence each of the different arrangements of bit patterns that can be achieved with seven bits are used to representation a letter of the alphabet, an integer number, a punctuation mark or a control character.

| Low 4 bits | High 3 bits | | | | | | | |
|---|---|---|---|---|---|---|---|---|
| | 000 | 001 | 010 | 011 | 100 | 101 | 110 | 111 |
| 0000 | NUL | DLE | SP | 0 | @ | P | ` | p |
| 0001 | SOH | DC1 | ! | 1 | A | Q | a | q |
| 0010 | STX | DC2 | " | 2 | B | R | b | r |
| 0011 | ETX | DC3 | # | 3 | C | S | c | s |
| 0100 | EOT | DC4 | $ | 4 | D | T | d | t |
| 0101 | ENQ | NAK | % | 5 | E | U | e | u |
| 0110 | ACK | SYN | & | 6 | F | V | f | v |
| 0111 | BEL | ETB | ' | 7 | G | W | g | w |
| 1000 | BS | CAN | ( | 8 | H | X | h | x |
| 1001 | HT | EM | ) | 9 | I | Y | i | y |
| 1010 | LF | SUB | * | : | J | Z | j | z |
| 1011 | VT | ESC | + | ; | K | [ | k | { |
| 1100 | FF | FS | , | < | L | \ | l | | |
| 1101 | CR | GS | - | = | M | ] | m | } |
| 1110 | SO | RS | . | > | N | ^ | n | ~ |
| 1111 | SI | US | / | ? | O | _ | o | DEL |

*Table 4.1 ASCII codes*

## Question 4.8

*What is the range of the ASCII representation for the control characters?*

## Task 4.5    PC 2                                                    *C2.4*

*Identify each of the control characters in the ASCII set shown in table 4.1. Explain the use of each control character.*

We want to have a simple check on each character transferred so we can be confident that it has been transferred successfully. The eighth bit is used as a **parity** bit to help ensure the character transfer has been successful, i.e. the bit on the left-hand side is set as a check to either a '0' or a '1' as is appropriate.

Parity setting on a character is a simple technique, but unfortunately several variations of parity settings are in use. The most common of these are odd and even parity. In the case of odd parity, the parity bit is set to ensure that the total number of 'ones' including the parity bit itself add up to be an odd number. Even parity ensures that the total number of 'ones' in a character including the parity bit is an even number. Both of these parity modes are common. Other methods such as space, mark or null parity are less frequently used.

On receipt of a character, a check is made to see if the parity is correctly set. If it is incorrect, the character transfer is assumed to have been corrupted and is discarded. In this case a retransmission of the corrupted character is required. The first step of this process is known as **error detection** and the second is known as **error correction**.

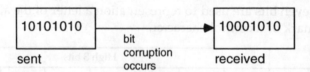

Figure 4.12 Serial bit corruption

The data communications installer would be responsible for ensuring that the correct parity setting was established between installed devices under his or her control. The suppliers or vendors of each item of equipment will identify the required parity setting for the individual interface. Both ends need to use the same parity setting approach, otherwise the technique won't work.

Consider the ASCII representation for 'A' which is 1000001. Using odd parity this would be represented as 11000001, i.e. we set the eighth bit (or left-hand bit) so the total number of bits is an odd number. Using even parity it would be represented as 01000001.

## Question 4.9

*What would the parity bits be for the ASCII code of 'B' and 'E' using odd parity setting? What would they be for even parity setting?*

## Task 4.6   PC 2                                            *C2.3*

*Construct a table of all the ASCII alphanumeric bit representations as bit patterns to show their parity setting when odd parity is used.*

This technique is good for detecting single bit errors, but if two bits were corrupted it would not detect the problem. Parity checking is fine at detecting those error conditions where the number of bits that have changed are odd (i.e. 1, 3, 5 etc.), but cannot detect the case where an even number of bits (i.e. 2, 4, 6, etc.) have changed.

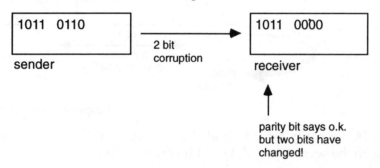

*Figure 4.13 Multiple bit corruption*

Data corruption often occurs in short bursts where many bits get changed. It will not surprise you to learn that more sophisticated techniques of error detection have therefore been implemented. It is critical that corrupted or erroneous data be detected. We are slightly less concerned that data becomes corrupted than we are in making sure we know when it is wrong, although we clearly strive to achieve error free transfers. At least when we know it is wrong, action can be taken to put it right. Undetected errors can create enormous problems, because we may believe the corrupted data is right and continue to use it afterwards in the context of it being accurate data.

## Question 4.10

*Suggest an example where an undetected error in a data transfer would be problematic.*

The faster you want to send data between two devices, the shorter the duration of each bit signalled on the transmission medium. A problem now arises at the receiving end of any data transfer. How does this receiver know when data is about to be sent and how will it know the rate at which the sending device will be transmitting? To recognise the incoming data and recover or record the data accurately, the receiver needs to read or sample the signal on the cable at a rate determined by the speed at which the data is being transmitted. Both ends must operate at the same rates and agree what that rate is.

### Start and stop bits

Let us first look at the situation where everything is idle, known as the **quiescent state**. To alert the receiver that a character (eight bits) of data is about to be transmitted, a **start bit** is sent at the front of the character. This tells the receiving station that the transmission line has become active and it needs to collect data bits off the line. The data bits then follow immediately behind the start bit and the receiver samples the signal level to determine whether a '0' or a '1' has been sent. Conventionally, we also send a **stop bit** at the end of the character. These start and stop bits also act as delimiters on the character so that the boundary points of any character being transmitted will be recognised and understood by the receiver. Thus, the stop bit is an important check for the receiver that the end boundary point of the character frame has been correctly reached and the receiver will expect to see a stop in this bit position. A typical transfer of a character in asynchronous mode would look like:

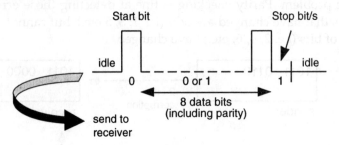

Figure 4.14 Asynchronous character representation

In figure 4.14 the parity bit is indicated as a zero, but it could of course have been a one, depending on the seven bits of data that it was checking.

## Question 4.11

Draw the asynchronous representation of the character frame for the eight bits 11000010.

## Task 4.7   PC 2                                                          N2.3

Draw the asynchronous representation of the character frame for each of the ASCII numeric data set.

Some systems may need more than one stop bit and a character will be terminated by 1.5 or 2 stop bits. This is usually for slower devices, typically with slow mechanical components and is becoming less common. If we send two stop bits to a receiving device that only requires one, it won't matter since the second stop bit will just appear to be the start of an idle signal level. That is because the voltage level of a stop bit and the voltage level maintained for the idle state are the same.

The form of transmission discussed above is known as **asynchronous transmission**. The receiver doesn't know when the next character is going to arrive and awaits the arrival of the next start bit. There is no information within the character about the speed at which it is being sent, so there is no 'timing' information (i.e. there is nothing to tell the receiver how quickly it needs to sample the incoming signal in order to recover the transmitted data). To clarify how important it is that the receiver should sample the transmission at the correct rate let us consider a simple example. A device is transmitting the character 01011010 at 100 bps (i.e. the duration or time cell of each bit is 10 ms) and the receiver tries to recover the data by sampling every 20 ms. Let's see what happens:

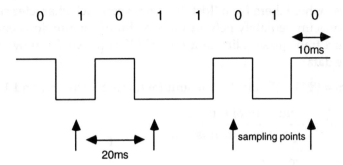

*Figure 4.15 Sampling the transmission incorrectly*

A receiver incorrectly sampling the transmission as shown in figure 4.15 would read the data sent as 0011. This assumes that in figure 4.15, the bits on the right hand side of the diagram arrive at the receiver first. Clearly this is not what we want. The receiver needs to sample the line at the same rate as the sender is transmitting it. To achieve this, the transmission interfaces of both devices have internal clocks, each of which, within a reasonable level of accuracy, are 'clocking' or reading the data at the same rate. Devices sending data to each other know the data rate between themselves, because the data communications designer will have established the speeds at one of the standard rates. So the arrival of the start bit at the receiver, starts its interface clock and instructs the receiver's interface when to sample the incoming signal.

Provided the sender and receiver clocks are running at the same rate, the data should be successfully received. We hope that the accuracy of the clocks is such that they maintain synchronisation and the receiver continues to sample the incoming signal near the mid-point of a time cell. If they are not accurate, it is possible that the receiver clock will drift out of synchronisation and will try to sample at some point off the middle of the time cell and misread the signal.

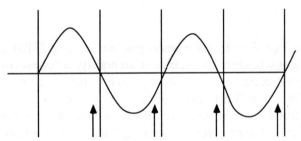

*Figure 4.16 Delayed sampling*

For relatively short lengths of data (in this case a character), the accuracy between the clocks is normally adequate enough for such drift not to be an issue. The faster the data rate and the greater the data length, the more difficult this issue becomes. As a check on the protocol, the receiver insists on seeing a stop bit in the tenth (and possibly eleventh) bit position. If that isn't present, there has been an error. In a typical character transfer, successive characters will have a short gap between them. It is possible for this inter-character time gap to be nothing or very small, especially when the sender is transmitting at a maximum rate.

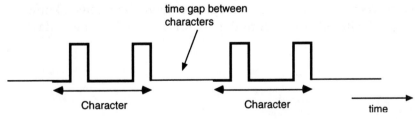

*Figure 4.17 Character string*

Consider a case where there is no 'lost' time between each character sent, i.e. a start bit for one character follows immediately behind the stop bit of the previous character. If 200 characters are sent down a transmission line at a rate of 1200 bps we can now calculate the time it takes to transfer the data.

200 characters = (200 × 10) bits to transmit (assuming 1 stop bit and 1 start bit).

$$\text{Time to transmit} = \frac{\text{Number of bits sent}}{\text{Speed of transmission}}$$

$$\text{Time to transmit} = \frac{200 \times 10}{1200} \text{ seconds} = 1.66 \text{ seconds}$$

### Question 4.12

*If we assume that each character could be sent without a delay between them, how long would it take to asynchronously send 100 characters down a line at 2400 bps?*

### Task 4.8    PC 1, PC 2          N2.3

*Investigate and report on the range of telephone line speeds to which a modem can connect.*

## Flow control

As we developed our data transfer concepts, we assumed that the destination is capable of receiving the data at whatever rate it is sent. In reality, of course, this may not be true. At a simple level, a personal computer is capable of generating and sending data much faster than a printer can handle it. For short bursts of data this can be managed by having a receiver memory or buffer to store incoming data until it can be handled. To prevent overflow occurring and the sender swamping the receiver by sending data faster than the handling capacity, we need to introduce the idea of **flow control**. If we don't use flow control, then overflow could occur and some of the data will get lost. There is an analogy we can use here. If you were pouring a liquid into a pot with an open tap at its bottom, once the pot was full you can only pour into the pot at the same rate as the liquid comes out of the tap. If you pour faster, then the pot overflows. If you were blindfolded whilst doing this pouring, someone could give you instructions to start pouring and stop pouring to manage the situation and prevent any spillage. These commands would be **flow control commands**.

A model has been developed that has an easy to implement flow control technique. Consider the positive acknowledgement system where additional new data will only be sent on receipt of a successful transfer acknowledgement from the receiver, known as an **ACK** (i.e. the data has arrived without error). Until this ACK is received, no more data is sent.

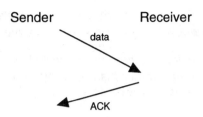

*Figure 4.18 Positive acknowledgement*

If the receiver wants to exert flow control at this level, we need an additional response. This could indicate that the last data element or character has been received OK, but not to send any more data elements until a future response indicates a state of readiness to receive more. **RNR (receiver not ready)** is such a response.

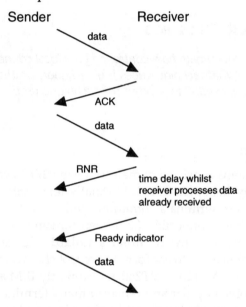

*Figure 4.19 Flow control*

## Question 4.13

*Why don't we delay sending a response rather than inventing the RNR response as a simple way of implementing flow control?*

The ready indicator notifies the sender that the receiving device is now ready to continue and data flow can be resumed. At the receiving end, the time delay between sending the RNR and the ready indicator permits the receiving device to 'catch up' with the processing of the information flow. Once it has emptied its buffers and is ready to resume receipt of the flow, it sends the ready indicator response.

When the connection between the two devices is a simple RS232C interface, the complexities of the flow control protocol outlined above can be reduced. RS232C uses two of the control lines within the interface to signal the flow control. When the sender has data to send, it signals **RTS (ready to send)**. If the receiver is ready to accept data, it responds with **CTS (clear to send)**. At any time that the receiver changes the CTS signal, because it can't cope with any more data just now, the sender stops. As soon as CTS is signalled again, data flow may be resumed. To some extent the CTS is like a red and green traffic light. Data flows when it is 'green' (or CTS is signalled) and stops when it is 'red' (CTS is not present). The lights only work when they are switched on by the RTS signal.

### Question 4.14

*Since the RS232C flow control technique is so simple, why don't we use it on all data transfers rather than the more complex protocol using additional response codes such as RNR?*

### Question 4.15

*Are there any other flow control techniques that can be used?*

### Task 4.9   PC 2, PC 3                                                    N2.2

*Investigate flow control on your local connections between a PC and a printer. What technique does it use? Report on the connection that is in place which is needed to support the technique used.*

### Terminal emulation

Early computing systems consisted of mainframe machines with users connected via terminals which were relatively unsophisticated. Normally terminals only offered text-based displays. The way in which these terminals communicated with the mainframe, using characters and control codes to establish connection (and keep transmission and reception of data operating successfully) was known as the **terminal standard**. Hence to communicate with a Digital machine, the terminal needed to conform to control character standards within the Digital terminal specifications, e.g. VT120 or VT240 etc. Similarly IBM and ICL had their own standards.

As PCs have become popular and replaced many terminals, the ability of the PC to also act as a terminal, when necessary, is achieved by running a piece of software which makes the PC look like the terminal. Hence it responds with all the control characters, etc. that you would expect from the terminal it is pretending to be. This is known as **terminal emulation**. The software may have a number of settings, to emulate the different range of terminal standards that exist. To manage world-wide interconnection, devices frequently conform to TELNET standards of NVT (**network virtual terminal**).

### Task 4.10   PC 2

*What are the control characters and sequences used on a VT120 terminal?*

## 4.1.3 Modes of communication

### Simplex

Where there is a single wire and data flows only in one direction, then we have the very simplest form of a connection. This mode of operation is known as **simplex**. It has many limitations, since the receiver cannot signal back to the sender. However, for some systems it may be ideal. For example, someone pressing a button which sends a signal to another device (e.g. to start or stop) would only transmit in one direction. There can only be one sender, one receiver and effectively only one signalling wire or channel in this mode.

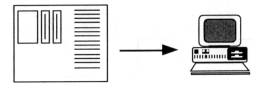

*Figure 4.20 Simplex system*

## Half-duplex

A slightly more sophisticated model is known as **half-duplex**. In the half-duplex arrangement the data flow is in one direction or the other, but not in both directions simultaneously. Hence, we still only need a 'single' piece of copper wire. (Electrically we need a second wire to complete the circuit and act as a voltage reference point, but for the purposes of signalling we can discount this). In a half-duplex arrangement, data can be sent in one direction. Once it has finished sending, the direction can be reversed and the device that was the receiver is now able to transmit. Typically this will be a response to the data just received, i.e. an ACK or a NAK. The responses of ACKs (acknowledgements) or **NAKs** (not acknowledgements, i.e. not received OK) are sent from the receiver back to the sender and determine how the sender is going to continue. Whether to send the next piece of data in the sequence, or whether to resend the last piece again because it wasn't successfully received, will be determined by the response. Half-duplex is the same principle as a single lane stretch of road controlled by traffic lights allowing traffic through in one direction or the other, but not in both simultaneously – otherwise we have a conflict of interests! Another example is a radio link, where an ACK is the statement 'Roger' and the release of control from one direction to the other direction is the statement 'Over'.

## Full-duplex

In a third approach we could introduce more than one circuit or wire between the devices, allowing data flow in both directions simultaneously. This mode of operation is known as **full-duplex**. Indeed, the RS232C interface which was introduced earlier, permits flow of data and signals in both directions simultaneously. In practice, of course, we would need more than two separate wires because we need to send control signals, etc. However, for the sake of clarity on the diagrams it is represented as a two channel circuit. The connection cable or ribbon used on systems can have up to 15 or 25 separate wire circuits within one cable, although less individual wires in a single cable is more often the norm.

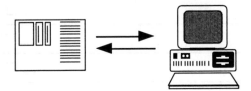

*Figure 4.21 Duplex transmission*

## Serial and parallel communication

The **serial** transmission approach is perhaps the most frequently-used technique. Each bit is sent sequentially along the connection. However, it does have the disadvantage that each byte of information takes eight time slots to be transmitted. Indeed, it takes longer when you consider the start and stop bits or other control characters that also have to be transferred.

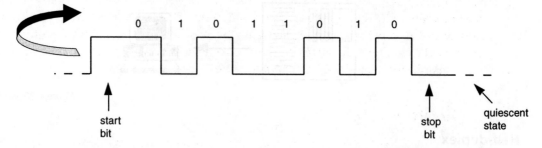

Figure 4.22 Bits transmitted serially

Over relatively short distances (e.g. between a PC and its attached printer) it is possible to have eight separate wires and to send each bit of a byte simultaneously. Each wire carries one bit of the character. This approach is known as **parallel** transmission.

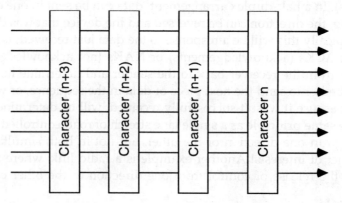

Figure 4.23 Parallel transmission

Because each individual wire has slightly different properties, there is a possibility that data could travel at marginally different speeds over each of the wires. This introduces the problem of **skew,** where the signal for each bit of the character arrives at the destination at a slightly different time.

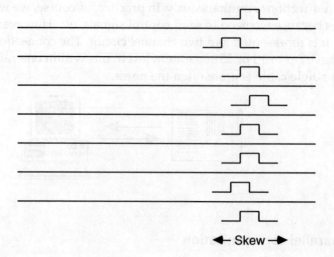

Figure 4.24 Skew

Ideally, we need to clock all eight transmission lines at the receiving end simultaneously, so we cannot allow any significant skew to develop. Hence, we tend to keep the length of parallel transmission fairly short so that the impact of any skewing is limited, and only a small time variation between each wire exists at the destination. This is coupled with the higher costs associated with the cabling and interfacing of the parallel approach. Consequently, it is normally only used over short distances between two devices where the advantage of speed over the serial transmission technique may be desirable.

## Question 4.16

*If you assume that the transmission speed of a parallel connection is 800 bytes/s, what is the shortest time taken to transmit 3200 bytes of data?*

## Question 4.17

*What assumptions have you had to make in answering the previous question?*

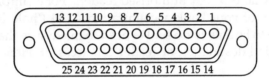

*Figure 4.25 RS232C 25-pin connector*

The V.24 or RS232C interface was originally designed to connect digital equipment to **data circuit terminating equipment (DCEs)** such as MODEMs. If we are connecting two devices together without using a modem then an RS232C connection typically uses a 25-pin D-type connection and can only be used to interconnect over short distances, typically less than 15m (50 feet). Remember that it is normal to only use a sub-set of the 25 wire connections and the connecting cable would frequently have less than 25 separate wires within the cable. Smaller D-types exist than 25-way connectors and are useful where space has been an issue. You can run quite successfully using four or five wires only. A typical layout of connection is shown in figure 4.26.

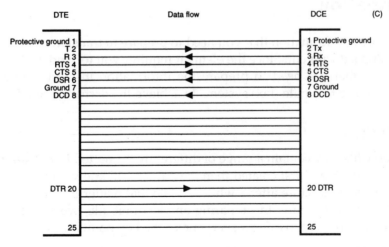

*Figure 4.26 V.24/RS232C connection*

223

# Use an electronic communication system

## Introduction

This is a practical element in which you can test out your understanding of some of the issues raised in Element 4.1. In this element we will look at the preparation of both an electronic file and a document to send across a communication system. You will also need to set up the communication system. To help make sure that each electronic file or document transfer takes place successfully, we need to apply accuracy checks which will detect if errors occurred during the transfer.

In the 'real' world the information being handled may be commercially confidential data or personal data which may fall into the category of sensitive data, i.e. data which needs to be kept secure and only accessed by authorised readers. For example, you would expect to be able to read some details of your bank account at an **ATM** ('hole in the wall') but you wouldn't expect other people to be able to do so. We need to make sure that the transfer is protected such that only the intended destination or reader can access it. Hence there may be security issues to such data.

## Question 4.18

*Can you identify two other types of sensitive data that may need protecting?*

The way in which you study this element will depend upon the equipment that you have available locally. Examples of one approach are included in the text as guidance to the way in which you may build up your portfolio of evidence.

## 4.2.1 Information

The two types of information that you need to prepare to transfer, receive and store are an electronic file and a document. Since the element requires you to send and receive the information electronically, then we need to prepare the information in electronic formats. The element requires us to use facsimile (fax) systems to achieve the exchange of a fax document.

### Electronic file

An electronic file may contain a range of differently formatted information, such as text or diagrams. When the file is first created then the author will know what it contains, but is likely to forget the content structure after a while. A potential reader may have no prior knowledge of the content or its structure. In preparing an electronic file, we should ensure that sufficient information is provided to inform everyone of the key points.

The name of the file (for DOS systems in particular) is structured to provide some of the key points. For example a text based file is called **name.doc** whereas an Excel spreadsheet file would conventionally be called **name.xls.** Other structured names also exist.

## Task 4.11 PC 1                                                                    C2.2

*Investigate and report on a range of file naming conventions.*

Files are often updated and changed. It is important to know exactly what is the status or version of any copy that is available. Many wordprocessing packages help by providing much of the framework necessary to capture the information.

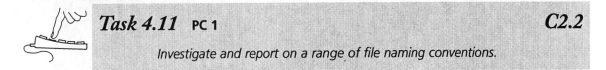

## Question 4.19

*What are the key points that someone reading or copying a file may want to know?*

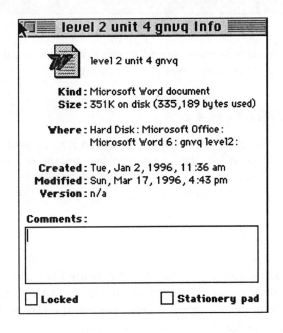

*Figure 4.27 File information*

The computer operating systems (DOS or MacOS, etc.) will also help by automatically capturing information about the file. Figures 4.27 and 4.28 are examples of the information that is available.

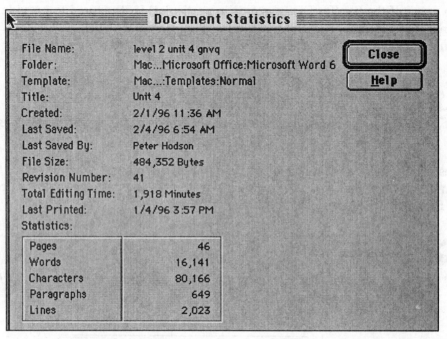

Figure 4.28 File statistics

You can see that the date last saved and revision number (equivalent to the version number) and file size are key components recorded in figure 4.28.

## Task 4.12 PC 1 C2.2

*Prepare an electronic file which is to be sent over a communications system, providing the key information points. The contents of the file should give directions on how to reach your college or school from major road or rail network points.*

### Fax document

To send a fax via a traditional fax system we prepare the document and then add a front page or cover sheet. The two elements are then transmitted through a fax machine to the destination as a single document. A paper copy is generated on the fax machine at the remote end.

## Question 4.20

*What information is needed on the front or cover page so that the destination fax office know who should be given the fax copy?*

## Question 4.21

*What information does the fax recipient need to know so that he or she may reply to the sender if necessary?*

## Question 4.22

*What simple piece of information should be put on the cover page so that we know that all the pages have been received and none have got lost?*

## Question 4.23

*A fax is received with some pages missing or incomplete. The fax operator contacts the sender and requests a retransmission.*

*Once the retransmission is complete, what information on the fax document distinguishes between the original fax and the second document?*

We saw, in the previous element, that recent developments have allowed us to have a modem/fax on a card which can be slotted into a PC. The document can exist at the sending end in electronic format, including the cover page. Hence a PC (with a fax/modem card) can transmit over the telephone network to a remote facsimile machine.

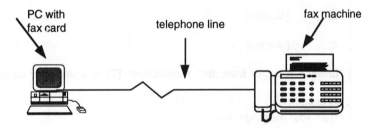

*Figure 4.29 PC fax system on telephone network*

We can take this one stage further. A PC with a fax/modem card can also receive an incoming fax and store the incoming fax document electronically. Hence the document may be created, transmitted and received in electronic format and never exist in paper format. Figure 4.30 shows the range of preferences that can be set up on a fax system on a PC.

```
                          Preferences...
        ┌─────────────────────────┐
        │ Personal Modem      ▼   │
        └─────────────────────────┘
        ☒ Show Fax Terminal window when sending or receiving
        ☒ Save fax image files that have been sent
        ☒ Turn off high speed (U.17) fax feature
        ☒ Turn off Error Correction Mode (ECM) feature
        ☐ Auto-Answer after: [2  ] ⬍ rings

        When Sending a Fax Fails:
        Retry: [1  ] ⬍ times   Time between tries: [5  ] ⬍ minutes
        ◉ Resend all pages
        ○ Resend only pages not already sent

        Received Fax, Manual Dial, or Error Notification:
        ○ None
        ◉ Display icon in menu bar 🖿         ┌─────────┐ ┌────────┐
        ○ Display icon and alert  🖿 ▢        │ Cancel  │ │   OK   │
                                              └─────────┘ └────────┘
```

*Figure 4.30 Terminal preferences*

You may have a software communication package that allows you to create the data for a cover page and automatically insert it onto a cover sheet that you have previously created and installed. Alternatively, you may create a template for a cover page and add it to the document you want to transfer. The combined document can then be sent. Such a cover page can be set up with any wordprocessing package. Indeed, many packages such as Word include a fax cover template as part of the package.

---

**[*Company Name*]**
[*Street Address*]
[*Town, County/PostalCode*]

## Fax Cover Sheet

| | | | |
|---|---|---|---|
| DATE: | 17th February 1996 | TIME: | 08:17 hrs |
| TO: | [*Names*] | PHONE: | [*Their phone number*] |
| | [*Company Name*] | | [*Their fax number*] |
| | | | |
| FROM: | [*Names*] | PHONE: | [*Your phone number*] |
| | [*Company Name*] | | [*Your fax number*] |
| | | | |
| RE: | [*Subject*] | | |
| | | | |
| CC: | [*Names*] | | |

**Number of pages including coversheet: [*Type number of pages here*]**

**Message**
[*Type your message here*]

---

*Figure 4.31 Example of fax cover template*

In the example above, a fax cover template allows a number of people at the sending end to use the same format. If this were installed as part of the fax communication software, then each individual person needs to enter their data via the software package interface. The next figure shows how my communication package asks me for the key information about myself. This key information is inserted into the fax cover template which is already installed on my system.

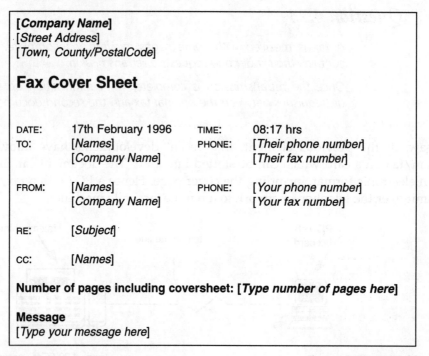

*Figure 4.32 Cover page data creation*

*Task 4.13* PC 2                                           *C2.3*

*Design a cover page for your centre. This may include graphics to represent the logo of your centre.*

*Task 4.14* PC 2

*If you have a software communication package that permits you to establish your own cover page as a standard, install your design from the previous task into this package.*

The document you wish to send by fax may simply be the cover page, because the message or note zone carries all the information you want to send. Alternatively, it may also have additional pages which were created in another package (wordprocessed text or drawings).

## 4.2.2 Set up electronic systems

The basic points that we need to consider in setting up an electronic system to achieve information transfers are:

- mode of communication;
- protocols;
- telephone numbers.

### Mode of communication

The first decision in setting up the connection is deciding whether simplex, half-duplex or full-duplex is needed. If a response to any data sent to the destination is required, then half-duplex or full-duplex is necessary. This is the normal arrangement in most communication links.

We must then decide if a serial or parallel connection is going to be used. Except for a local connection between two adjacent devices (e.g. PC and printer) it is normal to use a serial connection. Parallel connections allow a byte at a time to be transferred over short distances. For the vast majority of connections though, a serial connection is the only option. Most devices have a serial port connector to make an attachment to other devices. Relatively few have parallel connection ports.

### Protocols

The way in which both ends are expected to talk to each other, called **protocols,** needs to be the same. This includes making sure that the following features have been set to (and will operate at) the same value on both sides.

- Data bits: ASCII or EBCDIC representation? 7 bits format?
- Parity: Odd, even parity setting?
- Baud rate: Signalling rate e.g. 14400 bps or higher? (Note that baud rate is the signalling rate. Where only two signal levels are used, as in RS232, then the baud rate and the data rate are the same);
- Flow control: X-on/X-off or CTS/RTS?
- Stop bits: One or two stop bits required?

## Question 4.24

What is the difference between ASCII and EBCDIC?

## Question 4.25

What is **flow control** and why do we need it?

### Telephone numbers

When we contact the remote end, the communications software that we are using will require us to enter the telephone number of:

- either, the remote ends telephone number to link you to a modem connection (e.g. this allows an electronic file transfer to take place);
- or, the telephone number of a remote fax machine to transfer a document.

In many packages, the option is available to set up a list of telephone numbers that you frequently use. Figure 4.35 shows a fax and phone book in the bottom left hand corner, with two entries that I have already set up for my use. If I select one of the entries, then the full detail is displayed before I go ahead with the auto dial.

If this method is used, simply selecting the destination, checking the detail in the send to box and selecting the forward button is the only action required. Alternatively, the full telephone number can be typed into the fax quick send box.

## 4.2.3 Use electronic systems to transfer information

In this element we need to use an electronic system to transfer information. The electronic system includes the communication software, the computer system with its modem, a telephone network (or a substitute) and the fax facility. How you transfer an electronic file or fax document will depend on the system you have available.

### *Practical session and Task 4.15 for this element*   PC 3, PC 4

An example of a file transfer using **FTP (file transfer protocol)** is shown here.

NOTE: Messages in **bold** are those typed by the user. Messages that are *{italicised}* are additional comments to explain what is going on.

You need to configure your modem to 8 bits, 1 stop bit and no parity; commonly known as 8N1. The number for the University of Glamorgan is (01443) 482900 and there are four receiving modems which will handle up to 14,400 bits per second (bps). Note that the introductory stage is displayed in both English and Welsh.

*{Local Messages and Commands for dialling to 01443 482900}*

CONNECT 1200
<CR>
<CR>

*{Local Messages and Commands for dialling to 01443 482900}*

CONNECT 1200
**<CR>**
**<CR>**

DECserver 200 Terminal Server V3.0 (BL33F) – LAT V5.1
J152Q$70-A2

Please type HELP if you need assistance

Enter username> **gnvq**

Local> **connect a3500a** *{a3500a is an Alpha 3500 called "Alfi"}*
Local -010- Session 1 to A3500A established

*{The following is a start up message for all users of ALFI}*

> Welcome to OpenVMS AXP (TM) Operating System, Version V1.5
>> University Of Glamorgan / Prifysgol Morgannwg
>> General Purpose System / System Aml Bwrpas

WARNING / RHYBUDD

The programs and data held on this system are lawfully available to authorised users for authorised purposes only. Access to any program or data must be authorised by the University Of Glamorgan.

It is a criminal offence to secure unauthorised access to any program or data on, or make unauthorised modification to the contents of, this computer system. Offenders are liable to criminal prosecution. If you are not an authorised user DISCONNECT IMMEDIATELY.

Mae'r rhaglenni a'r data a gedwir ar y system hon ar gael yn gyfreithlon i ddefnyddwyr ar gyfer dibenion trwyddedig yn unig. Rhaid cael caniatad Prifysgol Morgannwg i ddefnyddio unrhyw raglen neu ddata.

Gall unrhyw un sy'n mynedi, neu newid unrhyw ran o'r system yma yn anghyfreithlon wynebu erlyniad troseddol. Os nad ydych yn ddefnyddiwr cyfreithlon DATGYSYLLTWCH YN SYTH.

Username: **GNVQ**
Password: **GNVQ** *{This would not appear when typed}*

*{The following is a start up message once a user logs on to ALFI}*

Good Evening ! *{or other appropriate greeting}*

> The IS Department is open during the following hours:
>> Monday to Thursday    08:15 to 21:30
>> Friday    08:15 to 21:00
>> Saturday & Sunday    09:30 to 12:30

> NIGHTLINE is available from 8 p.m. to 8 a.m. on 400333 if you're feeling stressed, upset or just want a chat. (*This is a student services support line*).

Have you logged in to do work for private gain ?
Please answer Yes or No **n**

*{GNVQ is a captive account which offers the following services}*
1. TELNET to GNVQ
2. FTP to GNVQ
3. KERMIT
0. LOGOUT from this session

```
Option ?: 2

220 Connected to www.comp.glam.ac.uk. { if you have web access you could
connect directly}
Name (GNVQ.COMP.GLAM.AC.UK:gnvq): anonymous
331 Guest log in, send E-mail address (user@host) as password.
Password: xxxx@comp.glamorgan.ac.uk {type in your e-mail address}

230-<Log on message for the FTP Server>
230 Anonymous login to 1 volumes. Access restrictions apply. "/pub".
FTP> pwd {pwd = print working directory}
257 "/pub" PWD command successful.

FTP> ls {ls = list files}
200 PORT command successful.
150 ASCII transfer started.
applications
incoming
publications
utilities
gnvq

226 Transfer complete.
49 bytes received in 00:00:00.03 seconds
FTP> cd gnvq {cd = change directory}

250 "/pub/gnvq" cd successful.
FTP> ls
200 PORT command successful.
150 ASCII transfer started.
gnvqcert.txt {This is an ASCII text file which certifies that a file transfer was
performed. Other files are not shown here for simplicity}

226 Transfer complete.
63 bytes received in 00:00:00.08 seconds
FTP> get gnvqcert.txt
200 PORT command successful.
150 ASCII transfer started (34k).
226 Transfer complete.
local: GNVQCERT.TXT remote: gnvqcert.txt
33464 bytes received in 00:00:01.14 seconds
FTP> quit
221 Nice chatting with you.

        1.   TELNET to GNVQ
        2.   FTP to GNVQ
        3.   KERMIT
        0.   LOGOUT from this session

Option ?: 3
```

You should select '0' here to logout, unless you are going to try a Kermit transfer as shown later in this element.

Another method of achieving a file transfer is to attach the file to an e-mail. The e-mail acts as an envelope to the file which is then delivered to the destination given on the e-mail header.

| | | From | Pri | Subject | Date Sent | |
|---|---|---|---|---|---|---|
| | ▤ | RADAVIES | - | RE: Resubmission fees for MSc dissertati | 02/04/96 | 12:32 pm |
| ⬗ | ▤ | /joshea | - | FW: Admissions and recruitment | 27/03/96 | 05:37 pm |
| | ▤ | /M.J.Rowle | - | Re: Exam moderation | 27/03/96 | 05:27 pm |
| | ▤ | BFJONES | - | RE: RAE | 27/03/96 | 04:56 pm |
| ⬗ | ▤ | /aevans | 3 | Syllabus+ Test Scenario. | 27/03/96 | 04:47 pm |

*Figure 4.33 E-mail file with two attachments (paperclip icon!)*

It is equally possible to use a file transfer programme (such as Kermit) to transfer a file between two PCs which are connected via a null modem cable. A null modem cable is a special arrangement where the wires inside the cable are set up, such that the two devices can transmit signals as though they were talking to a modem. However a modem isn't present and the two end devices are actually talking to each other with no modem in between. The transfer between the two stations looks like:

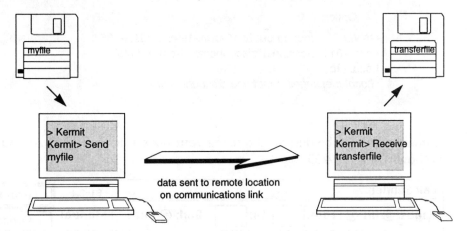

*Figure 4.34 Transfer using Kermit*

The remote user enters receive transferfile and now waits for a file to arrive. The command 'send myfile' causes the local PC to look for a copy of myfile and send it to the remote end. It may be sent as a series of smaller packets of data which are put together at the remote end to reconstruct the original file. A file at the far end called transferfile containing a copy of myfile from the local PC now exists.

If you want to try a Kermit transfer from The University of Glamorgan connection that was described above, the following sequence gives you the evidence you need for your portfolio.

```
C-Kermit, 4E(070) 29 Jan 88, Vax/VMS

C-Kermit>server
C-Kermit server starting. Return to your local machine by typing
its escape sequence for closing the connection, and issue further
commands from there. To shut down the C-Kermit server, issue the
FINISH or BYE command and then re-connect.

{On the local machine the user executes the following commands (The format for
these commands may vary for different machines:)}

Kermit> dir

Directory DISK$USER5:[COMP.MREDDY]
```

233

```
GNVQCERT.TXT;1 69 (RWED,RWED,RE,)
LOGIN.COM;16 3 (RWED,RWED,RE,)
MAIL.MAI;1 45 (RW,RW,,)
```

Total of 3 files, 117 blocks.

Kermit> **get gnvqcert.txt**
**

### Receive (KERMIT) gnvqcert.txt: 33464 bytes, 5:14 elapsed, 106 cps, 88%

Kermit> **finish** *{This tells the remote machine to stop being a server}*

C-Kermit server done

C-Kermit>**quit**

    1. TELNET to GNVQ
    2. FTP to GNVQ
    3. KERMIT
    0. LOGOUT from this session

  Option ?: **0**

GNVQ      logged out at 12-JUN-1995 18:01:10.36
Local -011- Session 1 disconnected from A3500A
Local> **lo**
*{Local messages about line disconnection}*

This document may then be despatched using your fax sender software. An example of a fax sender is shown in figure 4.35.

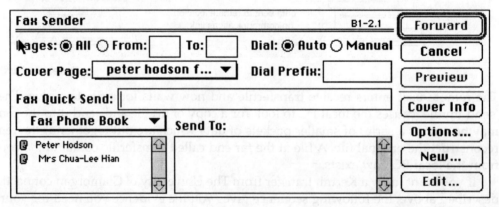

*Figure 4.35 Fax sender window*

 *Question 4.26*

*Why is a fax phone book a help and do we need a quick send facility?*

The fax can now be sent, either by selecting the recipient from your address, or fax book or by entering the destination fax number into the quick send field. A special transmission instruction to the system, such as delay sending this fax until a cheaper tariff rate is available, can also be set up. An example of selecting immediate or delayed transmission is shown in figure 4.36.

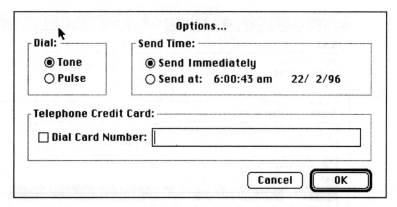

*Figure 4.36 Establishing despatch time*

Once the fax has been 'sent', its progress in transmission can be observed if you wish. The next two figures show two of the stages in the despatch sequence. The first figure is the software identifying the modem before scanning the document ready for transmission. Once the scan is complete then the modem dials the remote end to make a connection as shown in figure 4.38.

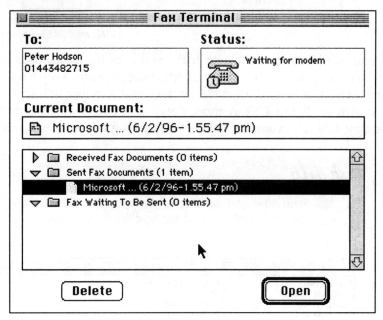

*Figure 4.37 Fax transmission status, scanning the document*

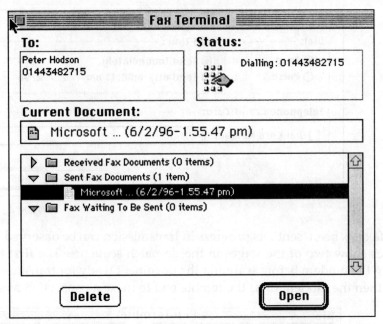

*Figure 4.38 Fax transmission status, modem dialling*

Normally you would not want to watch the status of the transmission, but simply want to know that the transmission was successful. Most fax packages keep a log which can be viewed.

If a simple check is needed, then the fax terminal window will show the list of sent documents, as shown on figure 4.38. A more detailed log is also available for inspection and is shown in figure 4.39. This contains details of how long the fax took to transmit, etc.

## Task 4.16                                                                 C2.4

*Send a fax and either track the progress of transmission or get a copy of the fax log to indicate that the transfer is complete.*

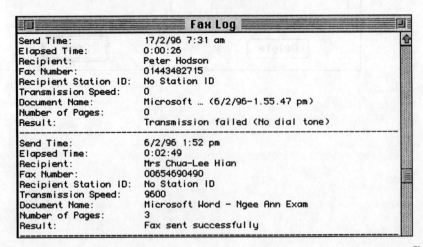

*Figure 4.39 Fax log*

## 4.2.4 Receive and store information on electronic systems

The GNVQ specification describes this as a separate activity. However, the transfer of information is often considered to include both the transmission and receipt. In the previous section of this element we looked at the way in which we sent information. If we want to consider receiving information and saving information, we can consider the other end of the link. In figure 4.34, for example, we looked at sending data using Kermit. If we had been at the other end of the link then we would have been receiving data. In our previous work on data transfer we have already covered the receiving activity, so we will not repeat the text here.

## 4.2.5 Accuracy and security

### Accuracy checks

It is important that any document or electronic file is accurately prepared and transmitted. Where we are entering text into an electronic system, the first accuracy check is the display on the screen. This is especially important where text is entered on a terminal, transmitted to a distant host machine and echoed back for screen display (i.e. the screen display is not directly linked to the keyboard, but is the data reflected back from the host machine). The user can readily undertake a visual check on the display.

It is normal to configure any communication link (local or remote) with an active parity checking mechanism. We saw in Element 4.1.2 how this functioned. If a device detects a parity error, it signals the incorrect receipt back to the sender so that retransmission can occur.

When we send a fax, the fax log will indicate whether the transmission was successful and what errors occurred if any. Figure 4.39 shows that a fax I sent on 6/2/96 was delivered to Singapore successfully, whereas the fax sent on 17/2/96 failed with no dial tone.

### Security checks

We have a requirement to keep data secure, indeed in Element 4.3 we will see there are legal requirements to do so in some cases. The range of approaches open to us are:

- encryption;
- password;
- privileges;
- user identity.

### Encryption

When we **encrypt** a file, we change its contents by applying a coding algorithm with a 'secret' word (**encryption key**) to reformat the data, i.e. the data is encrypted or **scrambled**. Normally that is done using the international standard encryption code. Anybody who illegally gets a copy of the data would need the encryption key to interpret the information.

### Passwords

Access to systems or applications can be **password** protected. Your password should be an alphanumeric combination, changed regularly and not recorded in a readable form (especially not on a 'sticker' on the side of the machine!).

In figure 4.40 you can see that the password set-up routine ensures that the password is kept secure during transmission by scrambling it. Note that the echo back of the password entered is 'locked off' and 'blobs' are substituted to give you an indication that a character has been entered.

**Task 4.17**  PC 5

*Set up a password system on a local application.*

**Task 4.18**  PC 5

*Encrypt a file before transferring it to a remote location*

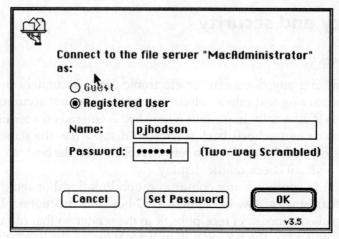

*Figure 4.40 Registration and password protection*

## Privileges

In accessing some data areas and applications, you can set up **privileges** or rights. Hence one individual or group may be allowed access, whereas others may not and access will be denied. In figure 4.40 I was registering as a user, but the administration have set up a closed group of people with such privileges, and so my attempt was denied as shown in figure 4.41.

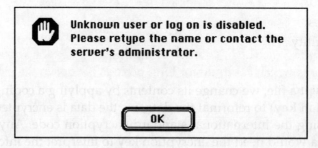

*Figure 4.41 Denied access*

## User identity

This can be established by a range of approaches that are covered in Element 4.3.5. We are simply noting here that this is an option we can apply at an appropriate level to ensure secure arrangements.

# Examine computer networks

## Introduction

In this element we will examine some of the basic features of computer networks. This element provides the background information you need to understand before you move on to Element 4.4 which introduces the practical issues. Some of the tasks that you are asked to do in this section will also provide the evidence you need for Element 4.4.

## 4.3.1 Types of networks

These broadly fit into the two categories of local area and wide area networks.

### Local area networks (LANs)

Anyone can set up their own **local area network** (**LAN**). It requires the purchase of the various pieces of hardware and software, installation of the cabling and operation of the service. You can operate the LAN over geographical distances that are limited by both the size of your premises and the maximum size of the LAN. A LAN can be as small as two users and as large as you wish within the previously noted limits. Typically LANs are one of the following standards, but there are very many other alternatives on the market. The first two of the following represent the major approaches:

**Ethernet** This was originally based on thick or thin coaxial cable, but has rapidly moved to twisted pair and fibre cable. It supports speeds of 10 and 100 Mbps. This is based on a bus topology and attached devices take their turn in sharing access time on the bus. To resolve any conflict when more than one station tries to talk at the same time, such that collisions occur, a technique called **collision detection** (**CSMA/CD**) is used. Ethernet is very good at handling short bursts of traffic such as file transfers, between engineering workstations, etc. Performance under heavy loads which continue for long periods is poor to the extent that little or no traffic may be transmitted.

*Question 4.27*

*If a network normally had a load of a 10kB file exchanged every minute, would an Ethernet LAN be a good network to use?*

*Question 4.28*

*If a network normally had a load of a 1MB file exchanged every second, would an Ethernet LAN be a good network to use?*

**Token ring** This is based on a twisted pair and operates at speeds of 4 and 16 Mbps. IBM are major supporters of the product. It is a little more expensive than Ethernet and is based on a ring topology. It uses a rotating token to resolve shared access conflict on the cable. It is good at handling fairly heavy loads up to its top limit. The performance under these heavy conditions is stable and does not deteriorate rapidly like Ethernet.

## Question 4.29

*Could the traffic levels outlined in the last question be carried successfully on a token ring?*

**Appletalk** This is based on Apple's own proprietary standards offering 230.4 kbps and used to connect Apple products together. It is a low level network designed to handle limited traffic cheaply (e.g. printer sharing).

The original need for LANs started when users wanted to be able to switch their terminal connections between different mainframe machines without the requirement to change the cable links physically. As relatively expensive devices (such as laser printers) became available, the option to share such devices between a number of users by connecting over a network became attractive. Finally and perhaps most importantly, the ability to share information and have a single source of any particular piece of data was enabled and supported by networks. This single occurrence of data is important in the updating and maintenance of information.

The helpful cabling layouts offered by LANs, allowing connection to a local cable rather than separate cable runs for every connection back to computer centres, made good economic sense and gave better control.

## Question 4.30

*Give two examples of advantages that LANs have given us.*

## Question 4.31

*Give two disadvantages of using LANs.*

Developments in LAN technologies include 100 Mbps Ethernet and a LAN implementation of **ATM (asynchronous transfer mode)**. Each LAN installation also needs a **network operating system (NOS)**. This provides the functionality and services whilst the infrastructure of cables and network cards etc. physically support the NOS by providing the mechanism for data transfer.

### Wide Area Networks (WANs)

In Element 4.1, we saw that **wide area networks (WANs)** are needed to achieve any data communication that needs to go outside the building or office complex, e.g. the use of telephone lines. We can think of a WAN as simply a network 'cloud' to which we connect. The 'cloud' [takes] data from the point of entry and delivers it to the destination point. How it achieves this [is not c]onsidered our worry, we just use the service. What we need to consider is how we con[nect to] the 'cloud'. A 'cloud' may require its own particular range of equipment. A typical

WAN protocol that will carry data to a distant location is **X.25**. Each network offers its own specific type of protocol connection.

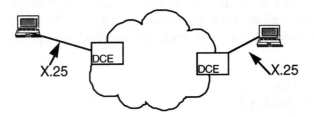

*Figure 4.42 X.25 interface*

For example, X.25 is a typical protocol between **end devices** (called **DTE**) and **communicating devices** (called **DCE**). It is available from most PTTs such as British Telecom. The DCE provides the connection facility into the WAN and accepts the specified input signals needed to use it successfully. If we were network engineers, we would need to set this link up correctly. The WAN is able to transfer the data internally to the specified destination.

### Public switched data network (PSDN)

The data network interface accepts packets, frames or cells of information and passes them across the network to the destination. This may involve using stations en-route to help get the data forwarded correctly. These data elements are often all referred to as **packets**, which is a generic name to cover all the terminology used.

Countries in Europe have been working together under the auspices of CCITT (Consultative Committee of the International Telegraph and Telephone), called the ITU (International Telecommunications Union). The standards which have become widely used are based on 64 kbps channels and network user addresses are defined by X.121.

Other standards for PSDN networks include Frame Relay, ATM and MANs. In each case, the original user data is routed across the network in packets which are normally smaller than the original component. At the destination, the fragmented packets are reassembled to form the complete data.

### Public switched telephone network (PSTN)

The PSTN is the general telephone network for voice traffic. Where data exchange between two points is required for a limited duration, it may provide the ideal communication facility. Connection via modems to the network has already been covered earlier in the unit.

Where the two devices (DTEs) are distant from each other, it is relatively simple to connect the two devices via their modems to the public switched telephone network. The modems provide a means of representing the digital signal as frequency tones. The basic idea behind this approach is similar to you whistling at different notes to signal the data. If two notes represent a '0' and a '1' in one direction and another two notes represent a '0' and a '1' in the opposite direction, then we can exchange data. All V.21 300 bps modems use this principle of using frequency shift keying to represent the data.

| Modem A to B | | Modem B to A | |
|---|---|---|---|
| 0 | 1 | 0 | 1 |
| 980 Hz | 1180 Hz | 1650 Hz | 1850 Hz |

In this arrangement, modem A is the originating modem (and therefore in originate mode) and modem B is in answer mode. Modems normally power up in the originate mode and switch to answer mode when they hear the ringing tone. The ITU V.21 standard operates at 300 bps, but higher speeds ranging from 1200 bps using V.22 modems, through to 9600 bps using V.32, and 19200 bps using V.32 terbo are available.

The PSTN offers a two-wire line and is the basic telephone network provided by British Telecom. Each country has its own services, e.g. DDD in the USA. A four-wire specification is also available. Most modems come with the standard telephone plug to connect to the telephone network.

## Question 4.32

*Is PSTN the normal telephone line provided to your home?*

### Integrated services data network (ISDN)

ISDN is a developing standard for digital communication allowing complete integration of voice, data, fax and video on a single system. In the basic format, it consists of two channels (B channels) of 64 kbps and one 16 kbps channel (D channel). This has developed into a megastream facility of 30 B channels and 1 D channel, making up a 2.048 Mbps system. Each of the B channels can carry voice or data. Larger capacity channels can be provided by combining a number of B channels together.

### Private wide area networks

Some WANs are established for the benefit of groups of people or organisations. These may be a series of telecommunication lines which have been leased by a company. The lines may be between their various countrywide offices and form a private network. All the company network traffic would be sent over these leased lines. Of course, if you lease a line then you have to pay for it whether you use it or not!

Banks will have closed WANs for managing their business, including Automatic Telling Machines. The universities have a closed network called JANET and Hewlett Packard have HP Internet as a closed Internet which operates across all their organisation. There are a range of closed wide area networks to which connection can be made. Typical of such an arrangement is:

- CompuServe: A commercial information service network. This is private in as much that it is a subscriber service, but public in as much that anyone can subscribe.

## Question 4.33

*Is CompuServe the only Internet provider available to the public?*

### Network services

With the state of current technology and digital communication, the range of services is already large and is getting bigger. If a network were to simply offer the ability to exchange raw bits without offering any software services or useful functions, then it is unlikely that much use will be made of it.

If the network now added some functionality, then users may be attracted to using the service. Added an e-mail or bulletin board service, then potential users will be attracted to using the service provided by the network and it becomes a realistic or commercially viable facility. We will consider a number of **network services** that are necessary for this unit, but the list is not exhaustive.

## Bulletin boards

**Bulletin Board Systems (BBS)** allow users to place messages, etc. in a central server or location which can be accessed by others. Many BBSs look like electronic versions of newspapers. Others provide free software which can be downloaded, although this has been the source of some virus prone pieces of software in the past.

## Conferencing

The facilities for conferencing have been evolving for a number of years. Perhaps the earliest of the conferencing facilities were those offered by BT when the telephone operator could interconnect a number of subscribers together to have a multiple-way conversation, known as **teleconferencing**. The evolution took us through a videoconferencing set-up where centres with studio facilities could have visual and verbal contact, although the cost of setting up and operating such a system was, and still is, quite expensive. Current developments involve PC conferencing where pairs of users can set up a conference. Each user's PC has a camera and conference board and is connected to other similarly equipped PCs by a reasonably high speed communication link. It is widely believed that the visual element coveys as much of the communication content as the written or spoken word.

### Question 4.34

*Why does the communication link between two PCs which are videoconferencing need to be a reasonably high speed link?*

The move to create a conferencing facility based on a central mini or a mainframe computer system, for all users registered on such a multi-user system, was a natural progression. The conference typically consists of one or more topic areas which people can read, add further data or comment on. These are frequently only text-based systems.

## Electronic mail

This is frequently considered to be electronic messaging, but we can exchange letters, numbers and images. Indeed anything that can be represented digitally could be part of an **electronic mail (e-mail)**. The normal arrangement is for a user to have a unique mail box to which other users can send their communication. A user can then connect to their mail box and retrieve any communications sent to them. Examples of e-mail services are:

- BT Mailbox (formerly Telecom Gold);
- Microsoft Mail, cc-mail, WordPerfect mail or other proprietary products;
- SMTP (Simple Mail Transfer Protocol);
- Viewdata.

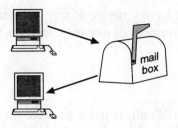

*Figure 4.43 Electronic mail*

If the mail box is available only to local users or a closed user group, then the format of the addressing can be quite simple, as shown in the following example of a Microsoft Mail message on a departmental network.

```
FROM: Hodson P J
DATE: 06/04/95 13:34
TO: Watkins M

CC:
SUBJECT: GNVQ IT
PRIORITY: R
ATTACHMENTS:
------------------------------------------------------------------
Is the schedule for the GNVQ IT development on target with our project plan?
Peter.
```

*Figure 4.44 Example of simple e-mail*

To send data to a wider group of people, then we need to structure the address. A typical format is pjhodson@comp.glamorgan.ac.uk, which is my e-mail address. The component fields show how to route the message across the Internet. This address means that I am a user at University of Glamorgan, which is an academic institution in the UK. Hence the structure of the e-mail address. Your mail service provider will give you your e-mail address detail. Of course not everyone uses the same e-mail package. If worldwide e-mail communication is to be achieved, then either everyone must use the same package or we must be able to interconnect and convert between the various e-mail services. Given that the former won't happen, then the provision of e-mail gateways, which provide standard structures, is inevitable.

Whilst many e-mail messages simply contain the text typed into the mail package, it is easy to attach an enclosure to the e-mail message. This attachment could be a wordprocessed document or a digital image, using the e-mail format as an envelope. Our example in figure 4.45 shows the attachments heading where the user simply specifies the name of the file to be 'attached' or enveloped.

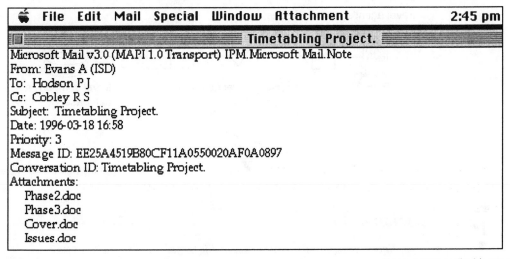

Figure 4.45 E-mail with attachment

## File transfer

This facility is frequently provided in a network system and allows users to transfer files, programs or indeed any digital data from remote locations to their own machine. A variety of **file transfer protocols (FTP)** exist. At a very simple level, programs such as Kermit permit the exchange of information between two systems. Other products (such as X-Modem) provide more sophistication to remote transfers. The larger protocol suites have inbuilt capabilities which achieve transfers without the user realising that it has been undertaken. Distributed File Systems such as Network File System (NFS) by SUN, are indicative of the developments in this area. Typically the following information could be specified:

- source and destination information including file names;
- mode of transfer describing how files will be created, appended or deleted on completion of the transfer;
- the quality of service;
- any security levels to be observed.

*Question 4.35*

*Was the transfer programme, Kermit, named after a little green frog?*

## Interacting with databases

It is common for interactive exchanges to occur which interrogate databases and update them when appropriate. For example, when you book a holiday at the travel agent, the normal activity is to query the travel company's database to check availability and costs. The database responds to the query with the current situation. A selection can be made and the database updated if a booking is confirmed. This is a typical example of an interactive session.

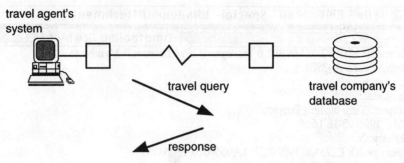

travel agent's
system

travel query

response

travel company's
database

*Figure 4.46 Interacting database*

## Question 4.36

*Can you identify another typical interaction with a database?*

### Task 4.19  PC 1                                                C2.2, C2.4

*Investigate and report on the range of networks provided by British Telecom.*

### Task 4.20  PC 1                                                      C2.4

*List the range of services you may find on a network. For each service identify
one implementation example. Indicate why you would use your example in a
daily situation.*

## 4.3.2 Benefits

### Central services

The issues of security, support and maintenance are often thought of as a problem. The wider
the geographic distribution of access points to a network (and potentially the data), the greater
the possible security risk. This is because you have less control when PCs are spread across lots
of buildings ... maybe in different towns or cities. If they were all in the same room you could
have a much tighter physical security policy. We can also approach security from the viewpoint
of access to data including logical access, or as a backup system and off-site copies.

With a corporate approach to security, the system could be established with greater security compared to multiple free-standing devices. For example, sensitive data can now be held at
a central point with appropriate access controls, rather than being located at the user's machine
location, where security measures depend upon people 'doing the right things'. In the central
location all the different security angles can be applied.

## Question 4.37

*Suggest two security approaches that can be taken for a system with remote PCs.*

The support and maintenance can also be centrally organised. All activities can be monitored from a central point on the network with benefits such as:

- ability to down-load software;
- ability to monitor and control access;
- ability to run diagnostic tests on remote equipment.

With the software tools now available, it is not too difficult to run maintenance software on all of the system from the central operation, regardless of how distant parts of it are.

### Shared resources

Before the PC became a popular workplace tool in the early 1980s, computer systems usually consisted of central mainframes. Suites of programs were written to handle particular applications and this often resulted in multiple occurrences of data, e.g. a customer's name and address might exist in several application program suites. Changes to the data required multiple updating and this frequently led to discrepancies between the various occurrences of the data. This problem resulted in the central database developments that we now see as a better approach. But PCs introduced another problem in the 1980s with 'private' user developments, including applications programs and data. Hence, we re-introduced the problem that multiple data sets may co-exist which were not compatible with each other. Data was created and existed within organisations that possibly only one or two individuals knew existed. Applications were developed that were locally produced, frequently undocumented and did not conform to organisational standards. These systems may have used a range of different software across the organisation (e.g. LOTUS 123, Excel, Quattro, etc.) and were frequently at different product version levels. These incompatible standards make it more difficult to move data between one PC and another.

Users can also make their own data available for access to others using access control fields. Hence, data created and saved from a database application by one user can be made readily available for other users to read. It is this aspect of data sharing capability that is attractive to organisations and achieves some of the objectives.

It is not only data that may be kept centrally and provided on a server basis. There are other types of device which an organisation is unlikely to provide separately for every station. For example, it is unlikely that every user would have their own laser printer, at least not a quality laser with a variety of paper trays holding company-headed stationary and blank paper of both A3 and A4 size. Nor is it likely that each station would have its own FAX, modem link or scanner attached directly.

### Question 4.38

*What multimedia device are you likely to find as a shared device on a network?*

In these cases, the organisation need only buy sufficient numbers of each type of device to satisfy the shared demand. Indeed, one of the benefits of installing a network is to provide the capability of sharing devices. The fileserver approach normally accepts requests for service from stations, and queues these requests up for action on a 'first come first served' basis (or whatever other algorithm is selected). To the user such access is seen to be immediately successful, but actually the action has automatically been slightly delayed until the request gets to the front of the queue.

Hence the benefits may be summarised as the sharing of software, hardware, resources and data.

### Team working

Where data is held on a central facility, the opportunity for people to work together on the same information (albeit with suitable updating and access control procedures) becomes an available option. It is common to see teams of people working on the same project or in the same area accessing the same data and files. A network allows easy and rapid sharing, rather than relying on sneakernet to transport data around. **Sneakernet** is an American expression where a user puts on his or her trainers (sneakers) and walks with a disk to another location!

### *Question 4.39*

*Do most businesses have computer systems developed by individuals or teams of people?*

### *Task 4.21* PC 2

*For each of the benefits described in this section, identify two advantages that networks have enabled. Are there any disadvantages?*

## 4.3.3 Network components

To physically set up a network service requires a number of components to be connected together. Rather than each manufacturer inventing their own rules or standards on how to achieve interconnection, a number of international standard interfaces have been agreed. If a manufacturer keeps to the standards, then interconnection of their equipment should be easier. This allows a user in one country to communicate with another country's user, both using different equipment. In this section we will define a number of the major components needed to achieve communication.

In a simple arrangement where two local stations which are sometimes called **data terminal equipment (DTE)** are connected, the physical structure may look like:

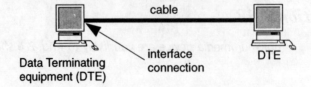

*Figure 4.47 Adjacent DTEs*

Of course, communication frequently involves a little more complexity and is not simply a direct link. In this case the communication structures are extended to include a **DCE (Data circuit terminating equipment)** and the ability to communicate over long distances is available.

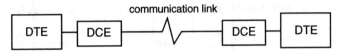

*Figure 4.48 Remote DTE connection*

Frequently the local configuration is based on RS232 and this can also be used to establish a remote link.

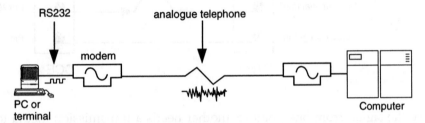

*Figure 4.49 Remote connection with RS232*

In the example shown here, the DCE converts the digital signals from the RS232 interface to an analogue telephone network. The DCEs in this example are the modems and the DTEs are the PC and computer. The interface has physical, electrical, functional and procedural characteristics. The connector and cabling provide the basic elements of these characteristics.

## Question 4.40

*Is the serial port that you normally find on the back of a PC an RS232 interface?*

### Cabling

To send data across a WAN, the connection is frequently via a modem, using a modem cable between the DTE and the modem. A modem cable has a simple arrangement of pin 2 at one end connected to pin 2 at the other end and similarly for other pins. It typically uses a D connector at both ends of the type shown in figure 4.25.

Where two DTEs are directly connected, we cannot use a cable directly configured as a modem cable, since the pins used to transmit at one end will arrive at the transmit pin and not the receive pin at the other end. Hence we have to set up a cross-over arrangement to ensure signals arrive at the right pin and the control signals work correctly. Such a cable is known as a **null modem cable** (i.e. there is no modem between the two DTEs).

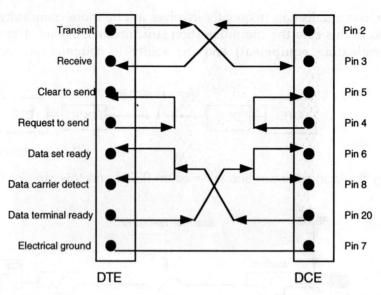

*Figure 4.50 Null modem cable*

To carry the signal from one point to another needs a transmission media to support the signalling approach taken. This could be anything from a piece of string or airwaves, to something more sophisticated. However, we most commonly use different forms of copper wire and fibre optic cable. Infra-red and microwave links provide more specialist services. Recent developments with wireless networks using **spread spectrum transmission** (**SST**) and microwave channels are appearing on the market place. The allocation of frequency channels which do not clash with the UK cellular operation of Cellnet and Vodafone has been problematic for the microwave developments.

## Question 4.41

*Is a piece of string a good transmission media?*

A range of cable exists, the majority of which provides a path for a one-way or two-way flow of a serial stream of bits. Alternatively, parallel ribbon or cable allows a multiple stream of data to be sent. As the desire to achieve high speeds of transmission have developed, then the types of transmission media have also developed. Typical of the range of copper wire is twisted pair and coaxial. Different types of fibre optic cable also exist.

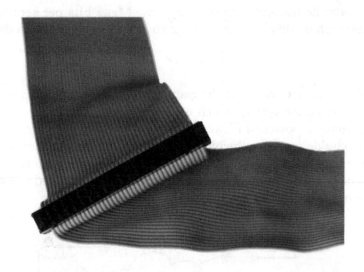

*Photograph 4.1 Parallel connector and ribbon*

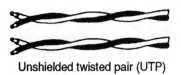

Unshielded twisted pair (UTP)

Shielded twisted pair (STP)

*Figure 4.51 Twisted pair*

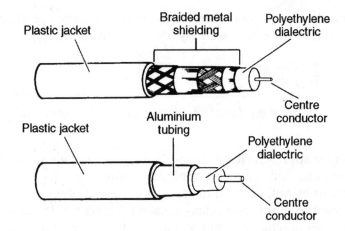

*Figure 4.52 Coaxial cable*
*(Copyright Ungermann-Bass Reprinted with permission)*

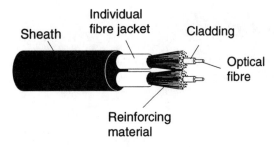

*Figure 4.53 Fibre optic*
*(Diagram courtesy of Cray Communications)*

Such cable can provide transmission speeds in the **Mega bits per second (Mbps** or **Mbit/s)** range with some high quality fibre able to transmit at much higher speeds.

### File servers

We have already seen that benefits can be gained by having a central approach to holding data. In a networked system, the way in which we keep data and software centrally is using a **file-server.** This is usually a powerful PC with a lot of disk space and frequently a lot of memory. It frequently also holds and runs the NOS. The other stations can access the fileserver to read the data or download the software held on it. The NOS controls the way in which this access occurs and can be set up such that access can be denied or restricted when security applies or privileges have not been granted.

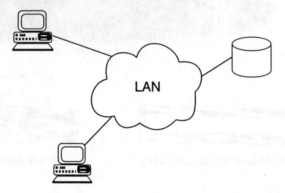

*Figure 4.54 LAN support for fileserver*

The fileserver is the key component in the successful operation of a LAN. Users keep their data on the server, so it must be kept securely with backup copies regularly maintained.

## Question 4.42

*How often should a backup copy of the server be taken?*

The central server approach clearly offers the organisation enormous benefits in creating genuine corporate data. Both data and application software can be accessed or downloaded to local workstations by authorised users as appropriate. It offers the organisation an opportunity of keeping control of software releases, exercising control to remain legal with the number of product licences purchased (and users attempting to use the product simultaneously) and can avoid too great a spread of products, thus achieving data compatibility. The user gains by having access to a wider data source with better data integrity.

## Question 4.43

*Are there any disadvantages to the server approach compared with individual workstations operating in isolation?*

## Network cards

To connect a device to the network we must be able to implement that network's access technique and be able to put the data to be transmitted into LAN packets. For LANs, this is via a network card connected to the device's bus.

Typically LAN cards provide either token ring or Ethernet facilities. Photograph 4.2 shows an Ethernet card with an RJ-45 connector.

*Photograph 4.2 RJ-45 connector o*

 *Question 4.44*

*Is the RJ-45 connection on the network card an RS232 interface?*

RJ-45 Modular Plug

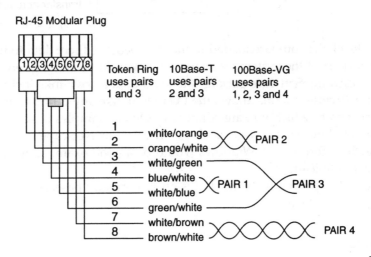

*Figure 4.55 RJ-45 plug*

## Network software

Software exists at many levels in data communications. The range of software includes:

- Application Software (e.g. e-mail or EDI);
- Application Software Tools or Calls (e.g. file transfer routines);
- Security and Presentation Software (encryption, compression etc.);
- Transport Software (between end points);
- Routing Software (using global addresses);
- Point-to-point delivery software and local error control.

Some of these functions are provided within the network operating system, some with the network driver software supplied with the network cards. Additional functionality provided by the application software (e.g. e-mail package or EDI, etc.) is user selected. Each interface or network card is normally driven by software systems. Some elements of this are embedded on the network card, having been developed in a low level language. Frequently the NOS has driver software which interfaces with the network card or whatever is used.

The interface card takes the data from the PC and formats the bits ready for despatch into the packet structures expected by the 'transmission'. On receipt of incoming data, it is able to provide the reverse operation. For example, the interface card could be token ring or Ethernet card creating or receiving token ring or Ethernet packets.

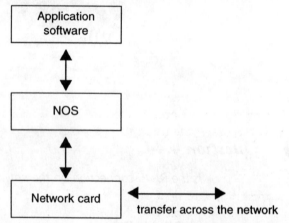

Figure 4.56 Layered approach to data transfer

At a higher level, the software loaded in the PC needs to direct data to the hardware interface. This could be part of the system software which would be serving requests to do so from the application software. Software packages to send data across links include terminal emulation software, e.g. Pacerterm. This allows the PC to look like any dumb terminal recognised by the computer system to which you are connected. Other examples of software that request transmission include Internet software, such as MOSAIC or Netscape or electronic mail software. Software such as Terminal in Windows would be a good example of the interface for users of electronic communications.

The layered approach to network design is normally based on a seven layer model and follows international standards.

## Print servers

If a number of devices are sharing access to a printer, it is common to provide a **print server**. The print server provides a queuing system in which the data to be printed is held. Any of the devices on the network can issue a print request, possibly at the same time The server will queue the print requests up and take each request off the queue when the printer is free to print. Control of this queue is available. Normally each print request is taken in order from the queue (i.e. first in, first out). However facilities to re-order or prioritise the queue also exist. The print server may be part of the main network server or exist as a separate device (such as an old PC with special software loaded) or as a purpose built device.

## Question 4.45

*Why would you want to re-order the print queue?*

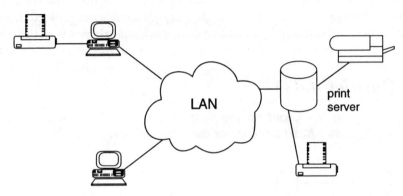

*Figure 4.57 Shared print facilities*

Control of the printer server will normally be a function of the network operating system. In many networks it is likely that a number of printers exist. If the user sends all printer requests to the print server, the option to select a specific print station for output exists. A default would normally operate if the user didn't specify or select a particular station.

### Workstations

The workstation can be a dumb terminal, a PC or a powerful station, such as a SUN microcomputer. The selection will depend on the funds available and the work to be carried out. Increasingly, to provide flexibility and allow for future developments, a PC or higher specification platform are normally selected for users. Remember, these are classed as DTE devices.

## Question 4.46

*What is an example of a DCE device?*

## Task 4.22  PC 3

*Describe how the various components combine together to form a computer network.*

### 4.3.4 Network topologies

In connecting devices together to form a network, we must consider the physical structure or layout of the cabling. The intention of a LAN is to bring order and management control to what could otherwise become a difficult problem. Consider the problem of adding another node or PC to either of the layouts shown in figure 4.58. It is fairly clear which of the two layouts will give us the most difficulty in establishing an additional connection to all the other existing stations. The left hand side is often called a **mesh** topology and, although unhelpful as a LAN structure, it is often found in WAN situations where multiple routes to other locations is useful.

## Question 4.47

*In the unstructured topology on the left hand side of figure 4.58 what do you see as the major problem of adding more nodes?*

## Question 4.48

*Is the layout on the right-hand side of figure 4.58 the only way to have a structured topology, or are there different layouts?*

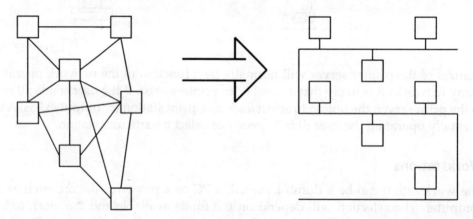

*Figure 4.58 Cable structures*

Cable structure is very important and its logical layout is a key element in supporting the different LAN approaches, such as Ethernet and token ring. The physical installation of the cable has been changing quite significantly over recent years. A structured cabling approach is now commonly implemented which may not resemble the logical layout we are fundamentally trying to create. Since it is important that the fundamental structures are understood, we will use the logical layout as a starting point.

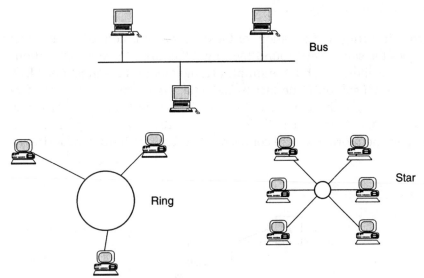

*Figure 4.59 Typical topologies*

## Bus

A **bus** topology consists of a 'single' communication channel. Each connected device is attached to the media at an interface point and has its own unique hardware address. Data transfers between the interfaces or nodes take place using these hardware addresses.

### Question 4.49

*Are both the following layouts a bus structure?*

Although we have represented the bus topology as a single cable run, in all but the simplest of installations the bus will have more complex arrangements with several interconnected segments. There are precise rules on how the interconnection of segments is arranged.

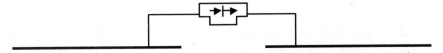

*Figure 4.60 Example of a more complex bus structure*

The two segments are joined together using a special type of network 'relay' device which could be a repeater or a bridge depending on the design. The advantages of using the bus structure include simplicity of layout and ease of connectivity. Locating cable faults on such a topology is also relatively easy and this is an important issue for network maintainability. The topology is ideal for one-to-many data transmissions since all connected devices 'hear' the traffic on the cable. There is a security disadvantage arising here since eavesdropping on other station's traffic is relatively easy.

### Question 4.50

*Can a bus topology easily handle broadcast messages where all stations hear the data transfer from the station that is sending?*

257

## Ring

It is normal in a **ring** configuration for the data transmission to be uni-directional i.e. the signal always goes the same way around the ring. Of course, there are exceptions to this when dual cable rings are operating, but the simple arrangement is uni-directional. Data transmissions are received by each station's interface as the data passes through the interface connection. As in the bus topology, each interface only copies the data from the network and passes it to the device (e.g. a PC), it connects to the network if it recognises the packet's destination address as its own. Each network interface connection has its own hardware address for identification.

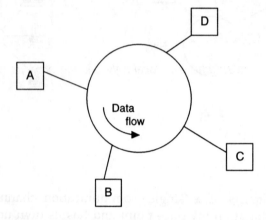

*Figure 4.61 Simple ring topology*

Larger networks may be constructed from a number of interconnected rings.

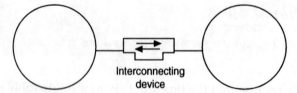

*Figure 4.62 Interconnected rings*

## Star

The normal arrangement for a **star** topology includes a central switching system or hub. In the figure shown, if a station wishes to talk to any other station, it does so via the hub. Early implementations based on this topology include systems using **PABX (private automatic branch exchange)** or office telephone switchboard. In the basic form shown here, the medium is not really shared and any new device requiring connection will need a cable to the central point or hub. If the hub was physically close to its connected devices then the individual cable runs would not be problematic.

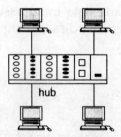

*Figure 4.63 Star configuration*

Recent advances in LAN design have resulted in star topologies providing the majority of new installation layouts. Purpose built hubs provide the central point. However, very different approaches within the hub occur depending on the network being created.

### *Task 4.23* PC 4                     *C2.4*

*For each of the three topologies write a brief report indicating which network standards are based on each structure.*

### *Task 4.24* PC 4

*Investigate your local network and draw its topology.*

## 4.3.5 Security requirements

The security level implemented will need to reflect the value of the information or system that is being protected. In a commercially sensitive environment (i.e. the stock exchange) the extent of the security will be different from a local college or school network where breaches of security, although unwelcome, ought not to end in the collapse of the organisation. Sensitive data may be encrypted to prevent recognition of content by unauthorised readers. This is particularly useful during transmission.

### User identity and passwords

Early computer systems housed in computer centres were able to control access almost completely by controlling physical access to the building. Access controls could be categorised as something you own, something you know or something you are. Typical controls include:

- identity cards;
- pass cards;
- passwords;
- control doors with security staff;
- coded locks with security code or simple swipe card;
- special devices, e.g. retina scanners, palm/finger print readers.

Each of these have advantages and disadvantages.

### *Task 4.25* PC 2                     *C2.4*

*List a possible advantage and disadvantage for each of the control approaches given above.*

Of course, communication systems have changed security requirements since personnel may be located outside the central office suite. Staff may be working from home, sales staff may connect in from remote locations and sales orders may be received via EDI. Hence a logical access control, in addition to the physical access, is required to support the security.

Security breaches are often caused by staff not following procedures. Raising the awareness of security amongst all users is important if systems are to be well protected. Leaving passwords written on 'post-it' stickers on the side of workstations is not unknown! Since there are statutory obligations to protect data, the security procedures will be the focus of meeting such legal requirements.

### Access rights

Logical access controls may be implemented by software or hardware controls. They can specify the various levels of access in terms of the range or permitted penetration into the system. In particular, the following permissions may be set up for access to data:

- read only;
- write;
- execute only;
- delete.

### Legal requirements

In any organisation holding data, there is a set of legal requirements with which there is a need to comply. Perhaps the most obvious area is the Data Protection Act. A number of important issues are identified in the act, including:

- individual's right of access to information held on them in the computer system;
- the requirement to keep information confidential and not to disclose it to others;
- the need to only keep information that is necessary and the requirement that it is not obsolete.

If you are holding information covered by the Act, then you need to register the database with the Data Protection authorities. Other legal requirements cover such issues as:

- copyright;
- licence agreement;
- computer misuse;
- health and safety at work.

Many organisations require staff to sign non-disclosure agreements as a condition of employment. Government Agencies may demand all staff working within the agency, or on contracts placed by the government, to sign the Official Secrets Act. Various levels of security vetting will be undertaken on staff signing the Official Secrets Act. Bringing a disk into some organisations and potentially introducing a virus is a sackable offence. Equally, the unauthorised removal of data from an organisation can result in the same outcome!

## *Task 4.26* PC 5

*How do each of the security issues identified in this element apply to your local network?*

# *Use a computer network*

### Introduction

This is really the element to put into practice the issues of establishing and managing a network. The approach you will be able to take will depend entirely on the network(s) that are available within your own school, college or organisation. Since there are very many network operating systems on the market it is not possible to cover each possibility here. Novell currently has a significant market penetration of the PC installations and many systems look like figure 4.64.

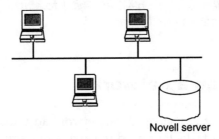

*Figure 4.64 Typical network server configuration*

Another popular route may be the use of a UNIX host to provide services to other client machines.

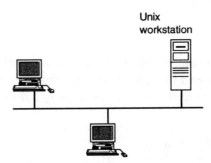

*Figure 4.65 Networked UNIX environment*

## 4.4.1 Access and security procedures

The security features that you need to demonstrate are:
- avoidance of data corruption;
- avoidance of data loss;
- copyright;
- login procedures, including passwords;
- maintain confidentiality.

If you have already accessed the University of Glamorgan's system in Element 4.2.3, you will have already collected the evidence needed for most of these. The issue of copyright means we must recognise that both the applications we have bought and the data owned by others is protected by law. Copying this may seem harmless, but it is theft.

## 4.4.2 Create subdirectory

A data file is normally located on a system by structuring the directory system. A hierarchical system, with a master user having pointers to the next group of directories, which in turn cascade down to lower levels, is a common structure. In this element you are required to create a subdirectory structure on your system.

**Task 4.27** PC 1, PC 2

*On your network create a subdirectory under your own user directory to hold the work you have in digital format for your GNVQ units. You may want separate files for each unit.*

## 4.4.3 Manage files on a network

A network doesn't look after itself and the network administration need to take action to manage the files. The regular tasks that need to carried out are:

- taking backups;
- copying files;
- deleting files;
- file protection;
- moving files.

We saw in the previous element that the frequency with which we undertake backups depends on the nature of the data and the rate at which it changes. Backup copies should be physically kept in a different location to the system, preferably a different building.

**Task 4.28** PC 3

*For the files you created in the last task, take a backup copy which you should take home for security. If you have an out of date copy, then this older copy should be deleted.*

## 4.4.4 Access network applications

The requirement is to access two network applications. This will obviously depend on the applications you have available. If you undertook task 4.15 on the University of Glamorgan's systems then you will have already used ftp and Kermit and therefore have the evidence of having completed this work.

## 4.4.5 Manipulate data files

For two network applications that you have available, you need to manipulate the files by undertaking the following activities:

- create;
- edit;
- save;
- print.

The creation and editing are normal functions of setting up data files and may be a simple word processing package or e-mail package. Saving and printing the files are normally menu driven options.

*Task 4.29*  PC 4, PC 5

*For two network applications create and edit a data file. Print the files and save the copies in the subdirectory structure you set up in task 4.27.*

# Answers to questions in Unit 4

**Answer 4.1**   Your answer may be completely different to mine but that doesn't make it wrong, as long as it is a valid example. Old broadcasting systems that come to mind are emergency services and taxi company radio systems. In the new area are mobile telephones and satellite television.

**Answer 4.2**   There are a number of possible answers here also, but fax is an obvious choice. The new video phones could be have selected or, for those of you who are technically minded, the X.25 packet switched network is an alternative.

**Answer 4.3**

1 0 1 0 1

**Answer 4.4**

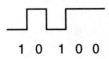

1 0 1 0 0

**Answer 4.5**   It is a little bit difficult drawing the line representing the last two zeroes to make sure it is the right length, i.e. the length of two digits. Just as you had a little difficulty in drawing this, the receiving devices have a little bit of a problem making sure they know how many digits are in a long signal at the same voltage level.

**Answer 4.6**   At 300 bps there is (1 divided by 300)th of a second for each signal, i.e. there is 3.33 ms for each bit signalled.

**Answer 4.7**   The answer is 0.625 ms or 625 micro seconds.

**Answer 4.8**   If you look at table 4.1 you can see that all of the first two columns are control characters and the start of the third row is also. We will forget about the odd character DEL at the end of the table. This means that the control characters are in the range 000 0000 up to 010 0001.

**Answer 4.9**
B is 42H or     11000010 with odd parity
                01000010 with even parity
E is 45H or     01000101 with odd parity
                11000101 with even parity

**Answer 4.10**   In the world of finance and banking, if the data got corrupted, then the wrong amounts of money could get transferred. If you were using an ATM machine to get money from the 'hole in the wall', you expect the right data to have been signalled back to your bank. What would happen if the transfer was the design of a road bridge and it was built on the basis of corrupted design data?

**Answer 4.11**   We are representing B with the following ASCII code … 11000010

Remember that the least significant bit is sent first. Hence the signal will look like:

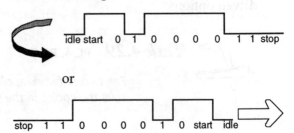

It is the order in which the bits are seen at the remote end that is important. Both of these give the same order, but you may see them drawn in either format in other texts.

**Answer 4.12**   100 characters is 1000 bits, assuming 1 start and 1 stop bit.

To send this at 2400 bps will take (1000/2400) seconds = 0.416 s

**Answer 4.13**   If we delay sending a response then the sender will time out and think that the signals haven't reached the destination. The sender will then re-send the data and the receiver will still get data arriving, which isn't what we wanted to happen.

**Answer 4.14**   We can use RS232 flow control where the number of wires in the connected are greater than just the data signalling wires. When we connect two or more devices which are not close together, then the cable doesn't have such a large number of separate wires. It is just too expensive. The wires in the cables used for long distances are only for data and no separate (or additional) wires are there for control signals. Hence we need to use other flow control techniques.

**Answer 4.15**   We have seen ACK and NAK plus RS232 as flow control techniques. There are other approaches which you may possibly have encountered if you have configured network systems, but don't worry if you couldn't answer this question. You may have X-on and X-off as an answer or even some of the protocol flow control commands from TCP or HDLC!

**Answer 4.16** In parallel transmission we transmit one byte at a time. In this case 800 bytes/sec. To transmit 3200 bytes will take 4 secs.

**Answer 4.17** There has been no delay between each byte and no error(s) have occurred which need retransmission.

**Answer 4.18** A range of correct answers exist here which include things like passwords, military messages or even examination papers!

**Answer 4.19** The file name, its size, its format any standards used for diagrams or other unusual data structures. Is it a Mac or IBM-compatible format etc? The date and version number are helpful to know also.

**Answer 4.20** This is a little obvious, but it simply the name of the person you want to reach. You would be surprised how many faxes are sent without this information.

**Answer 4.21** Simply the name of the sender and the fax number on which he or she may be reached.

**Answer 4.22** A count of the total number of pages sent including the cover page.

**Answer 4.23** Most faxes have the time sent stamped on them. The receiver can refer to the time sent stamp to distinguish between the two copies.

**Answer 4.24** ASCII is the way in which we can represent a range of alphanumeric and control characters using seven bits plus a parity bit. The layout of the ASCII set was given in table 4.1. Other ways of representing data were developed and ASCII isn't the only approach, although much of the world now uses it. An alternative representation was EBCDIC code which was used a lot by IBM.

**Answer 4.25** Flow control is the way in which we find a method of sending a signal from the receiver to the sender. This signal tells the sender that it wants to start or stop the flow of more data. It is the way in which we control the rate at which data is transmitted. Think of flow control on the roads. Traffic lights control the flow of cars across a junction and signal when to start and when to stop. This is the same idea.

**Answer 4.26** If you are sending faxes regularly, it is useful to have the frequently called numbers in a local directory. You can then simply select the entry, and all the detail of the name of the addressee and their fax number are automatically entered into the cover page. Once this is set up, there should be no possibility of sending to the wrong number because you mis-entered the fax number, etc.

Of course, there will always be numbers that you haven't called before and are one-off in as much that you don't expect to call them again and therefore don't want to enter the details in an additional directory entry. To support this you need the package to offer a quick send route, where you can enter the details for this one-off fax.

**Answer 4.27** 10kB is (10 times 1024 times 8) bits and this is sent every minute. An Ethernet LAN can normally support 10Mbps, i.e. (10 times 1024 times 1024) bits per second. In a minute it can send 60 times this amount. Hopefully you can see that the capacity of the LAN is much higher than the volume of data that you want it to carry. Therefore the Ethernet LAN will easily be able to carry this level. It will be like driving down a three lane motorway on a Sunday morning (I'm not sure this analogy works for the M25!).

**Answer 4.28** This situation would require the transfer of (10 times 1024 times 1024 times 8) bits per second. This is very close to the capacity of the network. Once you start reaching the capacity level of many systems the performance is not very good. What happens on a motorway when it is near capacity level! One small incident like a car breaking ripples through the system and delays start occurring. The same with networks. The Ethernet LAN would perform badly under such a heavy load, especially if that level of data was given to the network for any length of time. It would manage if it were only a short burst of heavy traffic, but not under constant load conditions.

**Answer 4.29** If the network was a token ring, which was working at 16Mbps, then the network would handle the data rate discussed in the last question. This is especially true because the token ring performs better under constant heavy loads than the Ethernet LAN.

**Answer 4.30** Possible answers include the access to shared information, which reduces the number of times you have to keep (and update) copies of data. Another advantage is the ability to share access to expensive devices between a number of network users. Of course there is the functional benefits that e-mail and file transfer brings. Also the ability to access other information services over the Internet become possible, etc.

**Answer 4.31** We now have another level of complexity and should the network fail, then all of the system may become inoperable. Indeed you may not be able to work locally very well, because you are dependant on access to servers to provide the application programs as well as the data. There is also cost of cabling and an overhead of staff salaries which are needed to manage the operation of a large network. You may well have thought of other ideas which are equally valid. They include the number of different LANs available, which make it difficult to join them together because they follow different standards.

**Answer 4.32**   Yes

**Answer 4.33**   No, there are many Internet providers and the list is growing (well at least changing!) on a weekly basis. CompuServe just happens to be one of the larger providers at the time of writing and are marketing their services pretty aggressively.

**Answer 4.34**   If the communication channel needs to carry images as well as sound, then there are many more bits of information to be signalled per second than a sound-only system.. Hence the communication link to support this service needs to be a reasonably high speed link such as ISDN.

**Answer 4.35**   Yes, the guys who wrote this software at Colombia University were fans of the Muppets.

**Answer 4.36**   A wide range of answers may be correctly suggested here. A typical application is an insurance office interrogating the car insurance databases to find you the best quote.

**Answer 4.37**   Security approaches can embrace some of the ideas that originally existed in mainframe systems. Hence ideas such as login passwords for identification, and automatic logouts for stations with no activity are amongst the possible answers to this question.

**Answer 4.38**   One possible multimedia device to be shared is a CD stack drive, in which a number of CDs can be stacked and mounted for a range of user access. For multimedia production it could be a scanner or digital camera or CD writer that is made available.

Other possibilities also exist.

**Answer 4.39**   Projects of any significance within an organisation tend to be team developments rather than solo efforts. Whilst there may be many exceptions to this, as a general guide it is true.

**Answer 4.40**   Normally yes.

**Answer 4.41**   Whilst string may act as a transmission media (indeed as a child I played in the garden with two cocoa tins connected by string which was kept taut) it is neither reliable nor does it support high data rates. Other than in fun situations, it is not a network media.

**Answer 4.42**   This depends on a number of factors, such as: how often does the data change, how important or valuable is the data, what are the consequences of losing data etc? For many systems backing up overnight is common, but for high security or high risk systems this may well be more frequent.

**Answer 4.43**   If the server or its network links develop a fault, then individual users at their separate workstations are also affected. In standalone mode, no matter what other work-stations do or don't do, there will be no impact on a workstation.

**Answer 4.44**   No, RJ-45 plug connectors and RS232 are different interfaces carrying different signalling conventions.

**Answer 4.45**   It could be that a particular print out becomes more important than other items in the print queue. In such cases the ability to push one or more print requests to the front of the queue and to prioritise the order is an important feature.

**Answer 4.46**   A modem is a good example.

**Answer 4.47**   Each new node that is added needs multiple new links setting up. The larger the network, the greater the number of new links that are required.

**Answer 4.48**   A range of structured layouts exist which are covered later in the element.

**Answer 4.49**   Yes, although there is a bend in the cable this is still a bus structure.

**Answer 4.50**   Certainly. If messages are passed in both directions from the point of contact on the media (i.e. bi-directional signalling), then a bus topology is fine for supporting broadcast messages.

# Unit 4 Sample Test Paper

1 Radio transmission is a form of electronic communication. What type of system is it?

A broadcast system
B local area network
C cellular network
D duplex

2 To make sure that a character sent across a network is transmitted without error, what approach is used?

A byte count
B parity check
C encryption
D encoding

3 Which device is needed to connect a PC to the telephone network?

A broadcast system
B telex
C codec
D modem

4 How do we send multiple bits at a time?

A half-duplex transmission
B serial transmission
C parallel transmission
D analogue signalling

5 What is the baud rate?

A the rate at which the signal changes
B the data transmission rate
C the speed of the network card
D the speed of the transmission cable

6 How is the speed of data transmission normally specified?

A milliseconds
B parallel
C serial
D bits per second

7 How would data be given additional security during transmission?

A encryption
B flow control
C emulation
D conversion to binary

8 What technique is used to prevent a PC sending data too quickly to a printer?

A disconnecting
B odd parity
C flow control
D serial

9 Which method can we use to send a copy of this page in electronic format to a location in London, taking only a few minutes to achieve delivery?

A broadcast
B facsimile
C local area networks
D telex

10 How does half-duplex work?

A by transmitting data in one direction only
B by transmitting data in only one direction at a time
C by transmitting data in both directions simultaneously
D by implementing serial transmission

11 Which of the following provides a user with a data entry accuracy check?

A echoing
B encryption
C flow control
D terminal emulation

12 Which of the following is a local area network?

A mesh topology
B half-duplex
C bus topology
D public network

13 Which topology is not likely to be a local area network?

A bus
B ring
C star
D mesh

14 A wide area network allows travel agents to connect to the enquiry and reservation system. What kind of system is the reservation system?

   A   print server
   B   Internet
   C   database
   D   router

15 Why do we need network cards?

   A   to connect devices to the local area network
   B   to connect remote devices to the local area network
   C   to terminate the network cabling system
   D   to provide the user with ID

16 Which of the following services is not provided by a file server?

   A   the ability to save files from your local station
   B   the ability to download files to your local station
   C   the ability to upload and download files to and from your local station
   D   the ability to save files locally

17 Which of the following devices can provide secure access to centrally held files?

   A   workstations
   B   locked central computer suite
   C   password
   D   file server

18 Why do we use local area networks?

   A   to use the extra capacity cable that has been installed
   B   to provide a secure environment
   C   to share data and devices
   D   to connect PCs to the cable

19 Which of the following is not an interactive database system?

   A   a holiday booking system
   B   an automatic telling machine (hole in the wall)
   C   the television teletext system
   D   an airline reservation system

20 A print server is used for which of the following purposes?

   A   controlling the print queue
   B   providing a queuing system to the printer
   C   providing flow control between the user and the printer
   D   charging the end user for the print facilities

21 Why do we use passwords?

   A   to prevent anyone from accessing a computer system
   B   to prevent unauthorised users from accessing the system
   C   to backup the system regularly and securely
   D   to prevent viruses from spreading

22 A file you have just created using a word processing package is likely to have which of the following access permissions?

   A   read only
   B   write only
   C   read and write only
   D   read, write and execute

23 You have bought a single user copy of a software package. What prevents you from installing the software on the network such that multiple users may use it at the same time?

   A   login procedures
   B   copyright laws
   C   Data Protection Act
   D   access permissions

24 How do you help make sure there is always sufficient space on the file server's hard disk?

   A   delete all files over 12 months old
   B   delete all files that have read and write access
   C   copy the unwanted files
   D   delete unwanted files

25 What should you do with passwords?

   A   keep them simple so you can easily remember them
   B   change them regularly
   C   write them down and keep the copy near the computer so you don't waste time looking it up during logins
   D   use your first name

# *Index*